MICHAEL

FOR THE

MILLENNIUM

MICHAEL

FOR THE

MILLENNIUM

THE FOURTH BOOK
IN THE MICHAEL TEACHING

Chelsea Quinn Yarbro

BERKLEY BOOKS, NEW YORK

MICHAEL FOR THE MILLENNIUM

A Berkley Book/published by arrangement with
the author

PRINTING HISTORY
Berkley trade paperback edition/December 1995

ISBN: 0-425-15074-7

BERKLEY®
Berkley Books are published by The Berkley Publishing Group,
200 Madison Avenue, New York, New York 10016.
BERKLEY and the "B" design
are trademarks belonging to Berkley Publishing Corporation.

PRINTED IN THE UNITED STATES OF AMERICA

10 9 8 7 6 5 4 3 2 1

for

G. W.

A. C.

S. C.

S. C.

J.

R. P.

L. C.

S. C.

and the rest of the Albuquerque gang

CONTENTS

MICHAEL

FOR THE

MILLENNIUM

INTRODUCTION

The Michael group has been in existence now for about twenty years. The people in it have been through a variety of upheavals and trials: deaths, births, marriages, divorces, the 1989 Loma Prieta Quake, the 1991 Oakland Hills Firestorm (which destroyed over 1,600 pages of Michael transcripts), health problems, and career changes. Members have moved away from the area and now participate on a phone-in basis.

I have now in my attic about five large cartons of transcripts, and that is less than half the material we have accumulated over the years. In going over it all for the preparation of this book, I was struck again by the singular consistency and character of the material. Michael has a distinctive voice; it does not matter who the medium is, Michael is still Michael, strange syntax and all. Editing the material isn't easy—there is so much of it, and so much of it is personal, that selecting the parts that will convey the most information without invading someone's privacy is a difficult thing to do. But after several months of reading, culling, and organizing, the stack of material is waiting by my desk.

For those of you unfamiliar with the material, I will go over the basic premises here: there are seven *roles in essence*, the thing you will be from the beginning of your lives to the end. These roles are: Slaves (about 25 percent of the population), Artisans (about 21 percent of the population), Warriors (about 18 percent of the population), Scholars (about 14 percent of the population), Sages (about 10 percent of the population), Priests (about 8 percent of the population), and Kings (about 4 percent of the population). There are five *cycles* on the physical plane: Infant, Baby, Young, Mature, and Old, with seven *levels* within each cycle. It usually takes more than one life to complete a level. For each life, you will choose *overleaves,* selecting one from seven *goals:* Retardation, Rejection, Submission, Stagnation, Acceptance, Growth, and Dominance; one of seven *modes:* Repression, Caution, Perseverance, Observation, Power, Passion, and Aggression (by far the most often encountered mode is Observation, with Caution the next most often encountered); one of seven *attitudes:* Stoic, Skeptic, Cynic, Pragmatist, Idealist, Spiritualist, and Realist. You will, by age three, acquire your *centering* (which is discussed in Chapter 3). By your late teens or early twenties, you will have developed a primary and secondary *chief feature,* the means by which fear controls you. Primary chief feature impacts the goal, secondary chief feature impacts the attitude. They are: Self-deprecation, Self-destruction, Martyrdom, Stubbornness, Greed, Arrogance, and Impatience.

According to Michael, we are all part of a group of essences called an *entity,* consisting of about 1,100 *fragments,* or individual essences, usually of three or four roles in essence in each entity. The entity is composed of *cadences* or groups of (you guessed it) seven fragments, all of the same essence. A cadence is the smallest complete unit Michael recognizes. A group of seven entities is called a *cadre.* All this has to do with *casting,* or where you are in the stack.

During lives you may have *karma* owed or owing from a past life in which you interfered with the life choices of another, or yours were interfered with. This is a major factor in any life, and not everyone has karma to contend with in any particular life. Karma is earned for such things as: murder, unjust imprisonment, abandonment of a help-less fragment, and what Michael calls mind-fuck. Karma is part of the balance of your evolution, and you may avoid it often, but eventually you will choose overleaves that will motivate you to burn the karmic ribbon. Not every life will have karma to deal with; there will be times you choose to reincarnate without karmic debts, usually in order to devote yourself to a specific task or talent.

There are lesser injuries that might be taken care of through *making amends,* which is not so compelling as karma. There are also *monads,* internal and external which are units of experience that are part of your evolution. Less binding but interesting are the *agreements* made between fragments for mutual assistance. These agreements are not crucial, and may be more easily *abdicated* than the more demanding monads and karma.

Most of Michael's vocabulary is explained in the first three books: *Messages from Michael, More Messages from Michael,* and *Michael's People.* If you have trouble locating these titles, write directly to the publisher, Berkley Books, at the address in the front of this book. The publisher is the one who decides when and if a book is reprinted, not its writer, and they will not reprint if they do not know there is a demand for a book.

Speaking of publishing, the newsletter we had started was discontinued when another self-proclaimed Michael channel threatened to sue us for publishing material that disagreed with what he had published. The company pro-ducing the newsletter sensibly refused to do more, and the group voted not to keep on, for my attorney advised us that a court appearance would mean the kind of publicity none of us wanted. We have, however, decided to establish an archive of the material and keep it in two places: the Bay Area in California and Albuquerque, New Mexico. It is possible that the New Mexico archives will be available for public review when an acceptable schedule of fees and royalties with the various mediums can be negotiated. I have already sent copies of half the transcripts I have—with personal information edited out. In the next year or so, I will finish supplying them with the material I have on hand, and then group members will do what they can to fill in the gaps.

To answer a question I have often been asked: no, I know of no other legitimate Michael group that is open to outside questions, and I cannot recommend any channels other than the ones who have worked with this group over the last eighteen years. Neither I nor the mediums of the group have endorsed any other channel. According to what Michael has told us, they have only two study groups in the United States: this one and one other, which is far more closed than ours. They also have a study group in Eastern Europe, and at one time had one in Russia, but as far as we know, that group has not been active for more than ten years.

That does not mean that there are no other mid-causal teachers like Michael—there are many of them. But if a medium purports to be channeling Michael, or anyone else, for that matter, let me urge you to approach with skepticism. My usual test when encountering such claims has been to ask for my overleaves. So far, none of those who have claimed to be channeling Michael have been able to give them accurately. There are other things to be wary of in any channeling claims: in all my years of being in the Michael group, I have never known Michael to predict anything, no matter how diligently group members tried to get them to. I have also never known Michael to tell anyone what to do, since, according to them, the whole purpose of life here is choice. If you find a medium whose teacher does either of those things, it isn't the Michael we know on the line. Let me also encourage you to avoid overleaves-shopping, that is, looking around for a medium who will tell you what you want to hear. There are very few Old Priests and Old Kings about, and only one of each was ever, when Young, Plato or Cleopatra. If it sounds too wonderful to believe, don't.

This book is almost all Michael, whose words appear in this typeface. Aside from removing personal material and arranging the order in which it occurs, I have done nothing to alter or edit the transcripts: this is Michael as straight as I can present them.

Chelsea Quinn Yarbro
Berkeley, California
November 1994

CHAPTER 1

The Care and Feeding of Planet Earth

The physical plane is distinguished by its description. It is physical. It has dimensions calculated physically, and it is described in physical parameters you designate "laws", although there is no legal consequence for attempting to ignore gravity or misrepresenting the apparent phases of the moon, at least not in your culture this century. We call these world truths, not laws. And there are many things that are possible only in physical manifestations, which is one of the "purposes" of reincarnation: that is, to experience the validity of physicality on the physical plane.

There are a number of ways that this is done, such as the acquisition of senses and a nervous system to have them with. The immediacy of physicality puts the information of the senses foremost in experience, which is modified by acculturation and "education" and the cumulative events of the life being led and all previous lives.

There is no way you can escape scathing. Scathing is endemic to the physical plane, the very nature of possessing a body. Life could not be lived without scathing. It is impossible. The process of birth itself, for the human being being born, is scathing. Scathing is a world truth throughout the physical plane, for only on the physical plane, with a body, can you be truly scathed. There are a great many experiences that can only be had while incarnate in a body, and scathing is one of the most persistent, and one that may be modified and "explained" by culture, but cannot be denied without true "insanity". The purpose of a body is to experience its validity, and because most fragments "trust" pain more than joy, scathing is often the means of "getting the message", as well as a world truth. This is a primary lesson of this and all lives. A fragment may try to deny or escape scathing, but that can lead to serious emotional difficulties and severe mental illness, which is, of course, scathing. That is not to say that scathing "ought" to be welcomed. We did not say that and we did not imply it. How you react to the scathing—as well as anything else—as we have said before but will repeat, is a matter of choice. You may not wish to define scathing as scathing, but the nature of experience, as many fragments do. You may acknowledge the scathing, you may deny it, you may label it philosophically or psychologically, you may demand revenge for it, you may rise above it, you may withdraw from the source of the scathing, you may direct your energies from it, you may become obsessed with it, you may sublimate it, you may be convinced by chief feature that the scathing requires more of you, you may take it out on yourself and/or others, you may embrace it, and so forth, within the entire scope of human experience. And, of course, there is no "need" for consistency in your reaction, which is apt to change over time, as well as in the event itself. There are as many ways to choose in response to scathing as there are fragments on the planet.

There is also the "reality" that the physical plane itself is scathed by its very nature. Mountain ranges are pushed up, seas drain and rise, and continents sink. Star systems are born, evolve, and collapse, as do galaxies. From time to time the physical plane itself collapses "in" on itself and another "Big Bang" occurs, with the "reversal of polarity" from the "matter" universe to the "anti-matter" universe, a "switch," incidentally, that has taken place more times than there are stars you can count with the most powerful telescope. This is part of the nature of evolution, and is neither a "good" nor a "bad" thing. It is merely the nature of the physical plane, and valid as such. There are no "judgments" passed in regard to these things. However, many actions undertaken by independently mobile, environmentally manipulating fragments, such as your species is, increase the scathing of the physical plane in a manner that is not allied with the process of evolution, and the scathing of these actions generally serves not only to disrupt some of the evolutionary process of your planet, but to bring increased scathing to your species as well. There is no "error" in this, it is only the expression of the nature of your species at this stage of evolution on the physical plane.

Nonpersonal agenda sessions happen about four times a year, and the understanding is that only questions not relating to personal issues will be asked. Some of the nonpersonal agenda sessions have covered a wide range of subjects, from epidemiology to possibilities for interstellar flight, from mass psychology to evolutionary biology, from public transit to acoustical engineering, from agriculture to metallurgy.

In 1975, Michael responded to a question about the very odd weather we had been having that year. Was it just El Niño, or was it something more?

It is important to remember, should you choose to do so, that all weather phenomena fluctuate, that is to say, there are changes that happen over time in regard to weather patterns. Your planet has just entered an approximately fifty-year pattern of unstable weather conditions that will lead to certain alterations in global weather. Those patterns will remain generally in effect for two to three hundred years, at which time another bout of instability will occur. The stresses of the planet itself cause these changes to take place. This has been going on for much longer than your species has existed, and is part of the nature of your planet, as weather is a factor on all planets of the physical plane. You may discover records of other minor shifts in the marketplaces of the world where accounts have been kept for long periods of time. Who was selling what from where indicates a great deal about prevailing weather patterns, which are well-documented if you choose to review the matter. Of course, these changes are part of larger cycles, such as pluvial periods, ice ages, and the like, but we assure you that no matter what the larger cycles are, these lesser cycles continue within them, and, of course, recent advances in technology have already created a destabilization of the atmosphere, so that these fluctuations are apt to be more dramatic than some in the past, and it is not only the question of pollution, but the presence of gases, such as, but not limited to, carbon monoxide and dioxide, in balances not previously encountered. It is important to be aware of volcanic activity in the ocean if the full impact of weather patterns are to be "appreciated," for it is the changes to ocean currents that begin the temperature fluctuations that are the impetus for weather changes. A two-degree change in an ocean current can have dramatic impact on weather across a continent, for the air above the ocean current travels faster and farther than the water beneath it. Volcanic dust in the upper atmosphere can also have a dramatic influence on weather.

The changes we have already discussed will, of course, continue, and more variable conditions throughout the world would not "amaze" us. The physics of the rotation and wobble of your planet accounts for these patterns of change and, of course, the same stresses that pull the air about also influence the oceans and land, but as the air is more "slippery" than liquid or solids, it is subject to faster and more frequent changes. That is not to say that your tectonics are on the same "schedule" as your atmosphere, but they do, of course, have cycles of their own that function independently from "human" intervention or strategy. Much as you might wish to control these forces, the problems involved might well prove insurmountable, as the complexity of the process and its necessity for all life on your planet makes any experimentation very risky. The atmosphere, by definition, is everywhere, and everything in the air has a bearing on it. You cannot isolate any portion of it in any "meaningful" manner. It is the only air you have, and compromising it through trying to "make a better use of it" is hazardous in the extreme. Of course, you may choose to try to "fix" the weather, and try to live with the results. Such things have happened before to other species on other planets, and approximately a third of them actually made their systems work, although we must add that their atmospheres are more dense than your own, and of different chemical and elemental composition.

Weather, by its very nature, is a genuine hazard of the physical plane and a world truth shared by many planets, although the composition of the atmosphere and the size and heat of the planet, of course, significantly influence the manifestation of weather, as do such things as the nature of radiation from the central star or stars, the number and nature of moons, rings and other "captured" material, the age of the system in which the planet is located, and many other similar considerations. Weather happens throughout the physical plane, and every planet-bound species has to find some means to accommodate it or lose its place in the evolutionary line.

When fragments claim they want to control the weather, they mean they want to control the weather in a specific way and a specific region, which is impossible. The weather is a planetary condition, and it cannot be "shoved around" without causing repercussions throughout the system, for the system is not a matter of discrete areas, but an entire, global atmosphere. A farmer in Illinois wants enough water for his crops to flourish, but not so much that they are drowned, and that farmer wants the water at certain times of the year in order to achieve the fullest and highest quality crops possible. But this rain, and its amounts, are born over the oceans, which are fed by rivers and other sources, and the characteristics of the oceans are the results of complicated interactions of currents and eddies in the air, and the farmer in Illinois is not able to change or control this from Illinois, even if there were some way to alter the patterns forming in the Pacific and Atlantic Oceans. Given the nature of your planet, everything that goes into the water also, eventually, goes into the air, which may be significant in regard to various pollutants that are slow to break down, such as certain metallic compounds, fissionable materials, chemicals with corrosive and/or poisonous properties. There is no part of the earth these will not reach as the weather stirs them around.

There have also been a number of major volcanic eruptions in the last several years, many of them in the ocean depths, so that many heavy metals and strong acids are in microparticles, to say nothing of two large mountains worth of pulverized rock floating in the air. In terms of human reactions to this, incidents of allergic responses, especially such things as pulmonary and bronchial distress, and skin conditions as well as alterations in the chemistry of certain plants, which can have long-term influences on the general condition of the species. And while it is true that there is little that you can do to prevent or avert a volcanic eruption, it is also true that many industrial wastes combine with volcanic effluvia in a manner that is harmful to mammals. A close monitoring of sewage in the area of volcanic activity might reveal much of interest, should you, as a species, choose to undertake such a study.

"**T**here have been many volcanic eruptions in history, and some of them have been enough to change global weather patterns for a short time; that much is accurate. Is Michael saying that because of the shifts in levels of carbon dioxide and carbon monoxide, the presence of these microparticles is more dangerous or pervasive than they have been before? Or that it will take longer to get them out of the atmosphere?"

That was part of our intention, yes. Because of deforestation and changes in various agricultural practices, we would have to say that there are now conditions where the levels of carbon dioxide are not at the levels often present on your planet. And because of various technological changes and the presence of machinery, levels of carbon monoxide have also changed from what they were three centuries ago, when the last weather shift—a weaker one than is currently under way, incidentally—took place. This, in concert with the volcanic activity, has brought about a level of atmospheric instability that is reflected in the dangers we have mentioned. With the alterations brought about by technology, the additional volcanic ash and acids and minerals can be regarded as causing a kind of backup in the air that will be present longer than would have been the case in times past. The events in Bhopal, India, "should" reveal the stakes more clearly than many others.

Incidentally, we would not call our answer gloom-and-doom; merely the answer to the question put to us by our student Roderick. We have in the past remarked that there were approximately ten scenarios likely for your planet. Now that nearly twenty years have gone by, we would have to say that the most "disastrous" is no longer as likely as it was then, or certainly not on the scale feared by so many, the choices made by those in world-influencing positions have modified stances that might have resulted in the deliberate rendering of this planet unviable to most forms of life as you know them. That is not to say that the possibility has entirely vanished, for, of course, as long as the method is there, it is within the realm of choice to do the act. Also, we would have to say that the least stressful, most generally pleasant of alternatives has also become less likely, so that of the ten possibilities we perceived when the question was first put to us, we would have to say that there are now nine left. We say nine because in the meantime another possibility has evolved and though it is not as "stringent" as some of the possibilities, it is not so "benign" that we could view it as a replacement for the most flexible of the alternatives. That is not to say that any of these alternatives are set in stone, or that any one of them "must" come about as it now exists as a possibility. We did not say that and we did not imply it. We are only telling you that, given the current vectors at work in your species, there are these nine general directions extant. In time they will change, and as the choices are made, other possibilities will emerge. For there is never only one course available to any fragment extant on the physical plane. There are always choices, even if one of those choices is to exit, and the others to accept conditions the fragment does not wholly "like" or "approve of".

"According to some scientists, there has been a decrease in the earth's magnetic field over the last several decades. Is there a cyclical pattern to changes in the earth's magnetic field? What is the impact of such changes?"

To begin with, we would agree that fluctuations in the magnetic field are indeed "part of the scheme of things". The most obvious effect is one we have already discussed, that is, the shifting of weather patterns. Weather patterns are more likely to fluctuate during times of diminished magnetic polarities and therefore shifts in the magnetic lines of force throughout the world influence the movement of air as well as, for example, the growing of crops. During such times, powerful waves of "industrial" origin can have a much greater impact on their immediate surroundings than during times of high magnetic field strength. Of course, there is a psychological impact not only on your species and the other species of reason, but within all other species as well, all the way down to bacteria and similar "living" things. In fact, we would wish to point out that mutations and shifts in virulency of many bacteria, bacterial agents, and to some degree viruses are more likely to occur at times of decreased magnetic "tension". We would also wish to point out that biological clocks are not as "rigorously" maintained at such times and certain physiological disruptions resulting from that are not uncommon. We would recommend consultation with a competent—and we stress competent—astrologer on the subject of magnetic effects of planetary movements in that they are apt to be stronger in their influence at this time and for the next thirty-five years. The magnetic disturbance will tend to diminish at that time but will undergo "predictable" fluctuations not only at this time and in the future but on, in fact, a "mappable" pattern that can be, to some degree, anticipated and planned for. The additional stress to the environment would tend to make this more emphatic in its impact just as some of the contributory factors in the shift in the ozone layer can be linked to this magnetic disruption as well as to the problems of passing comets. We would recommend that specific instances can be more easily anticipated and addressed in order to achieve a greater understanding of the nature, duration, and mechanism of these shifts. It would not be inappropriate to examine the records of farmers, merchants, and markets of the past to help in delineating other periods of magnetic field fluctuation, should you choose to make a beginning on such a project.

"Would Michael explain these cycles?"

Some of the fluctuation is directly related to the tidal influences described as "astrology", particularly with a number of planets occupying one apparent area of space. While this is significant to some degree, it is only a contributory factor. Shifts within the magnetic field are determined also by the phenomenon known as continental drift, which is directly related to the movement of certain crucial heavy metals in the "plasma" at the core of the earth. As these heavy metals rise and lower within the plasma, which is not uniformly one amalgam, as is currently believed, the dynamic of the field described as gravity also shifts, and with it the patterns of magnetic attraction. Areas where these fields are irregular on a more or less current basis can be seen in such regions as the area called the Bermuda Triangle, or the "Monster Sea" off Japan. There are eighteen of these areas within the earth, and the fluctuation of atmospheric phenomena around them is often indicative to shifts that affect and influence the upper atmosphere. The passage of certain heavy bodies such as comets and similar phenomena can indeed influence the upper atmospheric aspects, and crucial among these is the presence of what is called the "tails" of comets, which do more to influence the upper atmosphere than is currently understood or "believed". Let us therefore point out that knowledge of plasma metallurgy, along with the entire range of weather and upper atmospheric functions, can be related, along with "astrological" influences, to show shifts that are somewhat regular—and we stress somewhat—as well as anticipatable though not in the strictest sense "predictable". The presence of sulfuric acid in the upper atmosphere, such as is left after significant volcanic eruptions, can also play a role in the state of the ozone layer, as well as having impact on the air "we" all breathe. Volcanic activity, incidentally, is generally greater during times of reduced magnetic field activity, and less during the most heightened magnetic field activity.

In 1979, Michael had said: The quality of your life is directly related to the quality of the environment in which you live, in the physical, mental, emotional, spiritual, and perceptive senses. We do not say this trivially. We wish to remind you that when the air is not clean, the rain is not "clean", thus the ground is not "clean", and as a result, those creatures living from the ground are not "clean", and the plants on which they and you live are not "clean". We imply no moral or ethical judgment in the word "clean," incidentally, but only a state of being free of contaminants or chemically uncompromised. Most of you enjoy tasty food, and this is, in fact, Good Work. But the tastiness of the food is related to the quality of the soil that nurtured what you eat, and this, of course, has bearing on nutritional qualities as well as taste. It is not inappropriate to recall the old adage, should you choose to do so, that you are what you eat. While the "truth" of this is literal as well as figurative, it is also subject to social and cultural constraints that "color" the process of validation for all fragments. However, it does not mean that you will become bovine if you eat beef, or flowerlike if you consume plants, or that any diet is in any way more intrinsically desirable than another, but that you will partake of all that your food has partaken of through the process of consumption. And this may result in impacts on your body you do not antici- pate, from such things as allergies to the outbreak of more serious health problems due to the presence of certain modifiers in the food you eat and the water you drink. Your environment is internal as well as external, and there is no way that you can prevent the "outer" world from becoming the "inner" world as well.

────────

"**I**f we are endangering our environment as many fear we are, would Michael please comment on where they perceive the greatest danger to be, in regards to impact on the population in general?"

We perceive the danger in the population itself—its size and continued growth. We have said before but we will reiterate yet again that from our perspective, the single greatest danger confronting this world today is overpopula- tion. Almost all other environmental problems are directly related to the crisis in population. And make no mistake about it, the population of your planet has reached crisis levels. This is not imparted to cause you distress, only to remind you the scope of the problem. With increasing population comes increasing demands on all aspects of what you perceive as daily life. None of the problems confronting the environment that are within your powers to control are more pressing than overpopulation. We cannot emphasize that enough, for although there are many haz- ards confronting your species over which you have no control, in this one regard, the ability to bring the popula- tion growth under control is well within your power, and there are few genuine risks to reducing population by limiting the number of children produced.

Of course, we realize that there are social and cultural pressures that are brought to bear on all fragments, most of which are intended to keep the population increasing, a notion that has gone beyond any reasonable or justifiable limits. We would think that those who wish to serve your species at this time would elect to have two children at the most. Let us repeat that last again: two children at the most. Those willing to have fewer than two, such as one or none, are demonstrating "altruism" of no mean order, and we would have to disagree with anyone who is convinced that such a decision is, in fact, demonstrating "selfishness." In our view, any fragment knowingly producing more than two children is acting in an environmentally irresponsible manner, and displaying considerably more "selfishness" than those electing to bring one or no children into the world at this time. In fact, those who choose to have one or no child at this time we regard as showing genuine altruism. That does not mean that all fragments are not at liberty to choose to act irresponsibly in this or any other regard. All choices are equally valid and have no "right" or "wrong", only consequences. Any fragment is here to choose, and to live with the consequences of that choice. However, since you inquired in regard to our perceptions, we have given them.

———

"Is there anything else that is as crucial to our current state of the world as overpopulation? In regards to the quality of human life?"

In terms of the far-reaching influences throughout the whole of the environment, we would have to say that water is running a close second to overpopulation and deforestation, and is, of course, very much influenced by the demands of overpopulation. Since the quality of water has direct bearing on the health of the environment and everything you eat, as well as what you drink, its condition and cleanliness is extremely important to the quality of human and most other life on the planet. We have already mentioned the hazards of the air, which, in turn, appear in the quality of the water. As long as water is scarce and of questionable purity, the impact on human life will continue to have far-reaching effects. The assumption that water will somehow clean itself when the air is compromised is false and naive. We have said that deforestation has a strong impact on the quality of the air, and that observation is valid. It is also valid that the ramifications of deforestation has much to do with the state of the water, along with the levels of carbon monoxide and carbon dioxide. And, as the latter is a component of plant respiration, shifts in the levels of availability of this will have a bearing on the general recovery of water everywhere.

We are aware that the task of caring for a planet can appear overwhelming, and that much of what is recommended is stopgap at best. Recycling may be a minor thing for each fragment, but it does have some cumulative impact. Industrial cleanup is also a minor thing on a single-case basis, but without it, the situation would be far more critical than it has become. We would have to say that all of the actions alone will not, in fact, eliminate the environmental "problems" if population is not reduced. That does not mean such choices as recycling, finding nonpolluting fuels, reforestation, and other measures are futile and not worth pursuing, for this is not valid, and should you choose to undertake to plant trees, lobby to save the rain forests, or for more stringent regulation of toxic materials, there is much to be achieved through these measures. But again, we wish to point out that all the mentioned measures are not likely to achieve much until and unless your species chooses to reduce the birth rate everywhere, and by means other than oppression, chronic epidemic states, and war, which has been the "preferred" method in the past for reducing population, but are no longer as "successful" as they once were.

In the meantime, such measures as can be undertaken to reduce the impact of so high a population, such as the more efficient use of resources. This is not as easily accomplished as might be supposed, for in many instances, social and cultural expectations are such that it is not possible for any fragment to readily accept the notion that such measures are "necessary" or "correct". Many aspects of social position are revealed in what one may legitimately "waste", and as such, it is often perceived as a terrible imposition for a fragment to have to "pay attention" to using other methods of disposing of materials. There are a few options that would not make such social impositions on fragments. For example, we have said in the past that we find the use of petroleum for automotive fuel an extravagance when methane is much more readily available, could be cheaply produced with far fewer contaminants released into the atmosphere. It would also allow cities to turn a profit from waste disposal, and as many of the complaints about shifts in fuel supplies are regarded as too expensive, we are surprised that this one source is generally ignored. Also, it requires no major alteration of existing engine designs to accommodate methane fuels.

There are other "habits" that are less easily accounted for: we are "surprised" that the controlling of crop pests continues to be a method of "controlled" poisoning. From our point of view, this is a dangerous methodology for foodstuffs, in that it presupposes that a little bit of poison will not be harmful to the animals—which include your species—who consume it in food. Demonstrably this is not the case, and while current poisons rarely have the documented impact of DDT, they do build up in the system in such a way that the body becomes weakened in a variety of small ways, each "insignificant" on its own, but packing a cumulative genetic "punch" that might well have serious repercussions over time; these weaknesses might well be passed on to children, with severe results in two or three generations, with some of the same impact as the Romans of two thousand years ago reaped as the result of cooking in lead vessels.

Let us also remark here that the use of fissionable material that cannot be made less hazardous by its use as a source of power is extremely short-sighted, particularly when the exhausted fuel will remain deadly for thousands of years. We can think of no place on earth that has remained wholly stable for five thousand, let alone ten thousand years. What seismological influences have not done, political and military ones have. The truth of this is already apparent. As medical statistics will undoubtedly support, rates of the collagen disease you call cancer in those born after the military use of fissionables as compared to those born before, the introduction into the environment of radioactivity in highly potent forms can be seen to have a damaging effect on the population. It is not the fault of the radioactivity that this is so, for it is functioning the way in which it functions in accordance with the physical "laws" of the physical plane. The responsibility rests with those who chose to take the risk of using fissionable weapons, and who continued to test them in so-called peacetime. The damage done to the populations of countries involved in such tests are, in fact, cumulatively more disastrous than what the "enemy" has done.

Also, we perceive, in the general inability of cultures around the world to deal with the whole matter of garbage and similar waste, a lack of appreciation of the nature of garbage and its requirements. Garbage is the result of physicality. All the physical plane creates it in one form or another. Your planet would have some garbage with or without human activity, as all the physical plane does. There is no avoiding that truth while on the physical plane. Even ensouled fragments who are incapable of manipulating their environments have garbage to contend with, as do all creatures of nonreason, the manifestations of hive souls. As long as there is matter there will be garbage. There are those who would prefer to ignore the issue because garbage is "nasty". Let us assure you that garbage is truly appropriate to the physical plane and is not to be despised for being waste. It would not be amiss for those fragments eager to improve the general living conditions on the planet to learn to understand garbage in order to turn it to the advantage of the planet—which we assure you is possible—rather than to its disadvantage.

"**W**hat about space debris? Things we have put into orbit are increasing and are becoming more difficult to deal with."

It may be of use to remind all those involved that given the difficulty of "house calls" on the current condition, it might be "best" to anticipate and plan for as many hazards as possible rather than hope that the occasion for repair will never arise. In other words, you may wish to choose to approach from a position that a "plan B" is advisable, for it may prove more persuasive than reciting a list of horrors and dangers of outer space. Horrors and dangers are too ill-defined and too "frightening" to have the necessary validity to bring about the change in attitude that would establish a policy that would be of use in this context at this time. Such things as solar flares, comet tails, meteorites, and other frequent astronomical "clutter" could easily come into the picture [another example of Michael-wit] and given the fairly frequent occurrence of these events, a system of preparation to deal with them would seem a "reasonable" course of action.

There are other aspects to having such material overhead, and though falling is not the most immediate risk we perceive here, we would think that some design factor that would allow the space device to break up or be broken up in case of orbit decay might not be wholly amiss. Another aspect to consider in regard to these objects is what to do with them when they are worn out. We would think it might be counterproductive to have a large number of burned-out metal to deal with when new machines are launched to "take up the slack". It is also not beyond imagination that some of these machines could be pirated, that is, physically or electronically taken over by those not originally in charge of them, and their purpose diverted from the intended task to something less welcome. That is not to say all weather satellites are potential "rouge" machines, but that safeguards may be in order to keep the functions "on track".

"**W**ill Michael differentiate between those hazards of the physical plane we can do something about, and those we cannot?"

Those matters of the physical plane that you cannot control or affect might be described as follows: the disposition of the oceans, including currents and tides; its gaseous equivalent, weather; atmospheric fluctuations including to some degree, the hole in the ozone, which has cycles just as your weather patterns do; tectonics and related phenomena such as volcanic activity, earthquakes, landslips, tsunami, as well as all impacts from these activities, such as floes of volcanic ash; arid and wet, hot and cold cycles; the movements of glaciers and icebergs; the presence of life on the planet, from paramecia and bacteria to your species; the percentage of "space dust" impacting the planet; astronomical conditions, such as but not limited to passing through the tail of a comet with its attendant minerals and other debris, or the impact of a meteor; the activity of the sun such as sunspots and solar flares; suns and systems going nova. Incidentally, in this regard, it is not impossible that within the next one hundred fifty years your planet might well face impact from a large meteor currently moving on a line of convergence with you, convergence factored with gravitational influences, of course. We would think that some scientists are aware of this hazard and have not yet hit upon some means of dealing with it.

As to what you can influence: all forms of technology, from the lever and the wheel to the most sophisticated computer; sociocultural roles and organization; communications, from language to travel to commerce to information access; the number of your species on the planet and the conditions in which all of you live; within weather limits, the availability and quality of foodstuffs; the general state of the air and the ocean insofar as your activities impact them; the identification and treatment of diseases and other bodily conditions. Incidentally, we do not consider a broken bone a disease or a matter of poor health; it is merely something in need of repair: we do consider some form of mental "illness" diseases, but not all. Incidentally, we perceive within your western culture a tendency to label compulsions and obsessions diseases and/or addictions, which is inaccurate and misleading. For us, disease not only compromises the physicochemical integrity of the body, negatively affects all the body's "maintenance" systems. An addiction is a condition of physical necessity—for example, all mammals and a great many other forms of life on your planet are addicted to oxygen. To continue our list: the forms, structures, and "rules" of families, society, and culture; the manifestations of what you on the physical plane call the arts; the husbandry of flora and fauna; the creation of abstracts, such as advanced mathematics, aesthetics, philosophy, religion, law, politics, science, responsibility, obligation, decadence, perversity, social strata, and the like. The response to the exigencies of the physical plane. All the ramifications of choice including dharma and karma.

"Is there anything we might be able to do about such an event as discussed? Will Michael say more about this possible impact with a meteor?"

A renewed interest in space exploration would be a good place to begin, should you choose to undertake such a task. Then there are a number of options available to you, such as but not limited to blowing the meteor up before it comes too close—and by too close, we would suggest that the orbit of Mars is the nearest a body of that size would come without causing some problems for this planet, for it is accompanied by a "cloud" of "dust" that moves well in advance of the body itself, and, of course, behind it. It might also be possible to intercept the meteor farther out and deflect it into the pull of Saturn or Jupiter, where it would provide another moon for one or the other of them. It might also be possible to create space stations or planet settlements that would permit you to evacuate a significant percentage of the population of earth before the impact of such a body. Of course, this final possibility would tend to lead to the greatest loss of life for those remaining behind, including your fellow-ensouled fragments, the cetaceans. Undoubtedly, there are a number of other solutions to be explored if the undertaking is chosen. There is also the very distant binary of your sun, which has only recently begun to swing back toward Sol on a long, elliptical orbit. It is not apt to have much impact on your planet for several thousand years, but it is out there.

───────

"Will Michael comment on the urgency of the things we can change?"

The most pressing problem as we perceive it we have stated many times, but we will reiterate: overpopulation. Your environment is not currently being managed in such a way to make it possible to provide reasonable support for the increasing number of human beings extant upon the planet. We have said that, in our view, any parents with any option whatsoever in the matter might wish to consider the problem of world population before deciding on the size of family to produce. We repeat that any parent having more than two children is acting irresponsibly, and this includes those fragments whose societies allow for a plurality of spouses. In which case, we would recommend one child per spouse as a reasonable number, given the enormous scope of the problem. You may choose to have as many children as you or your society requires, but anything over two per parent imposes a burden on the rest of your species and on your planet. We cannot express it more directly than that.

───────

"Is Michael telling us not to have more than two children, period?"

Or course not. We do not tell any fragment what or how
to choose. We are only telling you how we perceive the
consequences of your choice. You are free to do whatever
you choose to do. The number of children you bring into
the world is as much a choice as any other you make. It
might be well to remember that the vast majority of fragments will be returning to this planet for more lives, and
the condition in which you will find it upon your return has
direct bearing on the choices you make now. While we do
not mean this in a genetic sense, you will be your own
grandchildren, and it is your future you are ensuring by the
choices you make now.

———————

"What about abortion? Wouldn't that cause karma?"

For over ninety percent of fragments, the soul enters the
body at the first breath. A few baby souls enter the body at
the beginning of full-term labor, but you will all agree that
is a trifle late for abortion. There is no karma in ending a
pregnancy before that time. In fact, those who compel
women to have children they do not choose to have are in
more "danger" of karmic consequences than are any
women choosing to abort a fetus for any reason whatsoever. To compel a woman to have a child the woman has
not chosen is a significant interference with her life choices,
which is, of course, the requirement for creating a karmic
ribbon, not unlike the ribbon created by unjust imprisonment or unchosen enslavement. We would also wish to add
that those who value females only for the children they
produce are responding directly to the impact of culture on
chief feature, which, as we have said before, promotes
anything that destroys true intimacy, which is the source
of all essence evolution. To relegate one half of the species
to being reproductive factories bars true intimacy from the
start and leads to fear-laden taboos that define sexual roles
and relationships in the narrowest possible manner and
therefore leads to greater reductions in intimacy.

"**O**kay, overpopulation is the first trouble we can change if we try. What does Michael see as the second?"

The quality of air and water is, we would have to say, the most directly and significantly compromised aspect of life on this planet that results from overpopulation. There is a direct impact on public health—and by that we mean the human species—resulting from the problems of overpopulation and the spread of disease, for, as you are aware, epidemics spread more quickly in densely populated areas than in less populated areas. Also, dense population provides an excellent opportunity for diseases to mutate more quickly and to become more virulent. There are larger issues of a planetary nature having to do with the most basic environment of all—the air. From the presence of carbon dioxide and monoxide as well as hydrocarbon levels in the air to effluvia in the water, these most essential "life supports" are in a precarious state. After that, the whole range and varieties of garbage become significant.

"**I**s there anything we can do about it? If we choose to do so?"

We would wish to remind you that with proper handling, today's garbage is tomorrow's "mulch". Much of what is now regarded as "useless" waste can, in fact, be reprocessed into materials useful to the environment. However, this demands most societies adjust their structure to include the reprocessing of garbage as a necessary and laudable effort, with rewards for pursuing the problem. It is the old question of who is more important—the garbageman or the physicist. The answer, of course, is that they are equally important, and represent two ends of the equation needed to bring about more progress in this endeavor.

"**W**hat about those nine possible futures Michael mentioned back in the seventies? Surely there have been some changes?"

It is no longer very likely that you will annihilate yourselves and your world in catastrophic nuclear war, which would have been the worst-case scenario fifteen years ago. While nuclear wars of a "brushfire" nature are not impossible, and their impact potentially devastating, we would agree that an all-out destruction caused by such a "conflict" is no longer a true probability. You have also missed an opportunity that presented itself about twenty years ago that would have made it possible to launch a program designed to promote and reward birth control on an international basis. That, in turn, would have made for an improved potential for peoples everywhere, which was the most favorable scenario perceived by us fifteen years ago. That is not to say that measures taken now would be "useless", but the problem is vaster and the general attitudes regarding fertility have become markedly more "conservative" in the intervening years. In this respect, we would have to say that what the attitude seeks to conserve is male superiority, not the earth or your species or some genuine cultural "truth", for those dedicated to conserving the earth are aware of the necessity of population control, no matter how unpopular the notion may be. However, in regard to the level of improvement possible in the "short run" with population limitation, there is a factor that colors the potentials: deforestation has been unchecked long enough that it now is presenting a scenario that was not as likely twenty years ago as it has become in the last decade—and while not as catastrophic as nuclear war, is potentially just as destructive, which has created a new not-quite-worst-possible scenario for your planet.

That is not to say that these scenarios are necessarily the ones that "must" be confronted. All is chosen, we assure you, and however you and those of your species decide to deal with these issues, there is nothing "right" or "wrong" in the choice. As choices are made, other scenarios will devolve from them, and the hazards will change as a result of choices made. It is the nature of the physical plane to change constantly, and all species within it, ensouled and otherwise, adapt through evolutionary or technological change or they become extinct. We remind all here gathered that doing nothing is as much a choice as doing something. No matter what happens, it will be the result of choice, as are all things.

━━━━━━

"About the general social attitude toward fertility becoming more conservative recently, that the conserving is of male superiority. Could Michael elaborate on that, please?"

The nature of society for your species, with two exceptions, has been dominated and shaped by males. Those advocating religious reasons for not limiting fertility are overwhelmingly male and seeking to preserve their long-held "privileges" in regard to procreation. Part of the reason for this is the physiologically greater strength of males, which gave them the advantage in any direct combat, and the nature of testosterone acting in the biochemistry of males. But if that were the sole factor, there would be no "social progress" possible, and the subjugation of females would be simply and directly sexual, not the pervasive cultural condition it tends to be. The more persuasive factor was the result of the long pregnancies that required females in early societies be protected while pregnant, and that the young be protected through the long childhood of your species, which early in your species development required an organized effort to ensure offspring were born and raised. When it comes to the first three years of life, human infants are essentially pouchless marsupials, in that the infants are not able to fend for themselves in any "survivalist" way, and require constant care to bring them to a point where they can function as individual fragments. As societies developed, the model for humanity evolved around the male. Females, as the name implies, suggested that those of the female gender were an imperfect version of the male model. Many languages indicate the females by modifying the word for male, such as happens in man, woman; don, doña. There is also a linguistic predisposition in several cultures to have the word for adult female be the same or nearly the same word as married female. This has resulted in a lopsided cultural development that has "plagued" your species from the start and will probably not be significantly changed until the average soul age on your planet is second or third level mature. At the moment, it is fifth level Young. Incidentally, in species with three or more sexes, the gender issues tends to be more diffuse. By having just the two, a great deal of attention is brought to bear on the differences between males and females, and judgments made based upon this "dichotomy".

━━━━━━

"Would Michael elaborate on that?"

This need to define all activities by gender definition is largely the result of having just two, so that the differences—which we assure you are minor at best—become focal to social and cultural expectations. In certain cultures it is a terrible thing for men and women to speak to each other if the woman is menstruating. This is not a sensible precaution. The man cannot "catch" menstruation from her. Speech is in no way related to the menstrual process, and is not "distorted" by it. So the reason for the restriction must be to emphasize the difference between male and female. In this culture, a male is often able to deflect legitimate inquiries from females by saying she is menstruating, or is about to menstruate, something he, the "right" version of a human being, cannot do. This is a way of ensuring the male that he need not pay any attention to anything a female says that he finds unflattering or threatening. We would have to say that there is no "logical" reason, bio- or otherwise, for such condemnation. Therefore, it is a cultural wedge of definition to alienate the sexes. We stress the male taboos because in all but two cultures, the males have defined the society, and have done so to their own benefit.

We would also wish to point out that while some very ancient cultural forms still exist in parts of the world, the cultural "rules" established for sexual conduct have long since been rendered unnecessary by the social changes wrought by technology and progress. And by technology, we mean everything since the lever. A fulcrum works as well for females as males, the block and tackle has no adjustment in function determined by the sex of the person using it. There is no reason for physics to change its "laws" to accommodate the gender or culture of the fragment employing its tenets. Time is a convenient method for dividing up the rotation of the planet in an agreed-upon manner, and it does not alter according to the gender of the human looking at a clock. Incidentally, time, conceptually, and by extension, mathematics, are female inventions; females in early human society needing to be more aware of the passage of specific units of planetary rotation than males, and in early human society females were responsible for specific items, which led to counting.

As long as these cultural paradigms exist, reinforcing the assumption that the proper role for a person to hold is a male one, there will continue to be sociological forms that will "compel" females to "earn" their rights to personhood by giving birth to males. Which, of course, contributes to the sociological demands to have offspring, as many male offspring as possible. We would think that it would be a useful study to learn what percentage of females throughout the world have felt they have had a significant improvement in "status" upon giving birth to a male child.

Incidentally, we would have to say that discussing population problems without discussing birth control and abortion is an exercise in futility. Of course, the strongest forces of culturation—organized religion—oppose such changes, for giving women the power of such decisions without social coercion would tend to undermine the authority of cultural patterns—organized religion. For most power-structures, those holding position in the power-structure fear nothing so much as the reduction of power, and would prefer to see the world "go to hell"—a fitting punishment for challenging the power-structure—than to reassess the role of the power-structure in the world.

We do not mean that all religion is destructive. We did not say that and we did not imply it. We do wish to observe, however, that most major religious organizations have become entrenched in the process of maintianing their influence and have ceased to examine either their own motives or the results of their demands. And in terms of potential major conflict among human societies at this time, we would think that religious idealism represents the single greatest social threat to world survival of any of the forces at work at this time.

◻━━━━━━◻

"Does Michael mean the fundamentalist movement in many world religions at this time when they say religious idealism?"

In a larger sense, yes, but we also mean the various exercises offered by religion in place of physical plane actions leading toward improved conditions on the earth. Many religions, while not advocating extremist positions, suggest that improvements and amends may be accomplished metaphorically. This is not Good Work, although many embrace it as such, which they may choose to do without the assumption of "error". For example, if you wish someone well, it is most effective to do so directly—by speech, letter, contemplation, or similar direct contact—instead of asking some extraterrestrial force—such as gods, angels, and the other disguises promoted to represent essence—to do it for you. And we would think that for most fragments serving one day a month in a public health clinic is a more effective way to express love of fellow humans than all the expensive luncheons to fund public programs; not that both do not have their places—just that working directly with people is more "essentially" altruistic than giving money for social prestige. The altruistic giving of blood is, to our perception, a more humanitarian exercise than protesting political decisions without any workable access to those seeking alleviation of the suffering. That is not to say all protest is without benefit. We did not say that and we did not imply it. We do, however, understand such actions in a less altruistic light than direct personal action undertaken for the specific purpose of assisting in the ending of suffering, which blood donation certainly facilitates.

Those fragments with life tasks related to political actions can be most usefully accomplished through political organizations. There is no doubt about this, and in a predominantly Young soul world, political action is at its evolutionary height. For Young souls it is in appropriate exercise in evolution. But for those fragments whose life-tasks lie elsewhere, political involvement often does little more than diffuse the focus of the task. All fragments are, of course, entitled to address their life tasks in any way they choose, just as they may choose not to address their life tasks at all, but many fragments, given the prevailing nature of Young-soul societies, will be "persuaded" to approach problems in a political manner, whether it is appropriate or not. That is not to say that political action is invalid in our perception. But political action is often selected as the means to address an issue because it provides like-minded support instead of tackling the matter in a more direct, less reinforced manner. We have said before but we will repeat: politics, by its very nature, creates false alliances, false victories, and false defeats, although it is the means by which Young soul societies advance. Also, we would wish to remind all here present that the purpose of politics is, by definition, compromise, and those seeking a solution without compromise will inevitably be disappointed with the political process.

Let us therefore recommend that the goal desired in any undertaking be understood in the context of its achievement. Where a consensus is desired, the political process is probably the most useful in a representational system. Where results other than consensus are desired, then the political process is probably not the most useful one to use. In terms of environmental issues, for example, clean air is not something that can be modified to the demands of different political-geographical regions. Air is worldwide and the same everywhere. The volcanic ash from South Pacific eruptions often spreads as far as Europe and America. The same is true of less "natural" pollutants. Adjusting demands for air restoration to the convenience of any particular country or other political unit is folly, for it presupposes only those in that region will breathe the air, which is demonstrably inaccurate. The same is true of standards for water, which is present everywhere in the world. The matter of such things as forestation is also part of the quality of air, though less-readily recognized as such because of the marketability of trees in a number of ways. That trees have benefits beyond the wood they provide is often overlooked in the sharp debates between those in the forest-clearing, wood-cutting industries and those concerned with the uses living trees may be put to.

The care of forests and seaweed beds is of tremendous importance to the preservation of many species on earth, your own included. The reasonable, longtime harvesting of kelp and wood is not an impossible achievement, but we would have to point out that the nature of profiting from these markets will require certain adjustments if the forests are to survive in any useful amount. This is something that "must" be established in the next generation, or the balance of oxygen-giving trees and oxygen-using humans may well become too severely unbalanced to be reparable for centuries to come. We would think that neglecting the trees would have far-reaching consequences. And when we say trees, we do not mean just the rain forest, but all forests, everywhere in the world.

"How does Michael see the international movement to plant trees?"

We perceive much use in such an effort, especially carried on in regions that were once forested and now are not, which includes large parts of Europe and the Near East as well as Latin America and Asia. In North America, the debate about the matter has alerted many to the scope of the problem. We also would have to say that most urban settings are not apt to lend themselves to such efforts on any large scale. That does not mean it isn't useful to plant a tree or two in a yard or in a park. All trees are useful, and many are decorative, which makes them doubly attractive. We do not see any "virtue" in planting trees without consideration of esthetics. In choosing a tree to plant, one that is adapted to the regional climate is a wise beginning, and selecting a tree that has a quality of beauty can do much to ensuring its longevity, for a tree is more apt to be "protected" if it is perceived as beautiful than if it is not.

Short of cutting population, concerted tree-planting and tree-gardening is one of the most useful things your species can do to help maintain the earth, for this benefits air and water as well as providing many secondary benefits, such as but not limited to additional foodstuffs, medicinal advantages, paper, shade, and aesthetic satisfaction. As we have intimated, there are many trees as well as other plants with medicinal properties that are worth cultivating for just those attributes. That does not mean any fragment is "required" to plant trees, but if a fragment wants to do something to aid the worldwide environment without embarking on political solutions, planting trees is a beneficial activity, and not so time-consuming or expensive to make it an unrealistic project for a great many fragments.

───────

"What about houseplants? Are they useful?"

On a small scale, certainly they are. A few houseplants are sizeable enough to qualify as trees, and they can do much to help keep the immediate environment "cleaner" as well as adding to the personal benefits brought about by the presence of living things. Also, there are "uses" for many houseplants, such as culinary and medicinal. Incidentally, for many children, the opportunity to grow a plant of their own is a good means of showing the benefits of responsible actions—you water the plant, it grows. You don't water it, it dies—without making an ordeal of the "lesson".

―――――

"What about pets? How does Michael view pets?"

All independently mobile ensouled species on the physical plane have pets of one sort or another. It is one of the behaviors that characterize all independently mobile ensouled species. Your planet, being toward the edge of the galaxy, has a greater variety of life forms to turn to that purpose, and there is great evolutionary benefit for both you as fragments, and the hive souls you interact with. We have said before but we will repeat, many species of animals would not be able to interrelate without the "human interface" you provide. For example, in their "natural" states, dogs and cats do not get along well. And there are those living as pets that still do not, though a great many do. The tradition of a goat in a horse stable is purely a human notion, not one carried over from "the wild". The responsiveness of various species to humans shows the degree to which the basic characteristics of the pet species may be adapted to human expectations. In this regard, cattle and dogs show the greatest impact, fowl and cats the least. This is in large part because herd or pack animals such as canines and bovines are already "hard-wired" to cooperate with "the leader", whereas felines, being for the most part solitary hunters, have no "hard-wiring" for cooperation, and fowl, having evolved from very ancient forms, retain a portion of the old dinosaur "echoes" more than most species do of their earlier forms. If caring for animals aids any human in a greater understanding of the true nature of the physical plane, it is Good Work to keep such animals about. If the purpose of having the animal is to promote a feeling of "human superiority" in the human fragment, the work is not an error, but it is no longer Good Work as we perceive it. Incidentally, for us, the maintaining of agricultural animals is as much a keeping of pets as is having a whippet in the house.

━━━━━

"What about the contention that it is improper to eat meat? Or poultry? Or fish?"

Dietary taboos have more to do with social and cultural expectations than any "larger" validity, including the assumption that any sort of food is more "honorable" than any other sort of food. Your species, being capable scavengers, is designed to eat almost anything it can catch, steal, or raise; if this were not the case, you would not have been able to evolve to a state where ensoulment became possible, for ensoulment "requires" certain survival parameters as well as physiological development allowing for social interactions in independently mobile fragments. There is no "moral failure" in eating meat, just as there is no "moral success" in eating only vegetables or fruits. Dietary conventions of all sorts reflect more of cultural values than spiritual ones. Various ethnic regions have evolved to certain diets, and the genetic nature of those coming from the regions in question will be more apt to digest foods from their ethnic regions than many others. That is not to say physiobiology is destiny. That is not the case, as the proliferation of international restaurants indicates. And many fragments have considerably mixed ethnicity in their genetic makeup, and attempting to find the "right" mix to accommodate all the various ethnic regions in a daily diet would probably prove more exasperating than useful, and provide little "improvement" for most fragments.

Proto-humans, shortly before ensoulment occurred, learned to follow leopards, bears, and other solitary predators, for the purpose of taking any left-over prey the predator might leave behind. Leopards, for example, often leave kills far up in the branches of trees and proto-humans were able to climb up and claim the kill for their own. Bears and leopards are far better hunters than human beings have been until the invention of gunpowder, and proto-humans were skilled and patient trackers and scavengers. In that way, the amount of protein increased markedly in the diet, and made it possible for the proto-humans to develop the necessary capacities for ensoulment to occur. This is not the preferred "image" of proto-humans, but it is far more accurate than the picture of a "Tarzan" swinging through the jungle catching lions single-handed and killing elephants with a spear and a knife. Incidentally, early humans most successfully lived near the water. Fish was a good source of food, and the water offered protection from many predators. It also aided in the evolution of the human upright posture and the distinctive lack of pelt that is characteristic of mammals of an aquatic or semiaquatic adaptation.

In regard to meat, however, pork and other hog parts tend to be the most easily assimilated meat for all humans. This is in part because the pig species has a strong similarity to the human "family" in terms of protein and diet, but is not so much like humans as to run into the "species barrier" present in many fragments, both culturally and biologically. Let us explicate: for those whose ethnic origins are in temperate climates, for example, the consumption of "lesser" primates, such as monkeys, has not developed in the diet because monkeys and apes are most often not found "naturally" in temperate or arctic climates. This is not true for many peoples living in tropical or subtropical regions of the earth, although in many places, the "species barrier" functions as a taboo, in that it is considered "incorrect" to eat anything that looks too much like humans. That does not mean that is it more "correct" to eat pork than any other form of animal protein, merely that it has certain "advantages" over other kinds of meat. You may, of course, eat anything you choose to.

Pork has another advantage in that it is the most "economical" meat source, in that in terms of what it costs to feed a pig, against the amount of "useable" meat and other

parts, the pig provides the best "rate of exchange". Early
cities where the major industry was making beer fed their
pigs on the spent grain, which improved the quality of
the pork and eliminated a major source of "garbage" at the
same time. You may regard that as an early example of
agricultural recycling, should you choose to do so.

———

"Is there any spiritual reason not to eat meat?"

Only if you choose to perceive one for yourself, and it is
not the imposition of someone else's choice, such as most
religiously based food restrictions are, although that is a
matter of choice, not of any greater validity. You may also
decide it is more "spiritual" to eat only what human beings
are made of—animal protein—and have that decision be
equally valid, and equally demanding on the body. It is true
that without meat or poultry in the diet, the available
energy level is generally reduced, and so a more "thought-
ful" approach to life may result because the demands of
strenuous physical activities are greater on a body that
does not have some form of animal protein—meat, poultry,
fish, and to a lesser degree, eggs—to draw upon to sustain
the activity. If this promotes an increased awareness of the
"thought" process, it may—and we stress may—have some
benefits, if it is in accord with the overleaves. We have
pointed out many times that it is not a question of being
more "spiritual". By the nature of being ensouled fragments, everything in life is spiritual, from meditation to
bowel movements. There is no reason to fear that your
activities lack "spirituality". The most difficult lesson for
all fragments is the lesson of being on the physical plane.
For ensouled species, spirit is easy. Bodies are difficult.

We would also wish to point out that in the matter of
selecting food, it is of use to consider the question of
enjoyment as a factor in nutrition. That is not a trivial
consideration, let us assure you at once. Enjoyment is a
part of nourishment as well as the balance of dietary

elements. A meal is not merely consumed to feed the organism, it is an occasion for communication and mammalian "togetherness"—the more enjoyable the food, the more convivial the meal is apt to be. To limit a diet to only the "healthy" things without an attempt at savor, taste, and gratification of the senses is to miss a good portion of validating the senses, which can only be done on the physical plane. Such validation is Good Work, for it brings to bear the access to self-intimacy.

"Would Michael care to elaborate on that?"

A significant "thrust" of lessons to be had on the physical plane comes through the validation of the senses. Of course, the senses are experienced only on the physical plane, and in that senses exist as discrete "knowable" characteristics when fragments are in the body. Therefore we would think it obvious that understanding the senses as discrete qualities of "human" life is, in fact, part of recognizing and validating the experience of and lessons from the physical plane. Since "feedback" as such is more important to those on Expression Polarity [Sages and Artisans], dedication to sensual recognition is often crucial to validating the totality of the life task, and it would not be inappropriate for those on the expression polarity to knowledgeably dedicate themselves to sensual assessment on a "regular" basis. That is not to say that all fragments cannot benefit from such a project and such a review. We did not say that and we did not imply it. All those on the physical plane seek validation of their experiences through the senses, as being a manifestation of independently mobile creatures of reason.

We have said before but we will reiterate: the natural "primate" tendency to trust pain more than joy is part and parcel of the non-validation of the senses and limits the experience available to essence, often in such a way that the true personality is only willing to experience negative sensual impact as valid. Positive sensual impact is relegated to areas of spirituality disassociated from the body and all its less-than-pristine functions. Many cases of sexual dysfunction, in fact, arise from the deeply held belief that nothing the body does can be "that good", and so positive experience must be regarded as intrusive and therefore negative.

Many religious teachings, as a means of gaining control of the fragment, make strict demands in regard to the senses. Fragments are instructed that the senses must be experienced in a certain way, at a certain time, and result in certain states of mind, or the fragment has erred; this perceived "failure" leads many fragments to condemn themselves for no cogent reason beyond the inability to subjugate themselves to a code of behavior that is inappropriate to their experiences.

Totality of the senses can, of course, contribute significantly to true intimacy, just as denial of sensual experience can lead to chief feature enhancement. Chief feature, being the source of fear, finds pain a useful tool in its manipulation of fragments. That is not to say that pain is invalid, but that it is only part of a very wide spectrum available to and instructive of the process of each and every life. Without the recognition and validation of such perceptions, many fragments "lose touch" with the world around them, and because of that "state", are unable to "relate" to the larger world in any "meaningful" way. In other words, if the senses are not trustworthy, the world around you is not wholly valid, and may be regarded with the "cavalier" attitude of any illusion. Not that recognizing and validating the senses will necessarily make a fragment more concerned for the world at large, for that is a matter of choice, but the chance of increased awareness of the state of the world, once the senses are recognized and validated as trustworthy, is more apt to occur in a nondogmatic manner as the "reports" of the senses are "reviewed".

Incidentally, there is no "error" in the senses. Each fragment perceives senses in the manner that is appropriate to the fragment. This is part of experiential differentiation, not a matter of "skill" or "virtue". If there were such a "right" way to sense, everyone would like the same perfume or the same sauce for fish. Each fragment chooses what certain sensory stimuli mean to the fragment, and that is the whole of the recognition. Validation is achieved when the fragment accepts the recognition as the fragment's own.

Of course, the senses "resonate" to the roles in essence, and there are seven of them. Slaves resonate to touch, Artisans to balance, Warriors to hearing, Scholars to sight, Sages to taste/smell, Priests to orientation, Kings to relationality. Not all species have precisely the same senses as yours, but the function of each is the same throughout the physical plane. Senses are the means by which the physical plane is experienced and interpreted, and each species is limited by the nature of the senses themselves. As is doubtless apparent, each species has a most prominent sense, one that is the "guiding sense" for all the others. For your species, it is sight. For the cetaceans, the most prominent sense is hearing. There are ensouled species with orientation as the primary sense, and those with balance as their primary sense, and so forth for all seven.

Where an appreciation of the senses exists, the fragment is more likely to be able to make choices that reflect the perception of essence. That is not to say that without an appreciation of the senses such choices are impossible, only that they are more difficult because of lack of "insight" of an "environmental" nature.

———

"**H**ow do the senses and our perception of the world interact? Supposing that they do interact at all."

Certainly they interact. The senses are the key to all physical-plane perceptions. Interpretation of the physical plane is based on how the organism "handles" information. For example, certain vibrations are processed by the human eye as light and color. There are vibrations the eye cannot "see" or process, and these things are therefore "invisible" and must be measured by instruments other than the human eye. The same things may be said about vibrations that impact the auditory nerves at certain levels, which are recognized by humans as sound. Not all vibrations are limited to the range of human hearing, so once again, the task of processing them must be left to other devices, such as other species or machines. There is nothing "wrong" in this. It is the nature of the physical plane to require limits of one sort and another. And the nature of the human nervous system "requires" a limitation on stimulus, otherwise the fragment could not function, being so constantly bombarded with sensations requiring immediate response. Much of the process of infancy is related to teaching the infant to "filter" sensory impact so that the "mind" can function without constant distraction. Some of what is seen as a shortness of attention or concentration is directly linked to lack of training in sensory filtering in the first three years of life.

It is of use to "review" the senses on a "regular"-but-non-ritualistic basis, should you choose to do so. We would think that taking an hour every few days and using it to concentrate the attention on one sense could do much to increase sensory awareness. Devoting an hour to hearing without the additional stimulus of radio, mechanical intrusions of all sorts, and similar "man-made" augmentation is a useful thing for fragments. Sitting quietly in a park may accomplish much if the fragment is willing to "indulge" in it, for the fragment will quickly discover that human beings hear quite well, and, in fact, have become adept at selecting what will be given hearing priorities and what will not. The same can be done with touch. A fragment might choose to spend an hour walking nude through the house, feeling textures on the feet and skin, the movement of air, the patterns of hot and cold that are present in all buildings. The sensation of a wooden seat as compared to a cushion might be explored. The feel of such things as leaves, leather, glass, plastic, and all manner of objects could be assessed. The texture of fabrics may be recognized more perceptively in this exercise, as well as the areas of the skin that are most sensitive to impact. Such an exercise would be most likely to provide insights when the fragment in question feels both safe and supported in such an activity. When exploring any sense but sight—which is predominant to your species—it might be of use to reduce visual impact by wearing dark glasses or a blindfold so that there is less "interference" from sight. There are many ways to accomplish valid sensory review and the methods we have proposed are not to be regarded as the only way, or the "right" way to manage the review, but suggestions as how fragments might go about it, should they choose to do so. That is not to say all fragments must undertake a sensory review, for all such things are a matter of choice. Doing a sensory review will not "make you better", or, for that matter, "make you worse". It will only enhance your understanding of your senses, and the environment in which they, and, of course, you function.

━━━━━━

"**W**hat would Michael recommend as something everyone could do to benefit the environment—other than planting trees and having fewer children?"

There is no one thing, for such choices are many. What we would think would be of use would be to select one or two environmentally improving things to do, and do them regularly. Let us emphasize that—do them regularly. Whether it is recycling, reducing the number and toxicity of household chemicals used, composting, using less polluting fuels, developing water retrieval methods, reducing "litter", planting trees, greenhousing, switching to nontoxic pesticides, reprocessing paint and other "hazardous" materials, developing and using heating and cooling systems with less negative environmental impact, and so forth. Should a fragment regularly recycle, compost, and reduce the use of toxic household chemicals, that would be a major individual contribution to maintaining the planet. If fifty percent of fragments should regularly practice two of these methods for a period of five years, it would make a measurable difference. That is not to say it would compensate for population growth, for it would not, though it would certainly have compensatory "merit". A fragment having three children who practices three of these methods mentioned has not, in fact, accomplished much. In terms of the world, having one fewer child would be a far more useful thing to the environment than greenhousing. Though it would be of use to do as much to minimize the "impact" of the extra child than to have the child and do nothing.

What would seem to be the "easiest" and the one that would show the most immediate "positive results" is the recycling of paper, which could help reduce the rate of deforestation by lessening the "need" for more cut trees. If large corporations were given incentives to recycle all their used paper, it would mean that the recycling industry would become an important component of the economic structure, and that would lead, in turn, to showing the way to recycle more, and more profitably. We would encourage all fragments to make a point of recycling paper, should they choose to do so.

In general, in most societies it is considered a misfortune for fragments to fail to "have a family", assuming that the family is the most necessary component of a society. While we would not dispute this, we would suggest that defining a family by the presence of children alone is unnecessarily dogmatic. There are many other considerations when it comes to defining a valid family, including friendship and every nature of support. We would suggest that those willing to have no children should be regarded as laudable, not sad or reprehensible. We would also think that providing incentives for family limitation, such as tax advantages, preferential rationing, and similar "advantages" could encourage families to "buck" the culture and have one child, or none. Those fragments electing to have few or no children and who practice two of the methods we have already mentioned can make a significant impact in a generation, by which we mean twenty years. And let us remark that without some immediate measures toward population limitation and reduction, the environment a generation from now will be severely compromised. This is not a prediction, for we do not predict. It is a simple mathematical extrapolation, and any fragment capable of the mathematical calculations can reach the same conclusion without our help.

━━━━━

"Michael, it looks as if you're harping on population."

We do not harp. We answer questions asked. You wish to know our assessment and we are providing it as succinctly as possible. Most of the fragments in our little group are aware of the risks inherent in "overloading" the environment, and for that reason, you have questions about them. Your planet is currently experiencing a crisis in population, and so when you ask about those conditions influencing the environment adversely, we cannot avoid discussing the issue of population. It is your questions that continually return us to this matter, for environmental questions must inevitably "factor in" population if the responses are to have any validity at all. We may also refer to the matters of public health that are concomitant with the population levels, if that would persuade you of our lack of intention to "harp". Should you choose to ask about other topics, we will not mention the question of population.

━━━━━

"Population is becoming a hot political issue in many parts of the world. Is this likely to help or make things worse?"

It would depend on what the political approaches are. And we do not regard this or any other issue as a matter of "better" or worse". You have asked about dangers to maintaining the environment. We have given our answer. This being predominantly a Young soul planet, we would think that a political approach is apt to be the most successful, or the least successful, if the political alliances support increasing population. We do see a few encouraging signs in that aspect of your planetary life—the lack of enthusiasm for statements made by many in high religious and political office for prohibiting birth control and abortion throughout the world. We would think that including birth control instruction as part of aid to impoverished countries might allow the fragments in question to choose for themselves. The habit of praising large families is another practice that might be reduced as a means of encouraging a limitation on children, should you choose to limit your numbers.

We do not intend to "cry wolf" or tell you how to make choices, but we do think that a great many fragments have not given the problem and all its manifestations any serious consideration. Not that such consideration is "required", but we think that many times decisions about children are made without any wider reflection then, "do we want one". While that is as valid as any question, it does not address the question of the sort of world the wanted child will live in—to say nothing of those children who are not wanted and are brought into the world with little awaiting them but hostility and lack and disease. If fragments are aware that they are condemning their offspring to suffering, they might be willing to have fewer of them in the hope that they will live in a world that is not so compromised as it may be if current patterns continue. We realize that there are many parts of your planet where such arguments have little validity, but we would think it would be worth the "effort" to be able to bring the numbers of humans down to a more reasonable level.

"**B**ut given the tremendous problem, isn't it kind of useless to reduce family size? What about places like India and Latin America? Shouldn't something be done there first?"

It is not Good Work to displace your responsibilities to others. Each fragment must make the choice for him or herself as to how the fragment will behave, and the choice

belongs to the fragment choosing. To say that others with
more serious population "pressures" have an obligation to
act first is abjuring the responsibility you have for your
choices. That is the stance taken by those who say, "We
can afford to have several children", forgetting that what
they mean by "afford" is that they have sufficient funds to
feed, house, clothe, and educate their children. They do
not mean "afford" in the sense of the species and the
planet, for it is clear that the planet cannot afford so many
people on it. It would be desirable for all countries the
world over to reduce their birthrates if the compromises to
your environment are to be lessened. Infants are most
generally had one at a time and therefore, every female has
the choice to increase the number of her children or not to
decrease the number. In some cultures it is more difficult
to exercise this authority, but as long as the lack of female
autonomy goes unchallenged, the problem will persist. And
we would think that for more reasons than number of
children, it would be useful for females to have autonomy
so that they can make all their life choices for themselves,
without the intervention of cultural ikons that require females to remain a male appendage.

There are, of course, overleaves to influence the choices
made in life and the manner of life led, but we would think
that given the option of deciding for themselves and being
the chattel of others, most fragments, male or female,
would prefer to decide for themselves. What is most unfortunate are those instances when the culture is so restrictive
that fragments are taught from birth that they are incapable
of making decisions for themselves, for this is a crippling
blow to autonomy, which, of course, mitigates the range of
choice available to anyone.

Let us tell you that there is no external "salvation",
there is only what you choose to do. We, and all teachers
like us, do not and cannot intervene on the physical plane,
for we are not of the physical plane. You are the ones who
will preserve or compromise your planet. You are the ones
who will preserve or compromise your species. You are the
ones whose choices will determine which of the futures

you will have. Whatever choice is made, it will be a valid one, neither good nor bad, but having consequences of far-reaching impact, as all such choices do.

———

"**D**oes Michael have any recommendations as to what we might—that's might, not should, Michael—do to help us get through this time?"

Given that all of the physical plane is subject to constant change, we would think that you would choose to be as flexible as possible if you wish to sustain yourselves, although no amount of flexibility will keep your species, or the planet in question, viable "forever". On the physical plane all things eventually become extinct. But that does not mean the process "must" be hurried. The experience of life is unique for every species and fragment within a species. With the variety of life forms on your planet, we would think that efforts to assess environmental impact on them would alert your species to what might develop for your species. An assumption that being ensouled removes you from the consequences of being mammals is not valid, and leads to the kind of thought that brings about irresponsible acts in regard to the planet. You, as a species, are part of the system of the earth. You have discovered ways to transform it, and have done so with, we think you would agree, mixed results. You may also discover ways to preserve and protect the planet, should you choose to do so, in a collective and individual manner. But we remind you that a collective manner is the result of many individual fragments choosing to act in concert. Each fragment is responsible for what the fragment chooses to do. It is not possible for fragments to make life choices for other fragments without karma resulting, no matter how noble the reason for the action.

All choices are valid and all choices are equally important from our point of view. If you seek to preserve your planet, choices made about recycling paper is as valid as choices about laws prohibiting industrial pollution. And while there is no karma as such for neglecting the environment, it is where you will return until such time as your species is rendered unviable or you finish your full cycles of lives, in which case you will ensoul yourselves in another species on the physical plane. But that cataclysm has not yet occurred. Your planet would have to sustain significantly more damage before it becomes uninhabitable for your species. That does not mean that the damage has no effect on how the planet will be in a decade or two or three. And you will have to deal with that when you are reborn. The condition of the environment you will grow up in ''next time around'' will be the result of the choices made now. We would agree that it is costly to correct various past abuses, but prolong those abuses will not make them less costly—in fact, it will tend to make the problems more far-reaching and the solutions more complex.

Probably the single greatest contributor to the non-population-based abuse of the planet is organized military hostilities. After that comes industrial factors. Both those factors have a population component, of course, but reducing the risk and impact of wars can be useful in lessening the abuse of the planet, as well as requiring stricter enforcement of environmental protections the world over, for pollution in Bangladesh will eventually wash up on all the shores of the world, as will Love Canal effluvia. Contaminants know no borders or nations. And the earth is a finite place.

''What about the current notion that the universe is a hologram? Is there any validity in that? And if not, why not?''

No, the universe is not a hologram, although it provides a useful mathematical reference. While holograms are indeed interesting artifacts, they are, in fact, illusional, and we wish to assure you that this—or any other—universe is not illusional, except in the sense of maya, which transcends all sense of time and space. If you wish to make an analogy

of the universe in terms of the human experience, consider
the complexity of genetic material in the human body, its
development and collapse, and magnify it many trillion-fold
and splatter it all around you as far as you can, and treble
that, you will have the beginning of some concept of what
you call the universe in its current function. And let us
assure you that while the universe is indeed finite, the
flip from/between positive and negative matter [Michael's
description of what the Big Bang is] has occurred more times
than there are stars visible in the sky that you can observe
with the most powerful current telescopes, and it will
certainly occur that many times more before any substan-
tial change in its nature occurs. Just as you will reacquire
genetic material for as many times as it is necessary for
you to complete the evolution of lives on the physical
plane. The contemplation of a single galaxy, from ''birth''
to ''death'' may provide some sense of scope and scale at
stake in this question, and galaxies exist in the multiple
billions and at distances that we cannot begin to convey to
you by analogies or figures.

———————

"Are there things man was not meant to know?"**

Of course not. ''Meant'' implies ''should'', and there are
no shoulds that are valid. If the mind can encompass it,
then the knowledge is available. The use you make of it,
and the consequences, are, of course, a matter of choice.

CHAPTER 2

The Clash of Cultures

While we would agree that all cultures are valid, that experiencing cultures is part of the "lessons" of the physical plane, and that it is a world truth that cultures exist, we would not agree that culture is immutable, for that can be perceived with a mirror review of history. Cultures change, albeit slowly, and often in response to tremendous pressures, such as, but not limited to, war, famine, plague, geologic disaster, flood, fire, and all the other "disasters" that are inherent in living on this or any planet. The immutability of a culture in such cases can be its "downfall", in that it possesses no mechanisms for adaptation to the altered circumstances, thereby making the members of the culture have to "deny" the change in order to preserve cultural integrity. Those cultures with "coping" mechanisms within the structure, such as religion and myth, have a better chance of "weathering the storm" than those that relegate such occurrences to the category of "outrage" and "heresy".

Many things can contribute to this pattern of "denial". Cultures have always "lagged" behind science and technology, and in the last century, the "lag" has become dramatic as the gap between technology and culture continues to widen. Unfortunately, it is unlikely that many cultures will "adapt" to these expanding changes without "travail".

Many factors contribute to this state of affairs, and few cultures have any "tools" to deal with the developments they represent, for such developments were not "anticipated" by the culture and "factored into" the cultural patterns. Cultures are based on useful habits and anticipatable conduct, which may no longer apply, thanks to satellite communication, fax machines, and other information sources that may strike at what a culture defines as "true". There are also traditions of conflict, often dating back centuries, that "require" cultural members to "resist" the incursions of others, often their longtime neighbors. This can be seen in the current collapse of the Jugoslavian state, where "feuds" of millennial duration are now being expressed with modern military technology. It is not likely that these "feuds" can be resolved through the machinations of diplomacy, for the "arguments" are "built in" to the cultures in conflict.

This does not mean that the conflict is "irresolvable", only that its resolution would have to include cultural "tools" for adaptations to a new relationship between the feuding factions. These "feuds" exist in many parts of the world. Let us choose another example: one of the many barriers to African "unity" is the long traditions of cultural conflicts between various ethnic units in that country, where rivalries have taken on the full weight of "tradition" and "necessity". The same may be said for many other parts of the world, particularly those regions with diverse ethnic or social groups living in proximity. Ethnic warfare has long been a factor in African, Arab, Eastern European, Russian, Chinese, Latin American indigenous peoples, and until fairly recently, North American indigenous peoples' lives. Now that the "need" for continental and similar cohesion has become apparent, the strains of longtime rivalry and hatreds make it difficult to achieve what is a "worthy" goal in any significant way.

We would think that some of these difficulties will continue to "haunt" traditional cultures the world over for some time to come, in that the myths and superstitions of the culture, as well as the "heros" of the religions, tend to support and encourage the patterns of hostility throughout the world, through promoting an ideal "ikoǹ" of an unvanquishable young male or malelike female whose main task in life is to rid "the world" of those disliked and/or feared by the hero's culture as manifested in myths and religion. This is most apparent in European cultures in the myths of the lives of saints, who, for the cause of religion, undertake great hardships on behalf of the "errant" members of their own culture, and for which they are held in awed regard and established as a model of behavior for all those seeking to live in a manner exemplary to their time and state of society. This pattern is by no means limited to Europe. Most "heroic" legends are replete with tales of the model young male of the group telling the tale overcoming hordes of his neighbors in combat with little or no help, due to the inherently "unheroic" character of the despised neighbors.

The situation in North America for those of recent arrival, including Europeans and Asians, among others—and we include Canada as well as the United States, and the significant Irish and French presence in Mexico, as well—is not so "fraught" with the problems that continue to roil in the societies of the "Old World", at least for those who came to the continent in the last six hundred years, for one of the reasons most of the fragments leaving Europe and Asia was a desire to break from the patterns that had locked the fragments into rigid cultural and social roles, which personal inclination or regional "calamities" had rendered unworkable. We would think that the process of defining an "amalgam" culture is still in the development process, for we are aware that there are many aspects of the Old World", no matter which "Old World" is in question, clinging to those who have come to this society as many as ten generations ago. Those fragments whose family traditions are more recently linked to the "Old World" have, of course, a stronger influence to contend with. Not that there is an error in such contention, only that we perceive the American immigrant culture to be, as yet, incomplete in its cultural "devices". Given the social paradigms of this culture, we would not expect this process to conclude any time "soon", for your social and legal "expectations" are predicated on a continuing influx of "new blood", which, of course, means an increasing variety of worldviews in the "mix". Let us also point out that with communications improving and ubiquitous, links between the "Old World" and the "New" are likely to strengthen, not lessen over time. This does not mean that there is anything "wrong", only that major adaptations are likely to be necessary as time goes by. The time is not far distant when it may be possible for all fragments on earth to have direct communication with all other fragments. We are not making a prediction, only commenting on the possibilities, given the nature of current choices.

━━━━━━

"Some time ago, Michael mentioned ten possible global paths that were the futures most likely to be open to this species. About two years ago, Michael said that the most catastrophic and most philanthropic of these possibilities had been passed over, and while still possible, were not as apt to happen. Would Michael comment on how things stand now?"

We have already mentioned a few of them, and so we will not dwell on them, but will remark that at this point, we would not be surprised to see an increasing among "Balkanization" of regions as one of the less pleasant possibilities, as is the potential for organized religionly-based wars. It would not be impossible for a robber baron international economy to arise using puppet governments to approve all manner of "shenanigans". It is also possible that an increasing division between those capable of and willing to be educated for the current societal needs and those incapable and unwilling of it will grow increasingly apart so that a "Mandarin-like" order of society could arise. If events in space exploration suddenly seem to make exploitation of resources within the solar system a feasible solution to various environmental problems on earth, the dispersion of peoples, especially workers "off-world," may come about. And the increasingly precarious general state of world health could well reach a crisis point that would demand the "lion's share" of the GNP for everyone for the return of a reduced (and traumatized) population. Those are the general overall trends as we perceive them at this time—and we stress at this time—as possibilities, and although there are offshoots to all of them as well as some other possibilities requiring specific events, we would think this is sufficient food for thought for the "nonce". Whatever path is chosen, it will be a valid choice, and whatever new paths enter "the lists" for future development, we would think that the choice will be made, as all choices are, on a fragment-by-fragment basis.

━━━━

"I notice that Michael is using more than their usual number of quotes when discussing cultures—is there any particular reason for this?"

There are cultural concepts that are so complex they cannot be easily summed up in a word or a phrase, but can be labeled without going into the "nature" of the problem. When this is our intention, we use quotes. We also use quotes when we lack specific words to express concepts and can only approximate them through the device of quotations. That said, we would wish to remind all here gathered that there are many concepts not easily contained in language—any language—and not only because language is very much a tool of culture, but because there are concepts not really "grasped" on the physical plane. Often we are hampered by the nature of spoken communication as much as by the nature of what we wish to convey. We wish to make it clear that we do not intend to confuse or mislead, but often we must answer your questions more metaphorically than we would wish to do because of the limitations of language, as well as cultural "constructs" that limit us to the "human" experience.

━━━━

"Is there some way we can get around this lack of conceptual understanding?"

During the astral interval, the matter does not exist. [Ha, ha, ha, the transcript says, making note of one of Michael's many bad puns.] We would wish to point out that experiencing culture, limits and all, is valid, and in fact, those who do not or cannot are regarded as insane. To achieve a "place in the world" is a part of being in an ensouled species, no matter in what form that species exists. But with such "benefits" comes restrictions as well, including the "natural" assumption of a predominantly Young soul world, that every culture has the "right" way and those who disagree are "wrong". This is usually enforced by various cultural institutions, such as courts, taxations, religions, and similar monolithic organizations that serve to enforce cultural rules as much as "benefit" the populace. The consequences of "going against" culture have often been severe to the point of fatality, although that is more generally enforced in single-culture "nations" than in multicultural ones. However, when multicultural "nations" suffer internal culture clash, the results may be civil war.

Only ensouled species or creatures of reason can experience culture, though most "parenting" animals have a "family" structure of sorts, dictated by the "hardwiring" of the hive soul of the species. Creatures of nonreason cannot experience culture. A dog will be a dog no matter which culture its owner may belong to, and while the owner may be able to train the dog to do certain things that are culturally acceptable or desirable, the dog will not, in fact, participate in the culture in any "valid" manner, and left to its own devices, the dog will behave as canines behave the world over. The same is true of cats, cattle, horses, sheep, birds, and all other so-called "domestic" animals, who have made some accommodation to "human" demands and have to some degree bridged the barriers of species through their interaction with humans, which extends to other species through the human "interface".

When it comes to human beings, there is, of course, a

component in the species of primate, since ensoulment took place in primates. Every one of you possesses primate qualities, and the experience of these qualities is valid, though culture does much to "distort" the primate experience, and shape it to the needs of the culture. Let us explicate: primates, particularly your nearer relatives, such as the chimpanzee, are skilled mimics, which is part of their species adaptation to living in groups. Human beings share this skill, but most cultures direct this skill to "magical" or artistic activities, such as, but not limited to, dance and theatre. Many cultures define when, where, and how mimicry may be "properly" done, and what the desired result may be. The voo-doo tradition of "being ridden" by gods—which, incidentally, is not at all limited to the religious culture of the Caribbean; many other religions include such "manifestations" of worship—has its deepest species roots in the primate skill for mimicry.

As we have said before, ensoulment of your species took place between fifty and sixty thousand years ago, and is marked by the development of abstract thought, which in turn led to language, esthetics, defined emotions and perceptions, "flights of fancy", anticipation, worry, intimacy, including self-intimacy, identity, and then to what you on the physical plane call art. That is not to say that proto-humans did not have rudimentary verbal communications, but so do chimpanzees, and like all "clever" animals, proto-humans could recognize a very wide variety of discrete sounds. But abstract "thought" widened all the potentials of the proto-human species. Without abstract thought, language, as compared to the vast "vocabulary" of mutters, shrieks, chuckles, and cries of primates, is conceptually "impossible", for it by its very nature contains information not immediately apparent. And while it is "true" that many animals have a number of "informational vocalizations", these do not contain abstractions, which are the cornerstones of all language. Language and the abstraction that must, of necessity, come with it, is the single most identifiable characteristic of ensoulment for your species. Many very intelligent animals are capable of "learning" many things from human beings, and as such may appear to have learned abstraction, but this is, in fact, incorrect, for without the human "factor," the observed behavior would not and could not occur.

Another factor of culture is what you might describe as cosmology, and its offshoot, religion; that is, the nature, purpose, affect, and perception of the universe. The Chinese cultural concept of the Mandate of Heaven contains a very different cosmological "construct" as does the Middle Eastern and Occidental Will of God, although the two may appear similar at first glance. A review of the cultural consequences of "disagreeing" with the Mandate of Heaven and the Will of God is revealing. Also, the manner of enforcing the consequences is carried on by very different bodies of cultural officials. Who has the power to maintain the culture and what they may "correctly" do to maintain it is always a valid approach to assessing the matter of culture. Both the Mandate of Heaven, which you might wish to view as the Order of the Universe, and the Will of God, which assumes that there is a Superseding Authority, are very ambiguous concepts, capable of being "taken" in a number of ways, which vary from time to time as the societies of the cultures underwent—and continue to undergo—many shifts and adjustments. Consider, also, should you choose to do so, the deities of the "pagan" Romans, who tended to embody civic virtues in their gods and goddesses, as compared to the forces of nature that were characteristic of the Greek versions of them. The cultural cosmology subsumed under the catchall of Hinduism is much more ambiguous than the Western archetypes in that most of the deities are embodiments of opposite qualities, such as fertility-and-destruction, carnality-and-asceticism, contemplation-and-conflict, philosophy-and-warfare, and so forth.

━━━━━

"Then, from your point of view, Michael, deities of all sorts are cultural archetypes or paradigms?"

Of course—what else could they be and retain any validity to members of a cultural group? By extension, religions are primarily cultural institutions, established to maintain cultural integrity through enforcing codes of behavior and establishing models of "virtue" and "vice" that then are used as paradigms of cultural continuity. Most religions that "travel" well have enough commonality to be comprehensible culturally to those not of the originating culture, no matter how great the Truth on which the religion may be founded. We have said before that the teachings of the manifestations of the Transcendental Soul and the Infinite Soul are valid as the "truth" only while the manifestations are alive to be questioned. Once the manifestations die, then the records of their teachings becomes literature, and it is in that form it must be presented to other cultures, if that is the choice of the fragments subscribing to its tenets.

"Why does culture have such a tremendous impact on us?"

Culture provides context, that is, the framework in which society defines itself and family units function, and every fragment has a family context of some sort, though the form a "family" takes is often a result of cultural and societal definitions as much as anything having to do with "blood" relations. Culture frames much of the perception of choice, and the beginning of recognition of choice takes place within families, which are microcosmic cultures. Even those children orphaned or abandoned have "family" contexts. In the most extreme cases—those fragments called "feral" children—the "family" is usually found in another species, but the concept of "family" is present, nonetheless. If you choose to think of a family as a small box inside a larger box, which is a society, and that is contained in a still larger box, which is a culture, you would be simplifying the matter very much; but the basic perception is a valid one, and may help in "sorting out" the levels of influence inherent in the experience of the life.

Of course, in a society such as the one of the United States of America at this time, the society forms a looser, larger whole in order to accommodate the many cultural "factors" brought into the society, which is essentially a societal branch of European culture, although it is far more flexible than the European culture from which it has "evolved".

In regard to "learning" in the educational sense, at least half of what is "taught" is the rules of the culture and society, as well of those of "caste" or "class", both of which are valid social constructs for young-soul worlds. The concept of "proper" behavior is one of the main thrusts of education, as well as providing what the culture deems necessary information for fragments to function "appropriately" within the culture in question, including the "popular" history of the culture, which is markedly different from the actual events, such as the famous fable of the cherry tree, which, in fact, never happened, and devolved from a remark made about the Mature Warrior in question—that he was so honest a child that he would admit to any wrong-doing, including chopping down his father's prize cherry tree. Education also explains the consequences of "improper" behavior and the ranges of "improper" behavior. How individual fragments react to such instruction is, of course, a matter of choice, and is often representative of the function of overleaves. A fragment with a goal of rejection may be more willing to question the "rules" of society and the nature of culture than a fragment with a goal of growth, who may, instead, choose to extend the limits of society and culture. Or not. For all ensouled species, choice is the most essential purpose of every life, and there is no "right" or "wrong" way to lead any life, no matter what a family, society, or culture may try to convince you.

Let us point out that cultural "expectations" are many times as stringent as family ikons [which are discussed in Chapter 4]. Such "expectations" may "require" a fragment to abandon the cutlure in question if the fragment chooses to break away from the "expectations" imposed by culture.

Breaking with society may involve conflict with the legal system of the society, and dealing with concepts of legality. Breaking with culture is a more "complex" act, and is more a question of "heresy" or "incomprehensibility" and does not always confront the legal "system", although it is often understood as "insanity", which, in the Young-soul sense, it is, although it is a fairly "normal" state of mind for Mature souls.

That does not mean that laws, as such, are invalid, or that there is no such thing as "true" insanity, or that those suffering from altered mental states are not, in fact, in an altered mental state. We did not say that and we did not imply it. Laws are the means by which society enforces "desirable" conduct, and it is valid for fragments to answer for conflicts with society. And while we would agree that there are always "reasons" why fragments choose to "break the law", those reasons do not cause a law to be unbroken. Inequities and arbitrary enforcement, which are "typical" of Young-soul species and cultures, have brought many laws into question, which reflects part of the rapid changes taking place in society, and the slower ones contributing to cultural evolution.

As to insanity, there are many cases, usually chosen as part of the life plan, that have to do with chemical or neuro-imbalances in the body, which causes information to be "processed" in a manner not in accord with the standard daily experience of the physical planet. All cultures, the world over, recognize that there are those with impairments of such magnitude and complexity that the fragments cannot "survive" as "regular" members of society. Schizophrenia is recognized by all cultures and most periods in time, but there is not necessarily agreement as to what the condition, in fact, is, since opinions on the nature and definition of insanity vary significantly, and are reflective of the cultural cosmology as well as religious traditions. In almost all cultures, insane fragments are accorded special "status", some of it privileged, some of it restrictive, depending on the paradigms of the culture in which the "insane" fragment lives. Such conditions as what has been called "split personality" or "multiple personality disorder" often evolve from incidents of trauma, and are apparent in all fragments, sane and insane, to a greater or lesser degree, and has to do with "realms" of activities and behavior "appropriate" to the "realms". When such "facets" become "discrete" to the point of non-congruity with the fragment and overleaves of the fragment possessing them, the condition becomes one that is regarded as a sign of "disease" and therefore subject to "treatment" and other societal "constraints" for the purpose of making it possible for the afflicted fragment not to be societally "penalized" for the inability to "function normally". We would have to say that this kind of "protection" extended to those trying to deal with such conditions often exacerbates the very problems it seeks to "cure", but that, again, is typical of Young-soul approaches to behavior that does not "adequately" reflect social and cultural "expectations".

Many cultures have little "slack" for significant deviation from what is perceived as "normal". Often, any significant deviation is regarded as a form of insanity and treated as such, although it has little to do with being "insane" as such, meaning one suffering from certain conditions, usually with a biochemical component, that result in what might be called "bad wiring". In some cultures, peculiarity of birth, such as multiple infants, or infants with instantly apparent "irregularities" are regarded as "intolerable", and are relegated to positions of outcasts. Other cultures have limited-but-privileged niches for such "deviations" from the "norm". The same may be said of the very gifted. In many cultures, obvious talents not already embraced by the culture are viewed with extreme suspicion, and can result in the fragment possessing the talent being "cast out" from the culture itself. And lest you think that this is limited to "primitive" peoples of the remote parts of the world where there are no telephones, we remind you that in certain societal groups—by which we mean more than one group, of course—within your own, multicultural nation, young men showing a predisposition to mathematics instead of guns are regarded with extreme "disapproval", and young women with similar abilities are often thought of as "unmarriageable" because they are not of the same "sort" as other young women.

─────

"Surely there are ways to overcome these problems?"

In a culture such as this one, yes, there are a few, though such choices often include a dramatic "break" with the base culture in question, and acculturation to other "expectations". Some of the dramatic "conversions" experienced by fragments in your society spring from this need for a "dramatic break" from the base culture. In general, such a choice "needs" overleaves, especially chief features, to impel the fragment to such action. And we would think that contemplating such a "break" without any suggestion of support would impose a tremendous burden on the fragment, although those with goals of rejection might find it somewhat less arduous than those with other goals. Again, in a culture with such diverse groups as this one, the possibilities are more readily perceived by all the fragments who choose to look. We would think that this is a "mixed blessing" for many whose base culture is restrictive in nature and "rigid" in expectations. In fact, we are aware of many cultural groups that are unable to accept the diversity of the larger culture and "draw in on themselves" in an attempt to be rid of the confusion presented by so many cultural possibilities immediately to "hand".

Oftentimes, gifted fragments born into socially and culturally restricted groups do so in order to "wrestle" with the limitations of culture as much to succeed with their "gifts". That does not mean that all gifted fragments in restricted cultures have chosen to overcome the limits of culture or that the sole purpose of being born into a restrictive culture is to wrestle with it in order to express certain gifts. We did not say that and we did not imply it. We only wish to observe that there tends to be more of that pattern here and in similar "johnny-come-lately" cultures than in those that have been established for many centuries, because in these multicultural cultures there is always an available alternative to the cultural "expectations" of the base culture, and often less stringent consequences from "breaking" with the cultural patterns of the family and immediate society around the family.

As general instantaneous information becomes more "universally" available, the rigidity of many cultures will have to learn to accommodate the Information Glut in order to preserve some semblance of congruity. This is not "easy" for fairly flexible cultures, such as the one encountered here in this country and Canada; for those more rigid cultures, adaptation is apt to be difficult and accomplished with more social upheaval than has been encountered in the cultural assemblage of North America. And many of you are aware of groups that have made it a practice to resist innovation and change even in this cultural context. We are aware of restrictive societies in many parts of the world where the "powers that be" have attempted to legislate against information, which is, we assure you, useless, though many fragments choose to make the attempt. It is also useless to legislate morality, for that inevitably interferes with choice and makes for considerably more "vice", or reverse-morality, than would have existed without the attempt to make moral issues legal or illegal.

Back in 1977, Michael said: In general, we consider "morals" to be a negative influence on the societies embracing them, for the imposition of such "codes" inevitably leads to a justification of cruelty. You have only to read history, let alone your newspapers to see the validity of this. We do, in general, think that an understanding of ethics is far less "intrusive", and provides fewer "excuses" for the kinds of actions that have marked "moral" actions. Of course, there are fragments who "disguise" their moral postures as ethical "dilemmas".

In 1979, Michael said: From our point of view, morality is cultural terrorism as practiced by those already in authority for the purpose of enforcing their "standards" as a means of control. Morals are also tools of chief feature to distort and deny perceptions through the infusion of fear.

In 1982, Michael said: We have stated before, but we will reiterate: morality is a "device" imposed upon fragments to justify the imposition of suffering, and inevitably leads to a proliferation of the very conduct it supposedly seeks to eradicate, by polarizing the choices available to be made. For example, sexual orientation is established beyond alteration by the time a fragment is three, well before any "moral" component is factored into the matter, which is part of the fixing of centering and the completion of the second internal monad, or the validation of individuality. By "pretending" the sexual fixation is a "moral" one, it "condemns" those with sexual orientations not in accord with the "moral" standard to social intrusions designed to humiliate and terrify the fragments. The most extreme "moral" cruelty comes when those with such orientation are offered a "fix" or a "cure" for their "aberration", a situation that often leads to karma for the supposed "fixer" for mind-fuck. And by establishing hard-and-fast definitions for "acceptable" sexual conduct, many fragments are "compelled" to decide to be "one or the other" in a manner not in accord with the life plan or the overleaves.

In 1984, Michael said: Morality is based upon fear, and as such, it is the societal bastion of chief feature. The underlying fear of all chief features [The underlying fear of Self-deprecation is fear of inadequacy; the underlying fear of Self-destruction is fear of loss of control; the underlying fear of Martyrdom is fear of worthlessness; the underlying fear of Stubbornness is the fear of dealing with new situations; the underlying fear of Greed is the fear of loss or want; the underlying fear of Arrogance is the fear of vulnerability; and the underlying fear of Impatience is the fear of missing something.] have "moral hooks" in them. To embrace "moral certainty", except in the legal sense, over the ambiguities of choice is to willingly embrace a cactus, and a philosophy of "better the pain you know".

In 1987, Michael said: Morality, as it is understood by

most fragments, is a more socially acceptable word for bigotry and intolerance, turning those who do not or will not accept the "standards" of the moralist into that "despicable" amorphous group called They or Them, whose sole purpose for existence is to make Us miserable, and whom We "must", for "high" "moral" "reasons" control/teach/correct/improve/subdue/transform/halt/eliminate. By embracing morality, fragments succumb to the demands of chief feature and allow their fears to frame their perceptions of others and to base their responses upon the supposition that character is contagious. Morality thereby provides an acceptable excuse to follow the dictates of chief features, and to block intimacy as "inappropriate" or "immoral". Ethics do not in general allow such simplistic depersonalization, and while the choices are "harder" in ethical contexts, they are based on an appreciation of shared "personhood", which does not as easily permit the imposition of "expectations" to the extent that morality does.

Morality presupposes that there is an external "authority" that "justifies" a response that is neither responsible nor informed. "The devil made me do it" is an eminently moral statement from our point of view in that it places "blame" on powers beyond the fragment's ken. Ethics, on the other hand, does not provide an external source of choice, and makes the fragment individually responsible for his or her actions, which, in fact, is the case.

In 1991, Michael said: One of the few workable challenges to cultural morality is the Information Glut, for it makes available immediately counter-arguments to any moralistic stance and reveals a pattern of other methods and standards of work, which in turn, reveals the cruelty of "moral" enforcement. This is one of the reasons "morality" is apparently "breaking down" all over the world. Be aware, should you choose to examine the question, that the people of Bosnia believe they have a "moral" obligation to kill one another, and only access to general world opinion for all fragments involved can reveal another point of view that questions the legitimacy of that "conviction".

There are, of course, aspects to the Information Glut

that are not as "desirable" as the usefulness in bringing "morality" into doubt. For one thing, many fragments, viewing carnage in Jugoslavia or Africa or Iraq or Latin America or China, may feel frustrated in that there is "nothing they can do" about these events, even though they are occurring as the fragments are watching or listening. This is not in itself an invalid perception, for your species is inclined to respond to evolving situations. There is the very "human" desire to intervene in immediate events. It is one thing to learn of a massacre or a similar tragedy a day or a week or a month after the event, for that displacement in time brings with it the consolation that it is now "too late" to do anything about it, no matter how tragic the event being reported might be. With the speed of communication as developed in the last decade, that is no longer true, and few fragments have developed skills to deal with the reactions they experience viewing or hearing instantaneous calamities.

It may be important to remember that human beings do not, in fact, move with the speed of information, at least not in this decade, and the demand for an "instantaneous" response is a fairly new one. For several millennia, it was the "usual" thing for "hard" information to move as fast as a human messenger could carry it. For example, at the height of the Roman Empire, a written message could be physically moved at the rate of eighty-five miles a day in good weather. Signals could move faster, of course, at the rate of about two hundred miles a day, again, in good weather. For most of human history, however, physical messages moved considerably more slowly and at increasing hazard as the distance to be covered grew vaster. Chinese Imperial messengers, in peacetime, could carry a message overland at the rate of sixty miles a day in good weather. But for the most part, physical messages, until the communications revolution of the last one hundred fifty years, have moved at an average of twenty-two miles a day in good weather, with about a ten percent increase in non-delivery for every five days in transit.

Most human cultures are not "prepared" to deal with

this transformation in the accessibility and volume of information, and some of the "strain" of this swift transformation has become apparent in recent years, both in social and legal senses. We have discussed culture "lag" in the past, and we remind you that it is nowhere more apparent than in dealing with the staggering increase of available, current information. Even those technologically "sophisticated" cultures, such as most of the United States and Canada and Occidental Europe, have few cultural "means" to deal with the constant bombardment of information, which many fragments find overwhelming, in large part because there are no true cultural "tools" for handling the plethora of information.

In those parts of the world where accessibility to information has been rigidly controlled, the degree of "shock" caused by the importation of information has been greater than it has been in those cultures where access to information is a more "regular" development, and one that the societal expectations have made "tolerable". For cultures and societies where efforts to control the availability of information is ongoing, the clash is becoming more severe, for we perceive the spread of such "nefarious" devices as "fax" machines and "dish" antennae as being the most "subversive" aspects within such cultures. As such, they represent not only the "evils" of the technological societies, but they call into question the purported societal "norms" by revealing developments that are not in accord with the cultural paradigms and are therefore "dangerous".

In many places in the world, where there is a single cultural "model", the problems of "sorting out" these differences become a more difficult issue, for diversity is not part of the allowable expectations. In such "binding" cultural frameworks, deviation from the "expectations" of the culture are often put in the context of insanity, for in the cultural "limits", the behavior is not "rational". In other words, if you yourself are Prussian and everyone around you is Prussian, it is not easy to deal with the world in non-Prussian terms, or with those who are not part of the Prussian culture and society, with those fragments who do not know the "rules" or the "right" way to behave, that is, the Prussian way. The same may be said of the Zulu or Saudis. For fragments coming from those cultures, the necessity of "adapting" to other cultural expectations is more difficult than those fragments belonging to multi-cultural societies can readily "understand", for although there are many instances of cultural "misunderstanding" in multi-cultural societies, there is also an appreciation of the functions of diversity, which makes it less "threatening" to the fragments in the society when they are confronted with cultural paradigms not in accord with their own.

"**D**oes the Information Glut make this better or worse?"

It is not a question of "better" or "worse" but of expectations and complexity. In societies of mono-cultural character, the introduction of information is usually a more "regulated" thing than in multi-cultural societies. There is also the degree to which the information is capable of "rocking" the cultural "boat". Mono-cultural societies are apt to address information that counters the societal model as "heretical" or "wrong" far more than multi-cultural societies. Culture is not wholly a matter of ethnicity, incidentally, although that is often a factor. There is also very much an aspect of class. The culture of the upper-class Hindu rulers of three centuries ago was as alien to a lower-class Hindu of the period as the culture of the Eskimos. In multi-cultural societies, the class lines tend to blur while the ethnic/linguistic/gender lines tend to sharpen. This has been true for nearly three thousand years of "human" experience and, while this pattern has been slightly modified in the last century, thanks in large part to the development of communications, the "lag" is very strong and quite pervasive, and we would think would remain a significant factor until the average soul age of your species has evolved to midcycle Mature. [According to Michael, the average soul age of the ensouled species on this planet at this time is fifth level Young].

That does not mean that those countries with an average soul age of mid-cycle Mature or older have necessarily an easier time of accommodating cultural diversity, although such national groups do tend not to react so "explosively" as those countries with younger souls predominating. We would think that patterns discerned in nonmetropolitan Russia and England, to name two Mature-soul countries, would show a few of the difficulties characteristic of Mature-soul societies. Just as the motto of the Baby soul is "Do it right or don't do it at all", and the Young soul is "Do it my way," we remind you that the motto of the Mature soul is "Do it anywhere but here". Oftentimes, Mature-soul countries have difficulty with eclecticism, not out of fears of "heresy" but dislike of "intrusion". In many Mature-soul countries, the Information Glut is a greater "imposition" on the fragments living there, as well as the cultural "fabric", because it becomes a significant "interference" with the nature of the Mature soul cycle.

There is much to consider, should you choose to do so, on the tapestry of culture and how it is generally impossible to remove one "thread" without "unraveling" the whole "cloth". That is not to say that all culture is therefore "immutable", but rather that the nature of cultural elements are complex enough to make it difficult to separate them in any "discrete" way. We would have to say that those who desire to "fix" a culture by ridding it of a single element or cluster of elements deemed to be "undesirable" are "doomed" to failure, for culture cannot be "fixed" through the elimination of a single aspect or group of aspects without damaging the whole and creating a kind of "make-believe" culture, such as, but not limited to, those attempting to re-create or reconstruct cultures of the past. These exist in many parts of the world today, and are inevitably dependent on the superseding culture around them to carry on a semblance of survival, and in this case, semblance is the operative word, for the apparent cultural congruity is, in fact, vitiated. Fragments living in such cultures often suffer many complex "personality" disorders due to the incomplete nature of the culture, for their definitions of their places in the world are not "whole". On the other hand, for those fragments seeking to acculturate or to "break" with a culture, it is easier to accomplish this in these "make-believe" cultures than in those of integral "soundness".

———

"Does the Information Glut contribute to these 'make believe' cultures?"

To a degree. In Western culture there is a marked "need" for entertainment as a means to break with the intellectual rigor of the culture at large, though society is profoundly anti-"intellectual" and siphons off most intellectual rigor to trade and commerce in many varied forms. This entertainment often takes the form of "playtime" identities, such as, but not limited to, role-playing games, various aficionado affiliations, revivals of traditions and customs from past times or other cultures, and any number of other "entertainments". Those with a more "stringent" need might express this "need" in extreme religious practices, rigid political activities, and so forth. The Information Glut is the "cannon fodder" for these "entertainments", and as such contributes to but does not create the "demand". Eastern culture exercises a different "hold" on those participating in it, and this "entertainment" need is not as demanding, though as the Eastern culture, perforce, is exposed to the Western culture, it is not impossible that the lure of "make-believe" cultures will be felt in Eastern culture as well, for such "make-believe" cultures do help in "blowing off steam" and help to diminish the "stress" of "culture shock" that is fairly pervasive throughout the world and is strongly influenced by the Information Glut. It is also significant that these "make-believe" cultures often play directly into the "hands" of those who take the "make-believe" cultures one step farther and found cults, which are "make-believe" cultures that purport to be "the real world" while all else is "make-believe". In the most extreme examples, cults destroy their members as a way of vindicating their "reality" in the face of clear demonstrations to the contrary. We would have to say that these cultish extremists often end up with karmic debts arising from mind-fuck and unjust imprisonment, which is often not carried out in an actual prison, but is encountered in creating a physical, financial, or religious "cage".

That is not to say that "make-believe" culture is or is not Good Work, although we are aware that it often leads to confusion before the fourth internal monad in terms of recognition and validation, and for those fragments who are very troubled, the introduction of such an "artificial" frame of reference can be severely "disorienting", in that it can add to the confusion experienced by the very troubled fragments.

Let us point out that Western culture has changed "dramatically" in the last fifty years, far more than Eastern culture, because although there have been extremely disruptive events in both parts of the world, the cultures have reacted very differently, particularly in regard to the information glut and all its permutations. In the Western world, where the dogma of "progress" has been woven into the cultural fabric for a long time, the changes brought about were not seen as "threatening" on the scale they are still perceived in much of the Eastern culture of the world, where "continuity" is the mainstay of culture, and where any "progress" must be inculcated to make it "acceptable" culturally.

There are also the cultures of Africa, the Middle East, the South Pacific region, Latin America, and other pockets throughout the planet that are factors in all the cultural clashes of the present day, although by far the most "visible" may be caled "East" and "West", and the umbrella-like result of their nature is readily perceived. We are aware that the inherent differences between East and West have a greater impact on other world cultures than do the other cultures on East or West. The surest sign of this is the degree to which these other cultures "mimic" Eastern and/ or Western cultures, and with what ends in mind.

In general, we are aware that the Information Glut has brought matters that had been minor considerations into situations of cultural prominence. We do not believe this is likely to change any time "soon": this is not a prediction, incidentally, only an observation. Fragments in those or any cultures are free to choose to change at any time, though most societal patterns in question are not swiftly transformable into a more "elastic" state. We would think that areas in which cultures are unable to adapt or accommodate the Information Glut are areas where the culture will have integral "trouble" in the next two generations: again, this is not a prediction, only a remark based upon the observations of long centuries of experience and a perception of social "structures", that does not necessarily subscribe to them. And by trouble with such cultures we do not mean anything so simple or overt as a poor fragment desiring the possessions and opportunities of those with more money, although the effects of this pattern are already becoming apparent and have shown repercussions in many levels of societies throughout the world. What we mean in this instance is a more complex problem, having to do with cultural "fluidity" and the "flexibility" to be willing to reject the dogmas of culture for the "models" of society, and to make it possible for information to be "processed" without "disruption" of cultural congruity.

Let us enlarge upon this: all cultures propose a "standard" of expectations directly related to behavior, and which is dependent on the culture being able to "deliver" on the promise associated with behavior—"Break the law, go to jail", "Save for the future, have a happy old age", "Marry well, advance in the world"—and enforced by shared "understanding" of what the "rewards" are and how they are attainable. When the culture is unable to "deliver" on the implied promise, there is cultural stress, often developing into open conflict, which, if it continues for any length of time, results in cultural change. That does not mean all cultural changes are brought about by conflict, but that the impetus for change is always the result of cultural stress. With the increase in immediately available information, the stresses tend to be more "instantaneous" and more "defined" than was the case a century ago. Think what problems would have confronted the James Brothers, for instance, if the regional sheriffs and marshals had had modems and fax machines, to say nothing of helicopters and fingerprints. Current preoccupations with "law and order" is as much a result of the awareness of the ubiquity of crimes, via the Information Glut, than any immediate individual danger, and the enforcement of law is one of the most ongoing promises of this or any culture, for "protection" is one of the essential functions of cultures. Where societal "crowding" is acute, the "promise" and "payoff" of a society is an issue of tremendous concern, for the repercussions tend to bring into question every standard within the culture, and response to a "defaulting" of the standard often results in extreme responses, which are apparent historically as well as currently.

We would think that the character of social protests of the last four decades has shown the validity of this, for much of the "nature" and "style" of the protests were based not so much on "moral" issues, but the perceived sense that the culture had failed to uphold the standard predicated by the nature of the cultural "fabric". The conduct of "law" has also changed, in part because of the Information Glut and in part due to cultural evolutionary "speed", all of which have contributed to the assumption of "failure" of society to "cope". The reason for those perceived failures had more to do with immediately available contradictory information than any increased "tenderness" of societal "conscience."

Culture makes it possible for fragments to experience the environment of the planet in different contexts and to "come to grips" with the reality that no matter what the world "does" to your species, there is a framework that makes coping with it possible. Cultures, of course, reflect the average soul age of the majority of the fragments living within its "framework", as we have discussed before at length. Where fragments of soul ages other than the average enter such cultures, there is bound to be some level of "personal" discomfort with the culture, although it is not "inevitable" that the culture in question be rejected. Many social critics and philosophers address culture from the point of view of one at a different point of evolution. In general, we would have to say that soul-age displacement is often the starting place for many sorts of what you on the physical plane call artistic expression.

Of course, there are many considerations that can influence or "override" cultural "demands", such as karma and certain monads and agreements. There are also bonds that, where recognized, will tend to transcend the limits of culture, such as Essence Twins, Task Companions, Cadence Mates, and the like. Where cultural requirements are very strong, fragments with karma, monads, or agreements to complete may, in that life, abdicate, and postpone the karma, monads, or agreements to a more "propitious" time and a more "adaptable" cultural context. There is nothing "wrong" in such a choice; it is as valid as all other choices.

⸻

"Does karma get worse if it isn't burned when you have it in the life plan?"

Karma is karma; no "better" and no "worse" in one life than another, although if fragments are having difficulty burning the ribbon, they might choose a life where the exigencies of the life are such that avoiding the ribbon is difficult. Such choices may be expressed in a wide range of options. We are aware of one pair of what you call Siamese twins where one twin owed the other a karmic debt of abandonment and had not been able to burn the ribbon in three separate "tries": in two, the debtor had more "pressing" demands upon him; in one, the fragment owed had successfully avoided dealing with the debtor. As a Siamese twin, abandonment was not physically possible, and the ribbon was completely burned in that shared life, though it was generally acknowledged that neither twin much "liked" the other. That, incidentally, does not mean all Siamese twins are karmically as well as physically linked. We did not say that and we did not imply it. But in terms of choosing a life in which abandonment was severely impractical, the two fragments agreed that cojoining was an eminently pragmatic solution to the problem.

Let us remark that dealing with culture is a "necessary" part of the experience of being independently mobile en-souled fragments. All independently mobile ensouled species throughout the physical plane have some sort of culture in order to maintain species cohesion. Those en-souled species that are not independently mobile do not "depend" on culture for context, and have other means of establishing context for the physical-plane experience. For a sense of "framework" is a part of ensouled life on the physical plane, life itself, as experienced on the physical plane, having a certain "course" that is not wholly that of the life plan, but reflective of the nature of the experiencing of life. In providing this frame of reference, the culture also shapes the limits the fragment will set upon itself as the "correct" way to live. Of course, once the physical plane is left behind, so is culture, as well as gender and species and all other aspects of physicality. There is no "Latin Quarter" on the astral or higher planes, as there is no such thing as male or female "energy" beyond the sexual tension experienced by your species in certain circumstances that vary from culture to culture, which is as much a result of the overall Young-soul evolution of your planet than anything inherent in gender itself. However, we have remarked before that in having just two sexes, your species has allowed that to become not a duality but a polarization, which is not Good Work. We have stated before but we will repeat that for independently mobile ensouled species, three sexes are more "usual" on the physical plane.

"**D**o the various essences have cultures? Are there cultures certain essences are more drawn to than others?"

We would not call them cultures as such, no, but we would think that there are institutions within cultures where certain essences—if overleaves and casting support such choices—tend "naturally" to gravitate. [This is another Michael joke. They think it is very funny.] Slaves, of course, are the most adaptable of all essences and can "fit in" anywhere, although support occupations are places where slaves find it easiest to fulfill the Common Good, whatever the individual Slave fragment decides that the Common Good is. Slaves make excellent teachers, doctors, nurses, politicians, attorneys, trainers, and diplomats. They, as a group, dislike open conflict where it can be avoided and are willing to devote themselves to a cause or a calling with little credit or recognition. Young Slaves run most of the major corporations of the world, and manage very well at it. Such fragments as Jonas Salk, Elizabeth II, Mikhail Gorbachev, Xavier Perez de Quellar, and many others in devoted public life are Mature Slaves. Slaves are "at home" in all parts of society and at all levels of function, and are, in fact, the only role in essence of which this is true. More winners of the Nobel Prize are Slaves than any other essence. Slaves come into the physical plane "prepared" for it, and do not need "time" or "special circumstances" to come into their own. Incidentally, this higher number of Nobel Prizewinners is not reflective of the naturally higher number of Slaves, but a significantly disproportionate amount of Nobel Prizewinners—in excess of forty-five percent are Slaves, which, we would think, any statistician would consider a significant deviation from the demographic "curve".

Artisans are the builders of society, and are much drawn [another bad Michael pun] to such things as architecture, construction, fashion, art, and athletics. They are also good at entertainment and cooking. Artisans seek structure in all things, from genetics to astrophysics, but prefer engineering and sculpture and dance for expression of that structure. Such fragments as John Travolta, Joe Montana, and Cher are Young Artisans, and Steven Spielberg, Frank Lloyd Wright, and Martha Graham are/were Mature ones. Artisans often appear somewhat "scattered" because of their constant "evaluation" of structure, and many fragments of other essence do not comprehend the wide-scale view that the Artisan nature has by definition. Artisans come into their own during the second, or Baby cycle of incarnations, and from then on are capable of achieving the full range of their potential, should they choose to do so. The current Chief Justice of the Supreme Court is a Mature Artisan. Botticelli and Michelangelo were also Mature Artisans. In general, Artisans do not like being tied to any one group for a significant length of time, unless the group itself is evolving, for it "interferes" with the evolving structure that is the focus of the Artisan essence.

Warriors are prone to inventing regiments for themselves, and are fiercely loyal to their regiments, be that regiment a family, a business, a profession, or, in fact, a regiment—anything that permits the Warrior to meet the challenge, whatever the Warrior decides the challenge is. The workhorse nature of the Warrior is often puzzling to Artisans and Sages, who are not "wired" for such front-line doggedness. Warriors come into their own in the Young, or third cycle of incarnations. Warriors are extremely protective of those they choose to protect, and only Kings are more implacable opponents. Incidentally, after the Young cycle, Warriors are inclined to dislike war and battle in all forms—experience has taught them that such endeavor is too costly and futile to be worth a great deal, though they remain very good at strategy and tactics through all their cycles of lives. Jessica Lange, Harrison Ford, and James Mason are examples of Old Warriors. Bram Stoker was a Mature Warrior. Marilyn Horne is a Mature Warrior. Abraham Lincoln was cast in the Scholar position of his cadence, Mature (Scholar) cycle, fourth (Scholar) level Warrior, who had more than his share of Scholar characteristics.

"I thought the early transcripts identified Lincoln as a Scholar."

These overleaves were asked very early in the formation of our little group and the medium called Jessica had not yet "honed" her skills to the acuity of the following years. When his overleaves were first asked, the medium picked up on all the Scholar, being a Scholar herself, and missed the Warrior completely, an understandable "lapse" in this case.

"What is the incident of medium error?"

For skilled and experienced legitimate mediums, the margin of error is about twelve to fifteen percent, depending on such things as fatigue, the nature of the question asked, and the available energy at hand. Incidentally, the medium called Jessica was able, after four years of channeling, to reduce her errors in overleaves to eight percent. For example, inquiring of Jessica on the nature of the society of the tenth-century, common reckoning, Bugandans might not be as accurate as information given on tenth-century, common reckoning, Greeks due to lack of accessible "reference points", particularly in regard to a nonliterate culture, such as the Bugandans had at that time. It is also important to remember that often minutiae of details are hard to get when there is general understanding of context, as any group of eyewitness accounts can demonstrate. For example, channeling information on the life of a miller in the twelfth century might not be easily differentiated with the life of a miller in the eleventh century or the thirteenth, common reckoning. Such matters often create margins of error in information, which is no one's "fault". Also, we are aware that our "take" on "time" is vastly different from yours and this is often a factor in apparent "errors" in this material, which is, again, not a matter of "fault". When we speak of margins of error, we include material the medium "blocks" for any number of reasons, including the problems of "past" experience. Most mediums are unable to channel information about the past in which they, in a previous life, played a role. In other words, if a medium had been a courtier at the court of Louis XIV of France, the medium would be able to get only "spotty" information about the court itself, although the rest of the French culture of the period would probably be more "accessible" for the medium.

━━━━━

"**B**ack to the cultural and societal attractions for the various essences."

Of course. Scholars are drawn to the classroom and, more significantly, the library. They obviously come into their own in the Mature or fourth cycle. When neither institution is easily accessible, the cloister is often a chosen alternative. In general, Scholars are more content with a solitary life than most other essences are, and aside from gathering in colleges for the exchange of information, Scholars are often inclined to "keep out" of groups, particularly in the Mature cycle, which is a "double dose" of Scholar. We would have to remark here that Scholars are also inclined to explore in order to gather more information. Scholars, being in the neutral position, are able to "mix" well with all other essences, but often would prefer not to have to be "bothered" unless they choose to gather information on other people, in which case they will tend to be intensely gregarious. Scholars also make excellent journalists, for they will be relentless in their pursuit of information. All Scholars relish learning things, although after the Mature cycle is begun, Scholars often have little patience with the strictures of "formal" higher education unless the information they seek is attained through higher education. Such fragments as Richard Nixon and John Knox were Baby Scholars; Young Scholars include Gay Talese, Leonard Wolfe, and Candace Bergen; Lord Byron, Richard Brinsley Sheridan, and Mary Shelley were Mature Scholars, as were Rossini, Verdi, Prokoffiev, and Sibelius.

The British actress Wendy Hiller is another example of
Mature Scholar, along with newsman Mike Wallace, as was
the physicist Robert Oppenheimer. Among the distinguished Old Scholars are author Reay Tannahill and actor
Anthony Hopkins.

Sages, who share the Expression Polarity with Artisans,
are lovers of drama, both in the observing and participatory
sense, and come into their own in the Old cycle. That does
not, of course, mean they cannot have "complete" lives
before the Old cycle. We did not say that and we did not
imply it. We mean only that the full range of possibilities
reaches the greatest potential in the Old cycle. Sages are
the most "comfortable" Old souls. They are at home in
courtrooms, theaters, circuses, and diplomatic centers all
over the world. Sages are the great communicators, and
tend to be drawn into the "spotlight". They are also
capable of many significant insights and genuine humanitar-
ianism. We would have to say that the Sages' attraction
to political life is "natural", for it combines high-profile
attention with high drama, an irresistible combination to
any true Sage. For these reasons if no others, Sages are
skilled diplomats and negotiators. On the other hand, Sages
experience the "needs" of audiences more keenly than
most other fragments do, and they are inclined to be more
"responsive" than many others, which can be exhausting
for all concerned. Sages make great raconteurs and wonderful hosts, but when deprived of an "audience," Sages may
turn close associates and family into audiences on short
notice or no notice at all. Noteworthy Sages include Bill
Clinton, Richard Chamberlain, and Bernadette Peters in
the Young cycle; Jack Palance, Diana Rigg, and Diane
Sawyer are Mature Sages, as is Tom Brokaw; Gene Hack-
man, Monserrat Caballe, and the irrepressible Sir Thomas
Beacham are/were Old Sages.

Priests, who share the Inspiration Polarity with Slaves,
always serve a higher ideal, whatever the Priest decides the
higher ideal to be. Priests always have a kind of "astral"
link in their nature, because as the sixth essence, they
never reach a state this is wholly their own on the physical
plane. This can lead to complications for those Priests who

are not aware of this "extra" realm of "consciousness" that is crucial to the Priest essence. Priests almost always have a sense of "inner purpose" to what they do, and often assume other fragments know what that purpose is, and, of course, share it, which is not often the case or appropriate. Serving higher ideals is the Priest's job, and not that of other essences, difficult as it is for Priests to believe that. Priests tend to create congregations for themselves, in the literal and figurative sense, which may be anything from a recreational group to a business staff to a union, and in the most extreme cases, a cult. They have an abiding need to realize the astral connection to all things "earthly", and find a number of ways to express this, many of which are baffling to fragments not on the Inspiration polarity. Incidentally, each Priest has his or her own higher ideal— they do not necessarily agree among one another what it is. Young Priests are often so zealous they are unble to see those who disagree with them as anything but deliberate heretics, and respond unfavorably to such fragments. Depending on the power wielded by the Priests, this lack of favor can mean anything from a cold shoulder to a hot stake. Apostasy is generally viewed by Priests as significantly worse than heresy, for apostasy means rejection of the Priest's higher ideal after it was accepted, which completely negates all of the Priest's "purpose in life". George Bush is a Young Priest, as was Indira Ghandi. Mature Priests include actor Peter O'Toole, novelist Anne Rice, and diplomat Anwar Sadat. Among Old Priests are numbered poet Theodore Rothke, entertainer Danny Kaye, composer Oliver Messiaen, and artist Mary Cossatt.

Kings, of course, have kingdoms, and these change their nature as the King essence evolves. The King is "connected" to the causal plane, just as Priests are connected to the astral, and there is always a sense of something larger or greater than the immediate in the nature of Kings. Like Priests, they do not tend to gather other Kings about them, but select their court, particularly their palace guard, which is most often taken from the other side of the Action polarity, from among Warriors, who are the single essence unlikely to be "pressured" successfully by Kings. Failure to demonstrate sufficient loyalty may result in banishment, which is the King's single greatest punishment. Kings tend to regard any perceived "desertion" as "treason", and will cut off the fragment, literally or figuratively, for this "unacceptable" behavior. It is difficult to put a King in a subordinate position unless the King has very accommodating overleaves, and even then, it is not easy. The single greatest trouble Kings face is that they will never be made to take full responsibility for the authority they exercise. This is especially true when Kings have been "permitted" to run a family since childhood, which happens fairly often, as you might suppose. Kings who do not learn to take responsibility for their authority are dangerous fragments, indeed, and we would have to say cause much trouble for themselves as well as those who have "bent the knee" to them. Young Kings tend to be highly visible fragments: the late Shah of Iran was a Young King, as is the CEO of Standard Oil. Mature Kings include Madeleine Albright, the U.S. ambassador to the United Nations, diva Dame Kiri TeKanewa, and actor James Garner. Among Old Kings are Sarah Caldwell of the Boston Opera, psychoanalyst Alice Miller, and actor Tommy Lee Jones.

Cultures provide the "context" in which fragments of all essences will work out the nature of their overleaves and their life plan, and for that reason, if no other, it is crucial to the nature of choices the fragment will tend to make. Those fragments of a markedly different level of evolution than the "average" fragment around them will tend to feel displaced and "out of touch" with society, no matter what overleaves are chosen, unless the fragment abdicates both third and fourth internal monads, allowing the family and society to define the personality rather than the overleaves. On the other hand, the culture into which a fragment is born is part of the life choices made before incarnation, and we would think few fragments ignore the "reality" of culture when making such choices about incarnation, although culture often turns out to be more of a "stumbling block" than fragments anticipate it will be when making choices between lives, when such world truths have less of a "hold" upon the "consciousness" of all fragments.

Culture is the "burden" fragments have created as a means of organizing survival skills. Without creating a society, your species would not have been able to gain enough of a foothold in the world to allow for the levels of evolution that led to ensoulment. It is not unlikely that your species would have remained at a "social" level similar to gorillas if the advantages of complex organization had not made themselves "apparent," leading to the kinds of adaptations that brought about sufficient development for ensoulment to be a "practical" addition to the nature of the species. For among primates, your species relies most heavily on group "solidarity" for survival, and given the many vulnerabilities of your species, developing "tribes" and "society" presented the only viable solution to the problems your species confronted as it made its way toward a point when ensoulment was "sensible". Culture has provided a "point of reference" for fragments wishing to have the "human" experience, as all fragments extant in your species do.

That does not mean that ensoulment is the "natural" end to which all species evolve, or that "culture" is an out-growth of ensoulment. This is demonstrably not the case. But given the variety of life your planet supports, it would have been "odd" if ensoulment did not become part of the "mix" during the long development of life on your planet. That you have a primate species ensouled and cetaceans are ensouled is a "modest" level of evolutionary "activity". We are aware of other planets with fewer available species where three or four of them are ensouled. This is due to high levels of interspecies interaction and inter-dependency, which is much less the case with your species, or for cetaceans, for that matter.

We do not intend to imply that capitulation to cultural demands is "required", for that would obviate choice. Culture is a context that provides fragments with a frame-work and a venue for the life task to be accomplished, and as such it is "necessary" for your species to do the tasks at hand in some way that will have "congruity" in impact and achievement. It also provides a "history" for all frag-ments to share.

CHAPTER 3

Gender, Sexuality, Biology, and Destiny

All fragments on the physical plane experience some sort of physical differentiation that can be perceived as gender. In your species even those with serious chromosomal and hormonal imbalances are generally identifiable as male or female, although there are very rare exceptions to this. In most instances, by which we mean among all independently mobile ensouled species, there are outward indications that make gender identifiable for species members, although it is not always something visible. It is the nature of ensoulment in your species that each of you is some mixture of what you call male and female, although this is not completely a "biological" matter, for much of what constitutes perceived male and female characteristics is more determined by culture than by such things as hormones.

As your science is well-aware, almost all very early fetuses are potential females. A hormone "shift" modifies the female to the male form. This alone should serve as a reminder that such things as rigorous gender identification is not as simple a matter as it might superficially appear to be. Because your species puts such heavy significance on gender differentiation, we are aware that these considerations tend to occupy more of the attention of all fragments than is "justified" by the nature of life as you experience it. For example, a burn burns males and females with

equal pain and severity. Sunlight exercises the same visual
opportunities for male and female alike. Oxygen is equally
important to both sexes, as is water, nourishment, protection, instruction, stimulation, health, and all the rest of
"human" experience. But, due to the apparent dichotomy
of male and female, all manner of assumptions have been
made predicated on nothing but a single, very minor varia-
tion within the species. We are aware that many fragments
view the "other" sex, whichever one it is, as not just
another form of human, but something so wholly alien, that
non-primate species are felt to be more like the fragment in
question than a member of the "other" sex, and this,
in spite of the fact that the non-primate species have the
same two sexes as well. To perceive other members of the
same species as alien, we would think is demonstrably
ridiculous, and yet it is evident throughout most of the
cultural structures of your species that this is precisely
what has happened.

━━━━━━━━

"Isn't gender and sex a little out of Michael's realm? Aren't
there things more appropriate to esoteric studies?"

Yes, we would agree that as we no longer experience
gender, or incarnation, for that matter, that we are not as
much "caught in the throes" as you on the physical plane
are. Which is, of course, a crucial lesson of the physical
plane. We have said before but we will state again: there
are lessons that can only be learned on the physical plane.
All the ramifications of having a body are the most "essential" [Michael puns again] of those lessons, and the "purpose", if such a thing is needed, for ensoulment in yours
or any species. Those on the physical plane, no matter
what form their incarnation takes, must deal with the
"reality" of physicality, and in terms of survival, gender
and sex are significant in their impact, and we would think
that most of the fragments currently extant on the physical
plane would concur.

As to what is appropriate to esoteric studies, anything that a fragment perceives is valid for esoteric studies, both as subject and realms of inquiry. We would think that those who are determined not to permit their physicality to "interfere" with their "spiritual" growth are, in fact, missing the point. Spirituality is "rife" in your species and in all ensouled species. The spirit has little or no need for your "involvement", for it is a constant more enduring than matter inself, but the body most certainly does. One of the most ongoing lessons of bodies is the whole matter of "up-keep". They must be nourished, protected, and a certain percentage of them need to reproduce in order to maintain the species, although, as we have often remarked, your species has gotten "carried away" with the "need" for reproduction. There is another aspect to including the body in studies with teachers like us—you can quickly validate that we are "on the level" with our information through physical experience. For example, a fragment may inquire the cause for headaches in that fragment's experience, or similar physical problems. Our diagnosis and recommendations can quickly be "checked out" and validated, which supports our less-easily validated teaching. This is true in matters having to do with gender-related matters as well. We have often been asked about choices made in this regard, and we will discuss gender identity and sexual orientation from our point of view.

In terms of sexuality, we would have to say that many fragments are so preoccupied with the nature of their sexuality, they have little sense of their personality beyond its impact on sexuality. That is definitely allowing the "cart before the horse", in that sexuality, while an important part of life, we would not deny, is a facet only of the complexity of personality, and as such, is no more or less important than which hand you write with. In fact, since many fragments spend far more time using their left or right hand at daily tasks than they do in overt sexual activity, we would think that "handedness" is in many ways more significant than the sexual orientation of the fragment possessing it.

Few infants are born with sexual orientation, although a few are, for reasons of life choices, and those choices tend to be manifest early in life. Most fixate as hetero-, homo-, ambi-, non-, etc., sexual at the time of the second internal monad, which occurs at approximately age three. Some accomplish this monad as early as twenty-six months, but there is usually trauma associated with so early a transit. In this internal monad, the differentiation of others takes place, the infant chooses lifetime centering, which is part-and-parcel of sexual perceptions. While much of this sexual orientation comes about through a sense of "trust" and "validation", it is essential to be aware that these decisions are made in terms of a very young person, and such concepts are not the complex philosophical matters they often become later in life, but a matter of physicality translated into "understanding". Many studies have been done on the effects of early treatment of children and subsequent development, and while we would agree that certain things will tend to be more "helpful" to the child than others, we would have to say that the essence and overleaves of the child are significant in terms of how any treatment, "good", "bad", or "indifferent", is perceived by the fragment in question. Obviously, starving and beating a child will be injurious to it, as it would be to any living thing, but there are aspects of family dynamics that exert subtle pressures on the infants that are generally wholly "insignificant" to the older fragments caring for the infants in question. What makes the infant aware of its sexual responses are of so wide and "odd" a range that we could not discuss it except in regard to individual bases, and the factors included in an infant's choice would tend to be perplexing to adults. There is no set of instructions regarding fixating your baby's sexuality, nor can one be developed, for that would abrogate choice, which is, as we have often reminded you, the "point" of living.

═══════

"**W**hat about the concern that school instruction might make a child choose a sexual orientation by creating an air of approbation for all sexual orientations?"

Let us assure you that by the time a fragment is in
school, sexual orientation is fixed. Sexual orientation is not
something that is "catching" like the flu; it is a choice
made at the completion of the second internal monad. Just
because there is no overt or obvious expression of sexual
orientation, it is inaccurate to assume it does not exist.
Your concerns in this regard are invalid. By the time formal
education begins, the "damage" has been done. Those
fragments who believe that lessons in school will change a
child's sexual orientation are deluding themselves, and
attempting to create scapegoats for something that is in no
way a matter of "indoctrination". In fact, for those fragments who have chosen an orientation not generally supported by the society, we would think that some indication
of tolerance and viability would not be amiss. We would
also have to observe that for some fragments, who sense
familial ambivalence of various sexual orientations, exposure to a more diverse perspective may save the fragment
from many long, uncomfortable hours of self-criticism and
indulgence of chief feature over issues of sexual orientation, their own, or the orientation of those around them. It
is also of interest in this case to be aware that societal
"norms" have little to do with the reasons a fragment
chooses the sexual orientation it does, for at so young an
age, societal "norms" are not an understood concept.

That is not to say that some youngsters will not experiment out of curiosity with sexual expressions not in accord
with their orientation. This behavior is not uncommon
in all youngsters, and is not in any way remarkable or
"blameworthy". We are aware of a fragment who was at
one time associated with a member of our little group
who had, at age twenty-four, decided it was politically
advisable, as a feminist, to have her sexual alliances with
women, although her chosen sexual orientation was em-
phatically heterosexual. Sexuality may be an issue in the
many difficulties between men and women, but sexual
orientation, we assure you, is not an aspect of species
politics. That this Young Artisan was unable to sustain her
sexual alliances with women does not surprise us, just as

we are not surprised that the former sexual partner of one of the women in our little group has had difficulty in finding the "right" partner among the women he has pursued, since his sexual orientation is toward his own sex. In his case, a great deal of religious blackmail has distorted his ability to recognize his sexuality for what it is, and this has caused him a great deal of misery, which, inevitably, he shares with his female sexual partners. Let us also point out that gender, as such, has little to do with what you call romance. Romance is not the product of sexuality, but of cultural expectations and the conduct of intimate friendships of a sexual or nonsexual nature. We perceive that in this culture, as in all Young-soul cultures, there is a tendency to assume romance and sexuality are necessarily the same thing, which can lead to dramatic misunderstandings and occasionally to hostile activities such as assault and what is being termed date rape. Romance can be "indulged in" on many levels, some of them more tenuous than others. We would think also that many fragments would benefit from "getting" the romance "rules" straight from the start. That way a couple whose sexual orientation is not compatible can be able to enjoy a romantic association without misapprehension on anyone's part. We would think much could be learned by all parties in such an endeavor.

"Then it is possible to shift sexual orientation?"

If by that you mean is it possible to have sexual contact with those who are not the truly desired gender, of course it is. Ask anyone who has ever been in prison if you suppose otherwise. Or make inquiries of those running educational institutions where postpubescent fragments are rigidly segregated. There are many, many fragments who have let their social conditioning override their original choices that we would have to say that at least fifteen percent of the adult population experiences some form of sexual orientation distortion because of societal pressure, although this is by no means limited to pressure for those attracted to their own sex to form sexual alliances with members of the "opposite" sex. Oftentimes, those fragments, especially males, who are abusive to the females they live with are actually attracted to members of their own gender and are angry with the females for making it unacceptable for them to follow their inclinations. Of course, not all abusing husbands or wives are repressed homosexuals, but such orientations often contribute consciously or unconsciously to the treatment of the fragment of the "opposite" sex with whom the abusive fragments cohabits. There can also be religious factors in continuing abuse, based on the staunch belief that sexual behavior is sinful and that the fragments who tempt the abusive fragment to sin is deserving of punishment. These are not the only issues that bring about abuse of a sexual partner, but at least one factor is usually a component in any continuing abusive relationship.

Such alliances, that is, those alliances to a fragment who is not one of those to whom the partner is sexually oriented, need not be "unpleasant". For example, we are aware of Task Companions who have lived together as sexual partners for a decade, although one of the two men is heterosexual in terms of his original choice. However, the satisfaction of his relationship with his Task Companion is comprehensive enough that the sexual aspect of their alliance does not present a "problem" for him, and he is truly content with his life with his Task Companion as he was not content with his eight-year marriage to a "temperamental", female Young Sage. This choice in later life was not made to slight the Sage, as she has often accused her former husband, it was made out of a "need" for a supportive general environment, which living with the Task Companion provides far more comprehensively than did the marriage with the Sage. And in this case, the most significant aspect of both relationships was that of living together, not sexual expression and activity, but all the other hours when sexual expression was not the focus of the alliance. To assume that all sexual activity is the result of sexual orientation is to take an overly stringent view of the nature of the human experience, at least as we understand it.

———

"If that choice was made later in life, wasn't it a moral one?"

Let us suggest that it be examined ethically instead of morally, for, as we have stated before, the question of morality is not valid in this, or almost any, context. We have realized that there are many of you who find accepting this new frame of reference "troubling"; let us assure you that once the concept is examined, our "take" on the matter can be "grasped". More karma has resulted from fragments doing the "moral" thing than those who have chosen to do the "ethical" thing. We would think it far more ethical to accept a supportive relationship over one driven almost wholly by chief feature, no matter how outwardly "correct" the relationship might appear to be. There are those who would recommend that a divorce is immoral and therefore encourage partners to "stick it out" together "for the sake of the children", which only serves to reinforce negativity in the partners and to demonstrate to the children that "marriages" are unhappy. To remain in a negative "spiral" because it is more societally accept-able in terms of apparent sexuality may suit certain limited moral precepts, but is ethically invalid. To be willing to end the negative "spiral", we would think is Good Work. And we would have to say that there is much commendable in the validation of positive bonds. Had the sexual orientation of both Task Companions been actively homosexual, we would think the transition would have been easier for all concerned.

———

"What about transsexuals? How does that fit into the 'scheme of things'?"

First we would have to remark that such a choice has not been possible until the last thirty years or so, and the impact on the culture in general has not yet been fully assessed, nor will it be for at least three generations, or a period of sixty to seventy years. We would agree that certain family perceptions can "skew" the expression of sexual orientation for many fragments, and that it is not uncommon for fragments to feel they have somehow "got it wrong" in regard to expressing sexual orientation, though rarely in the matter of sexual orientation itself. In such cases, an assessment of sexual conduct between the parents might reveal certain sorts of behavior with which the child did not choose to identify as part of its own sexual orientation, which led to a desire to "break" the "pattern". That there are a number of (predominantly) men who wish to become women we find an interesting choice, especially for those who were raised as males and had made heterosexual choices in terms of their sexual orientation. This is reflected in the number of transsexual males who, once surgically altered to females, continue to be sexually attracted to females, delineating the "problem" of identity in relation to sexuality with remarkable clarity. That does not mean that the "transsexuality" was a "mistake", only that sexual orientation is not something that is dictated by "equipment". This continuing attraction to females for males who have become female is not so unusual a development as might seem apparent for, as most homosexuals will tell you, few of them want to be the "opposite" sex simply because they are attracted to their own. The assumption of incipient heterosexuality in all sexual expression is an erroneous perception, and obviates the validity of sexual orientation by denying it has any true form but one.

Let us also point out that there are lives in which sexual orientations are chosen as part of the life-plan, whether they are societally "correct" or not. Until fairly recently, in Western culture, the choice of a celibate life in religious communities was seen as admirable and something that was favorable. Now such choices, and the underlying compulsions often associated with such institutions enforcing this behavioral code, have come under scrutiny that has shown much of the celibacy was, in fact, a facade for activities that were regarded as "unacceptable" by the society as a whole. Often the fragments entering the constraints of a religious life did so in the hope that their compulsions could be "diverted" into more "acceptable" expressions. That does not mean that all fragments choosing to live in celibate communities suffer from "aberrant" sexual inclinations. We did not say that and we did not imply it. There have been any number of fragments who choose a nonsexual "lifestyle" for any number of reasons, just as those who express their sexuality in some active way do so for a vast array of reasons. And not all those who choose celibate lives do so in the context of religion. We are aware of a great number of fragments in professions of so disruptive and "demanding" a nature that sustaining a sexual alliance becomes an intolerable burden for the fragment in question, and in order to do the "work", the fragment has little or no actual sexual contact of any kind. Obviously, there are fragments who use a demanding occupation as an excuse to avoid the hazards of intimacy of any kind outside the context of occupation. That, of course, is a matter of choice, as is everything in life. And from our point of view, all choices are equally valid.

There are fragments who perceive all sexual choices as "tainted", and believe that to express sexuality reveals a "loss of innocence", which is not a valid perception, although they are certainly free to choose to have it. To equate innocence with ignorance, as the "loss of innocence" assumption does, places the whole matter of sexuality and sexual orientation into an area of behavior where it becomes the method of self-condemnation. Those who choose to believe that children are incapable of sexual perceptions are permitting their chief features to sentimentalize the experience of childhood and the reality of the nature of sexuality as it develops in the young humans. All fragments experience sexual stimulation of an oriented sort after the age of three, when the second internal monad is complete; the ability for adults to dismiss this comes from the fact that before puberty sexual stimulation is not "limited" to the genitals, or to an orgasmic focus, but instead is bound up in sensuality and gratification. Sexuality, in and of itself, is not an issue of legal responsibility, and therefore the whole concept of guilt is inappropriate to the matter and to the choices made at the time of sexual orientation. There are ways in which fragments conduct themselves sexually that are not responsible in a legal sense, and that conduct may be described as guilty, but not because it is sexual—because it is irresponsible. This distinction may prove "difficult" for certain fragments to "grasp", due to the expectations of their cultural indoctrination and the blandishments of chief features. But we assure you that sexuality is "natural" to your species, and your choices in its regard are all valid.

The opportunities to confuse sexual activities with aggression are many, and those who perceive all sexualized forms of aggression as sexual in purpose have allowed their own preoccupations with sexuality to distort their understanding of the nature of aggression. This is most apparent in the highly ambivalent attitude held in most human societies regarding the question of rape. Although it is generally legally recognized that rape is a crime of aggression expressed sexually, most fragments do not fully "believe" it, as the relatively small number of complaints reveal, to say nothing of the much smaller number of prosecutions and the relatively minor percentages of convictions. This is in large part due to the belief it is morally incorrect to sexually attract those who might be aggressive in their response, hence the tendency to "blame the victim".

This is also a clear pattern in the matter of aggressive sexual exploitation of children, rendered the more complicated because most children have few personality tools to accurately assess the acts they have endured, particularly as sexual perceptions in the young are not as bodily specific as they tend to become in adults. And often recollections in adult life are "colored" by adult perceptions that were, of course, not part of the "picture" when the fragment was a child. Not all those compelled to express their sexuality through acts upon children can be summed up in a few phrases, but there is some commonality in most of the patterns these fragments display: those who have a compulsion to vent their aggressions in overtly sexual ways on children are in large part confused about their response to children and the nature of intimacy, in that the aggressive fragments not only dread criticism from a sexual partner, their terror at the threat of intimacy is so great that chief features "require" sexual "partners" who have no comprehension of the focus of sexuality in adults and cannot therefore respond in any way that would lead to valid contact with the aggressor. Not all fragments wish to actively participate in such activities, no matter how much they are drawn to children in a sexual sense. Intimacy of any variety assumes "access," which is not possible across the gulf of childhood and adult sexuality. Those who find "kiddie porn" stimulating are often intensely ashamed of their own adult sexual vulnerability that to validate the "erotic" process with adults is too terrifying to make the contact "rewarding" except in the inappropriate context of children, who are not yet able to focus their sexual orientation in any valid way or have "cognizance" of the nature of what is taking place. The fact that many children find the initial approach of a sexually interested adult flattering does much to "complicate" such contacts, for in this case, it is only too easy to "blame the victim" and have the victim accept the blame without question.

We are aware that many—not to say most—fragments have occasional "inappropriate" sexual perceptions, and fantasies based on these perceptions are not only a common occurrence, they are a sign of good mental health in almost all instances, for it reveals a balance in the fragment. It would be a very troubling sign if a fragment never had such perceptions, for it would mean there was a dangerous lack of self-awareness that could lead to emotional "problems" due to a "failure" to conceptualize physical responses, or a "need" to disown any impulses that are not under strict mental control, which is, of course, impossible in a "healthy" fragment. Let us also mention here that those fragments who are unable to recognize fantasy for what it

is—a fantasy—and insist on responding to it as if it were
reality, put themselves into precarious states, although
such responses in puberty are not unusual and are only
alarming in our preceptions when they carry over into
"adult" life. There are many, many fragments whose curiosity is roused in sexual contexts, and the nature of discovery in regard to the questions raised is most generally
expressed in experimental sexual activity. In other words,
most fragments will, at some time in their lives, have
occasion to feel a sexual "thrill" triggered by a fragment
who is not an actual "target" of sexual activity. There is
nothing "dreadful" about this, for most human fragments
have such experiences. What we advise, however, is that
these occasional perceptions be recognized for what they
are and not "condemned" or "dismissed" or "denied" or
used to "justify" activities that exploit the body and deny
the intimacy of a sexual partner. To use the "guilt" stimu-
lated by sexual thoughts about a neighbor's teenage daughter as an excuse to beat up your wife is not Good Work in
any sense of the word, and the triumph of chief feature, for
it takes the preferred method of human intimacy and turns
it into the most intense betrayal, the repercussions of which
are reflected in choices throughout the life.

―――――

"Are there independently mobile ensouled species for whom
sexual contact is not the preferred method of intimacy?"

Of course. For some species, the taking of nourishment
together is the most intimate form of communication: there
is an independently mobile ensouled species for whom the
mutual consumption of redundant body parts is the most
intimate act possible. There are species for whom an exchange of body odors is the height of intimacy. There are
species where what you would perceive as a cross between
athletic competition and massage is the most intimate act:
for this species the activity itself is the source of sexual
expression. There are species where vocalizations are the

most intimate exchange. In fact, there are intimate expressions in various species that would appear so "bizarre" to your species you would not recognize the intimacy taking place if you were able to observe it. And there are independently mobile ensouled species for whom sexual activity—that is reproductive activity—is no more intimate than the recreative processes of salmon.

———

"**H**ow important is gender and sexual orientation to such species?"

That question has no single answer, for each species, as you might suppose, is different, and there are many aspects of intimate activity that cannot easily be identified in what you would perceive as "gender-specific". Which is why we say that in regard to the sexual center in your species, the physical excitation associated with sexual activity is the nature of the center. The function of physical excitation is essential to those in moving center, or either the emotional or intellectual part of moving center, for without the physical response, the possibility of movement becomes haphazard. Let us assure you that there is no ensouled independently mobile species that does not have some expression of intimacy that in some way reflects a biological predilection of the fragments involved, no matter how "peculiar" that is manifested. For independently mobile ensouled species, gender in some form or other—and many of those forms are notably "strange" from your point of view—is always a factor, for it is something that can only be experienced on the physical plane and therefore is "germane" to the physical plane itself for those fragments ensouled in independently mobile species. The requirement of reproduction does not, in fact, "demand" more than one sex, but the acquisition of diverse genetic material to prevent "in-breeding" is necessarily a factor in evolution. Even the most stable of ensouled species has a "compulsion" to gather genetic material from more than one source for the purpose of evolutionary "elasticity".

Let us remind you that the physical plane has experiences to offer that can be had nowhere else. Gender and its ramifications is one of the most "significant" experiences of the physical plane, as much a part of the nature of "survival" as nourishment, rest, and safety. And while we would not think that fragments "must" deal with gender in every life, we would think the choice not to do so might well be far more "consuming" than would appear to be the case at first review. The very experience of having gender is a valid one only on the physical plane, and we would think that for that reason alone, if no other, that all fragments would be inclined to understand the effect and affect of gender in all valid contexts, as well as to determine what contexts are not valid. For example, there is no biosexual reason why females should receive lower wages for the same work than males do, but you are all aware that this is a relatively common practice. There is also no biosexual reason why females with athletic abilities cannot openly compete with males in many events, such as golf or tennis. The real problem in such instances is, of course, cultural, and a reflection of the manner in which cultures "parcel out" power and recognition. Most males in this culture would not like to have to face a female in equal competition, for fear of intolerable chagrin that would result if the female prevailed. There is no biosexual reason why intellectual skills may not be developed in either gender, though there are many cultural "excuses" not to, and many rewards for accepting these paradigms; for example, males and females are both equally capable of understanding astronomy, and their observations are equally valid, although many cultures will predispose culture members to think otherwise. There is also no biosexual reason why such things as enlightened teaching "must" come from either gender, for such teachings, like us, have no gender. We lack bodies to do gender with. Those that claim validity for sexual identification and orientation beyond the physical plane are not presenting valid insights of those planes beyond the physical and those insights beyond the body.

Bodies, being physical, are subject to "wear and tear",

as are the garments you put on them. This continuing use
of bodies has a component of the most basic experience of
the physical plane: time. Time, as experienced linearly,
which is the nature of the physical plane, brings about
demands that can be encountered nowhere else in all planes
of existence. One of the most compelling aspects of incarnation for fragments in the process of evolution is the
experience of time in a linear manner and dealing with its
many impacts, from birth to death.

When you address matters of physicality and "biology",
you are at the heart of the "significance" of the physical
plane. We would want to remind you that this experience,
with all its difficulties, is unique to the physical plane and
has its own "virtues" that make its validity an essential
part of the evolution of essence. To appreciate your physicality is the beginning of what you call enlightenment.
Those who seek to attain a state "beyond" the body while
still ensouled in one are "missing" the "point". To abjure
the body is to deprive yourself of the validation and recognition of the physical plane. Without such validation and
recognition, what you call enlightenment becomes unattain-
able, as well as giving the chief features more than a little
power through the effort to "rule out" the experience of
the body. When what you call enlightenment takes place,
the body is experienced as what it is, neither pandered to
nor neglected. Hair shirts have no spiritual merit and often
lead to serious health intrusions. Flagellation, by oneself or
by others, does nothing beyond harming the flesh. Yes, it is
true that making the body hideously uncomfortable may
lead to out-of-body experiences; the nature of escaping
pain, by its very nature, makes attaining a state of enlightenment impossible.

━━━━━━━

"But isn't it Good Work to realize the maya in our existence
here?"

If by maya you mean the lack of recognition that essence
is eternal in the face of the finite body, then, yes, we would

agree it is Good Work. But disavowing the body with the mistaken impression that it is an illusion is not Good Work at all, for it leads to many misconceptions, particularly about the nature of life, the passage of time as the physical plane experiences it, and the whole process of growth and aging in a body.

━━━━━━

"If time isn't the way we think it is, what does that say about choice? Isn't everything in place somewhere on the higher planes?"

Let us answer this way: if you will picture a cable strand composed of many filaments, some of which, but not all, are being braided into the cable. The cable is the lives you have completed and the result of the choices you have made. There are occasional knots in the cable brought about by karma, when life choices were taken away either by or from the fragment in question. Where the braiding is taking place is the current point in the life. The filaments are of different lengths, substances, and textures, and some tend to be more "central" to the cable than others, but at each and every choice, the filaments are braided in or out, depending on the ramifications of the choice made. Which is why we do not predict: we do not predict because we cannot. Each choice is made by the fragment in question, and each brings new form to bear on the cable. From our point of view, all the filaments are valid—though some are likelier than others—until the choice is made. That is also why there is no destiny, only vectors, which tend to tangle filaments—because the tangling is caused by choice. In other words, you may be on vectors with another fragment and would have met at the concert that night, except you chose to look after an injured friend instead. That does not mean such a meeting will "never" take place, but if you choose to have it happen, it will be in a different venue, under circumstances that were not part of the original agreement. Not being part of the original plan is not crucial, any more than changing the time of a luncheon appointment to accommodate shifts in schedules.

Some of you who are more visually oriented may prefer to think of the difference between a sketch and the filled-in fresco painting, the sort that is made on new plaster. The sketch, often more than one sketch, or portion of a sketch, is just a suggestion, one of many options, which is not an actual "picture" until the paint is put on the surface, which is, we need not remind you, the result of choice. Some modification can take place afterward, but not much, as the paint soaks into the plaster quickly and is not easily altered. This analogy is not wholly accurate, just as the cable-and-filament one is not, but between the two, some sense of how we perceive your lives is possible.

Let us offer a third analogy, to accommodate the moving as well as the intellectual and emotional centers: there are a number of connecting routes to the same destination. A few are more direct than others, but all are equally effective. Where the traveler is on this complex series of routes is the present. The option to select other routes at every junction (choice) and every resulting aspect of the journey (ramifications of choice) are the valid experience of life. We would think that this might make it easier to comprehend the exigencies of life, as well as the importance of choice. It can also show how you can complete your journey without arriving at the destination you had in mind at the beginning. And perhaps it can show some of the nature of how such things as detours, rough roads, and the intrusions of the physical plane can do much to make the journey as "unpredictable" as it is. It is not amiss to keep in mind that roads do not wash out to ruin your day, they wash out as part of the hazards of the physical plane. Dealing with the hazard is as much a matter of choice as any other aspect of life. Confronted with a washed-out road, you may attempt to go back to the last junction and take another route, you may curse the road, you may blame yourself for making an erroneous choice, you may start off beside the washed-out road to keep as much to the old course as possible, you may choose to do something entirely different than what you had been doing, you may sit down and wait for the road to be repaired, you may try to find help over the washed-out part, you may invent some means of getting across, or any other of the myriad choices available to you in this predicament. All the choices are valid and any choice you make is as valid as any other. We remind you yet again that doing nothing is as much a choice as any action or decision you may choose.

———

"**All** right, all choices are valid. But aren't some better than others? Aren't some more likely to advance you in terms of essence evolution than others?"

From our point of view there is no "better" or "worse", only the ramifications of choice. It is true that some choices bring about more karmic ribbons than others, but if that occurs, you will in time choose ways to burn these ribbons. Let us remark that it is the purpose of the overleaves to make it possible for the fragment to complete the life task chosen for the life in question. There are times that the means to complete the life task does not come readily to hand, or that events on the physical plane intervene in its accomplishment. This is not an error, as we would think "should" be evident by now. There are times that the thrust of the life task is not in accord with the culture. For example, we know of Task Companions who have a monad to accomplish in this life—should they choose to do so—having to do with reciprocity and social responsibilities. Both are Young souls. One is a very dedicated policeman, the other is an accomplished criminal. They have been "locked" in a legalistic "waltz" for more than a dozen years and both of them have an "inexplicable" fondness for the other. A successful conviction of the criminal would tend to have a devastating effect on the policeman, who has defined his importance in terms of how he interacts with the criminal. And the criminal would not like to have to set his competition with the policeman aside. Both of them, without the activities of the other, would be likely to feel "useless" and "bored". That is not to say that all police and criminals are Task Companions working on monads, for that is demonstrably impossible, by numbers alone. But in this particular instance, a significant factor in their on-going relationship is the actions and the consequences of actions in relation to the law. In another life they are likely to choose to deal with their relationship in a different way, possibly one with fewer social intrusions or perhaps with less stringent consequences for the cardinal fragment.

========

"You said that certain choices in life were more likely for individual fragments. Is this in some way essence-specific?"

We would have to say in a general way that it is: Slaves are more apt to choose the filament that serves the common good than one that does not; Artisans are more apt to choose the filament that integrates structure; Warriors are more apt to choose the filament that responds to a challenge; Scholars are more apt to choose the filament that provides the greatest information; Sages are apt to choose the filament that makes the greatest degree of communication possible; Priests are apt to choose the filament that tends to serve the higher ideal; Kings are most apt to choose the filament that unites the kingdom. We are aware of more than one King who nearly worked him or herself to death in order to advance the kingdom; in fact, a few of them succeeded in dying. That is not to say, however, that such choices are always going to reflect the needs of essence, for such is not the case. In what we have just said, "apt" is the operative word, and cannot be viewed as revealing more than an inclination without any modification of such things as soul age, overleaves, stage of life, the circumstances concerning the choice, cultural and familial aspects, and all the rest of it, including mood, weather, astrological influences, physical conditioning, physical surroundings, other demands on the fragment, and caprice.

It may also be of use to remember that the physical plane, by its very nature of matter and time, is the only place that accidents can happen. A few fragments have some skill in sensing the approach of certain accidents, but for the most part, the accidents arrive, their impact major or minor is intrusive. Dealing with these developments is one of the most valid experiences on the physical plane, though all experiences are valid.

———

"Is there anything we can do to increase our ability to deal with accidents?"

It might be useful to recognize and validate that they do happen, that you do not have to be responsible legally, ethically, spiritually, or psychologically for the event, except in regard to your own response. If you are struck by a run-away bus, this is not necessarily an indication that it was part of your life plan or that you "needed" to be hit by a bus. It may be that the event was an accident. Few fragments injured in traffic accidents do so for life plan reasons. Almost all are the subject of accidents. We would have to say that dealing with your response in this, or any, context, it is not unreasonable to suppose your experience will be a complex one—assuming you survive. Attempting to present a uniform reaction to any accident, particularly over time, will not serve anything but chief feature. Responses are multilayered and as such manifest in a wide variety of ways, and have a tendency to change over time. To continue to view an event, any event, as if it had just occurred is to deny the validity of time, which is not Good Work on the physical plane.

For those who seek to have some insight to their own vectors, we would think that consulting a competent—and we stress competent—astrologer or reader of tarot cards or similar "divinatory" practices. Astrologers, to be competent, need to have a "talent" for it as well as special knowledge from study. Those relying on computers will not have the perceptions that those who actually do the work themselves would provide. Of course, all areas of endeavor are more effective when the fragment doing the activity has "talent" for it, from composing symphonies to welding engine parts; from abstract mathematics to composting fields. We would encourage those of you who choose to do this to take notes and evaluate them critically, for in what other way can you determine the competence of the "expert" consulted? It would not be amiss to review the commentaries of such "experts" from time to time for the purpose of analyzing the material, not only for accuracy but for content and impact. For example, such an "expert" may tell you that you are likely to receive a large amount of cash and property within the next six months. In and of itself, this means little. You will, we would think, also want to know the source and reason for the "good fortune", which would be, we suspect, more welcome coming from a lottery, an advancement in your work, or other "favorable" experiences, than if the "good fortune" came from wills or court compensation for the loss of all your possessions. A degree of circumspection is not amiss when using these methods of discerning vectors in the life, and would have the additional benefit of making it possible for you to assess the worth of such consultations. The only reason such "divinatory" arts are of any interest whatsoever to us is that they make it possible for you to choose with a little more insight, if you choose to use such "experts" to enable you to have some sense of how influences around you are developing. If you choose to regard such material as "fate" we would have to say it will not aid you in choosing, for it moves your responsibility outside your own choice to the nebulous regions of "destiny", which, as we have informed you in the past, does not exist. That does not mean you cannot choose to do it, for all is chosen.

―――――

"**W**hat about those individuals who seem to be able to predict the future. What is going on with them?"

As we have already said, some fragments have an ability to sense vectors. There are a few—and we cannot make that few a small enough figure—who are able, being sixth or seventh cast at a sixth or seventh level in whatever cycle they occupy who can, under certain circumstances, become aware of encroaching events in a sufficiently coherent way to make it useful as a reliable prediction. However, much of what is assumed to be prediction is nothing more than a good statistical guess. For example, to predict a drought in west Texas is not a major achievement, as is predicting earthquakes in California or Japan. Statistically, such events are going to happen. It is more significant if a "prophet" predicts a snowstorm in May in Atlanta or Rome, and the event occurs, for that is a statistically unlikely event and something that can be judged in a framework of time. Those fragments who experience what they suppose is precognitive powers might do well to keep a journal of the impression, with as much detail as possible, and then review the journal and update it as to accuracy. This will accomplish two things: (one) it will enable you to determine whether you are picking up on something "genuine" or only reacting to chief feature and, (two) it will make it possible for you to develop a sharper understanding of the nature of the precognitive experiences you have and hone your recognition skills.

—————

"**A**re there such things as psychics? Real psychics?"

If you mean are there fragments who are able to gain access to the Higher Intellectual and/or Higher Emotional Centers with some regularity and with some discipline, yes, of course there are. But they are not often encountered, are often "shy" of attention, and we would think that those unwilling to be reviewed for results or whose prices are more than a week's salary are not without agendas having more to do with profit and cult status than actual use of psychic talents. There is a great deal of credulity around what is sometimes called the "paranormal", and there are many fragments willing to exploit the credulity. That is one of the reasons we encourage you to question our answers and evaluate the information with "realistic" parameters, for otherwise you will not be able to recognize, let alone validate what we have to say.

We wish to remind all here gathered that the possession of such talent is rarely a pleasant thing, and those whose gifts are genuine, due to such things as position in casting and evolution and soul age, often choose to "underplay" the talents they have than be subject to the kinds of emotional and personal demands that can be made over time, to say nothing of having to "live with" the things they perceive. It would be of use to consider the burden of the talent as well as any supposed advantages. There is good reason to perceive genuine psychic ability as at least as problematic as a chronic but low-level disease—a thing that demands constant attention and may flare up without warning, but which gives you an "edge" on the world by making you more aware of potential hazards. Incidentally, a great many psychics can "read" for everyone but themselves. This is occasionally a life choice, but is more often the result of chief feature interference, just as most true mediums can get information about everyone but themselves, past and present. For those fragments choosing psychic abilities as part of the life plan, we would think that the overriding reasons for such a choice would be karmic, generally to enable a "pay-back" for the karmic ribbon of "mind-fuck".

"**W**hat about all those accounts of parents being told that their infant child would be a world leader, and it turns out to be true?"

Think, should you choose to do so, of the number of times such a prediction was made and the fragment did not become a world leader. We assure you that this is a far

more common occurrence than the fulfillment of the
"prophesy". Not many fragments "come equipped" for
such work, and it would not avail the infant or its parents
much to "push" the issue. It is a fairly popular prediction
for infant males, and the one predicting is more likely to be
well-received if he or she has such a message than one
more accurate in nature. That is not to say that occasionally
such predictions are right—statistically, if for no other
reason, such would be the case. We would have to say that
once in a rare while a "reader" makes a "prediction"
based on a sense of overleaves and life task that lends
legitimacy to such pronouncements. We would think it
would be more significant if such a thing was predicted for
a female infant, although the cultural climate accepting
such a notion is changing in some parts of your society.
Incidentally, we would wish to point out that the prediction
of greatness has missed a few significant figures: the Mature
Sage who was Josef Stalin was never predicted to rise in
the world, and in the context of his parents, he never
accomplished what they expected; the Old Sage Angelo
Roncalli, who reigned as John XXIII, was not expected to
go far, as much because of his peasant origins as his
unorthodox approach to the Church; the Baby Scholar
Richard Nixon was thought to be as unsuccessful as his
father, and all his life dreaded it might be true; the Mature
Warrior Julius Caesar was expected never to amount to
much, and until his mid-thirties and the fourth internal
monad, fulfilled that expectation; the Mature Slave Jonas
Salk was believed to be an unpromising child, and the
family had very high standards for all members to meet;
the Mature Priest Dante Alighieri was predicted to be a
disappointment, and in the eyes of several of his relatives,
he was; the Young King Catherine the Great of Russia as a
minor German aristocratic female was not expected to
achieve much beyond a good marriage, which was assumed
to be the most she could do; the Young Artisan Steve Croft
was not expected to go far, and his journalistic leanings
were not at first encouraged. There are many other notable
figures who could be included in this catalogue, major

historical and current fragments for whom there were no extraordinary prophesies at birth. It would not be inappropriate to keep this in mind when dealing with prognostications in infancy.

Hindsight being what it is, it is possible to look at the examples cited and feel "smug" because the choices of the fragments in question were made apparent from the course of their lives. Consider the parents, who were confronted with a child whose potential can only be guessed at, and the guesses must, of necessity, reflect the parents' understanding of the world as well as the victories and disappointments of the parents. Let us remind you, however, that there are any number of fragments around you who are children now, who are burdened with the expectations of their families in ways that may not be appropriate to the children in question. Not that this is "avoidable", for it is not, and where such family "frameworks" are lacking, the child becomes what is called "feral", and unable to find a place in general human society. The nature of the experience of life is such that such incidents as the ones we have related are to be "expected". We will later discuss the family ikon and its impact on the fragment, but suffice it to say at this point that the nature of anticipation for children can be as much a hampering force as a support, no matter how "well-intentioned" the family is in making the choices for the infant. The "function" of the child within a family is generally established before the child is born, and it is not uncommon for children to think of themselves in terms of family "role", which is part of the process of living in your species. For as we have stated in the past, you are as much primates as you are ensouled fragments, and the experience of the dichotomy is wholly valid. We would think that many fragments find this difficult to understand, largely because they wish to "establish" which is more valid—primate or essence. The answer is that they have parity on the physical plane, which is, of course, one of the most significant "lessons" of life on the physical plane.

Destiny is, as we have indicated in the past, a lie, for it implies that choice makes no difference, that a predeter-

mined course is in place, like a rat's maze, and the life is
nothing more than a race to the cheese. This does not mean
you do not have choice about the nature of the life before
it begins, or that it is wholly without "direction", for that
is not the case, either. There is the life path, which you
may choose to follow or to abdicate at any time in the
course of a life. There are internal monads to transit or
abdicate, as you choose. There is karma, which you will
eventually choose to burn, but that is choice, not fate, and
a part of the evolution of essence. If there were true fate,
that is, a set "scheme of things", choice would be the lie,
and each and every fragment would be nothing more than a
kind of robot arm of an external force, less independent
than members of hive souls, and in no way answerable for
anything the fragment does, or anything that is "visited
upon" the fragment. Where there is choice, and we assure
you, choice is the only validity, there is responsibility. You
may decide to do anything you choose to do. And you are
responsible for it.

"Responsible to whom?"

Why, to essence, of course, to the core of your current
self and the core of all the selves you have been in the past
and will be in the future. It is essence that chooses the
overleaves and life tasks, life path, makes agreements, sets
up vectors, and all the rest of it. Then essence ensouls the
body and the whole matter of choice passes to you, meaning the person the fragment ensouls. Essence is what most
fragments perceive when they "see God", although it is
not God, nor are we, for that matter. It is the "light" you
go to in the process of death, just as the perceived "tunnel"
is the physical plane. It is also what some call the "Guard-
ian Angel". Prayer, as we have said before, is the personality, true or false, petitioning essence to intervene. Essence
never compels, incidentally. Essence impels. We cannot
stress this firmly enough. Essence will not "force" you to

do anything, for that obviates choice and is not Good Work; no one can be "ordered" to evolve or "conned into" growth. Insight, recognition, and validation are the processes used to grow, and as such, give access to essence. Essence is a function of love, and as such, will not "require" anything of the fragment. Chief features, on the other hand, are the distillation of fear, and are manipulative and very, very seductive. Chief features can present their fears in most persuasive guises, which is one of the reasons they are so good at ruling your lives—they do not "seem" to frighten you, only to "save" you. Essence is the only thing capable of "saving" you, not that any fragment actually needs "saving". We would think that those willing to recognize the validity of essence can do much, should they choose to, to "come to grips" with chief features. Incidentally, it is not "necessary" to extinguish chief features in order to evolve, although fragments occasionally accomplish this. Essence contact, or what you call intimacy, is the means of evolution. However brief essence contact may be, and however fiercely denied by chief features after the fact, all essence contact is valid, and the true means of the evolution of fragments ensouled everywhere on the physical plane.

CHAPTER 4

The Family

It is often assumed that a family is a microcosm of the society around it, but we would think that society is, in fact, a macrocosm of the family, and more "cogently" recognized in this light for the things society attempts to accommodate. This is not merely a bit of semantic sleight-of-hand, but a valid representation of our perceptions on this subject, and we would think that some of you may choose to consider examining it. The "purpose" of society is to provide context, congruity, opportunity, and care for its members, which is precisely what families are supposed to do. We are aware of familial patterns going back to first ensoulment, and where the family has survived. Those familial patterns that have protected their members have in all instances have thrived and been more successful than those that have failed to do so.

This is more easily perceived in the development of what you call civilization than by immediate observation of the current world, for the confusion of elements that regularly impinge on what you call real life can lead to distorted assessments due to the multiplicity of factors. Real life, for those in multicultural societies, has more of a "stretch" to achieve societal "familyhood". Extended families already existed with your species when ensoulment occurred. And those extended family groups quickly became interconnected family groups, that is, tribes, which, in turn, as nomadic life gave way to agrarian life, hamlets, and then villages. At the village level, the family model is still more or less "visible". But once towns develop, so does bureaucracy, and the position of elders, or village parents, become officials, and the family model becomes institutionalized and therefore less able to manage familial conduct on an individual basis, although "social" needs for the first time can be efficiently and comprehensively met. By the time villages become cities, the habituated "division of labor" has led to a class structure and the development of societal archetypes, which are the cultural equivalents of family ikons, which in turn bring about enhanced "self-awareness" of the culture as an identity as much as a structure, and a context in which all of the physical plane may be interpreted.

Families have "obligations" beyond nurturing their members, although this is surely the basic essential. To exist as a member of an ensouled species, a fragment has to know more than how to talk, what and when to eat, and how to tie its shoelaces. Those families where nothing more than basic survival skills are taught can be said not to be a family at all, but a kind of temporary bivouac for fragments of all ages. To the extent a society or culture does this it has failed in its "first obligations": to "imitate" the family. That does not mean that political coercion is Good Work, for it is certainly not; in fact, political coercion, with its labels and epithets is very like a permanent political familial ikon, arbitrarily assigned to groups by the political units of the society, and given the same sacred status as familial ikons are within a family. Many times, the labeled groups— Senior Citizens, The Homeless, Young Hispanic Males, Unwed Mothers, Radical Leftists, Radical Religious Rightists, Suburbanites, Rural Blocs, etc., to select some of the currently popular ones in your society—share the veneration of their ikon in that it removes their individual responsibility for their choices: "I couldn't help what I have done—what else can you expect of African-American Street Kids?" "I am not responsible because I come from a Dysfunctional Family.'', "It wasn't my fault because I had an Abusive Childhood," and so forth. The purpose of these statements is to invoke the ikon as much as to provide an "excuse" rather than a reason for action. We remind you yet again, that reaction to all events in life, no matter what they are, is a matter of choice, and the choice and its ramifications is the "purpose" for your life. Also, all things chosen in life have a "reason", which may or may not be "rational" or "appropriate", but is nonetheless a reason, and generally have little to do with group ikons or other cultural "labels". These group ikons, if recognized for what they are, can be broken free of, just as the family ikon may be broken free of, with recognition and validation.

Infants learn all they will ever "believe" about a society, a family, and culture by the time of the second internal monad, which, of course, means before they have been taught to "think", and before they have developed a significant vocabulary, which, in turn, indicates that these things are learned by what is observed, not what is taught. You as a parent or adult supervisor may spend hours "telling" a child how a member of this family behaves in the most proper sense, but if the instruction is not in accord with daily action, it is for "naught". We would think that those working with young children would agree with this statement. A child observes more attentively in the first two years of life than at any other time, and although it may not appear to be concentrating, we would wish to remind you that those in "trance" do not appear to be "thinking", either. It is not inappropriate to review your actions with your instructions when dealing with very young children, should you choose to do so, in order to minimize the inconsistencies that can be perceived. For example, a young child may be told repeatedly that hitting people is wrong, but if "daddy" beats up "mommy", particularly where the child can see it, the child will never fully accept such behavior as "wrong".

While we would agree that often the exigencies of the physical plane have made familial protection problematic at best, we would also think that where familial care has ranked the "highest", the family, and hence the tribe, has advanced more "effectively" than those where familial care of all members has not been a high priority. The family faced with environmental catastrophe, if the family structure is based upon continuing mutual support, is more apt to preserve their family members and maintain cohesion than those families where the continuing mutual support is absent. We would have to add that families, in any time of crisis, will tend either to "work as a team" or "fall apart," depending on the way in which the family has "performed its duties" to family members in the past in less "trying" times. Incidentally, from our point of view, multiple spouse families are not designed to care for all members responsibly. The redundancy of spouses, and therefore the higher birthrate, is generally linked with family structures where the multiple spouses are "replaceable" as are their children. Where partners have one spouse at a time, we would think that concern for that spouse will be of greater familial significance than where there are a plethora of spouses.

Let us remark that families constitute the basis by which a newborn learns or does not learn trust, which may seem obvious, but upon reflection, you will find is a complex matter. And trust is essential in developing a basis for intimacy, and the means by which it is achieved in later life. Without trust, essence contact, including self-intimacy, becomes almost impossible, and the access of fear to the personality increases dramatically. We cannot emphasize this enough—a child who does not learn trust before the second internal monad will have a very difficult time in ever being able to trust other fragments for the rest of that particular life, or to understand it when it has been given to the untrusting fragment. The single most important manner trust is created is through direct personal response to the child when it cries; response to crying will not, in fact, "spoil" the child, particularly before the second internal monad. Even whining is a sign of distress or malaise, and a child left to deal with such "nameless dreads" as are represented by whining will tend to be beset by fears throughout life. A child who is not held when it cries, no matter what the overleaves, will have a far more difficult time than most later in life where intimacy is concerned, for the perceived risk in intimacy will appear far greater to such fragments than it does to most, and most fragments find the initiation of true intimacy frightening at best. This is as much a factor in being primates as being ensouled, for as you will observe, should you choose to do so, a neglected baby chimpanzee will never truly "belong" in any context, due primarily to lack of trust. Trust, incidentally, permits a fragment to say "no" without endangering support or fear of ostracism, which is a fairly rare thing in this or any young-soul world, where no is generally perceived as defiance, and which, if support is withdrawn because of it, it quickly becomes.

To consider families as merely accidents of breeding is, from our point of view, a misconception [very funny, Michael]. Families are often the products of agreements and "old habits", and while it is relatively common to have family associations with those fragments with whom the fragments have some established "history", it is rare for immediate family members to be part of the same entity, for that bond is also fairly familial in its nature and this often produces a "double whammy" of tightness which is not necessarily desired. That does not mean such things do not occur, for, of course, they do, but we stress again that the instances are infrequent. It is, however, relatively common for fragments to have entity mates at one remove, such as uncles, aunts, cousins, grandparents, and the like, or occasionally parental life-long friends will be entity-mates with the children in question. Essence Twins are very rarely incarnated in the same family, although it does, very, very, very occasionally happen. Task Companions may incarnate in the same family slightly more often than Essence Twins do, especially when their shared task "requires" life-long preparation.

Within a family, there is an understanding based on alliances formed by what you call blood, which, in fact, has to do with DNA, biologically, and acculturation, psychologically. These alliances are primary to determining a sense of identity, which is set at the second internal monad, when experiential differentiation is truly possible for the first time. The first internal monad—that is, birth—is a familial concept, though not necessarily a reality. The second internal monad—the establishment of individual identity—is often more "fraught" with complexities, depending on familial structure, reality, and expectations. Let us mention here that where an infant has not been permitted or encouraged to have a sense of self but instead is encouraged to be a "cog in a wheel", the possibility of completing and validating the second monad is not great, and as a result, all subsequent monads will of necessity remain incomplete, and the hold of chief features is apt to become stronger over time. For a fragment to have an individual identity, the second monad, which, we have stated, occurs by age three, must be validated not only by the fragment but by the family as well in order for the fragment to be able to learn to make choices of an individual nature that are truly in accord with the life plan.

All families, without exception, are subject to various forms of disruption, from the birth of a child to the death of a family member, to fluctuations in fortune, changes in living conditions, problems of health, restructuring of family relationships, marriages, divorces, criminal activities, political and military shifts, and all the rest of the developments that are part of the way a life is led. We cannot emphasize enough that such fluctuations are part of life as lived on the physical plane, and dealing with them—or not dealing with them—are valid choices. With the disruptions come choices that are not always welcome, but generally "necessary", and as such, difficult for all family members. It is important to know that there is nothing "wrong" in disruptions, and that in fact it is "prudent" to expect them, for they are going to happen, and to be aware that when they come, a response of some sort will be "required". This is not a prediction, incidentally, but a simple observation on the nature of life as it is experienced, and you have only to review your own lives to perceive the validity in what we say. The only way a fragment may escape disruptions is to become catatonic, which a few fragments choose to do from time to time, but we would like to point out that in such a state, the continuing care and support from others is absolutely essential to survival, and therefore cannot be said to actually exclude the fragment withdrawing from familial function, either in the microcosm or macrocosm sense.

In order to maintain a "sense of identity" as a family, it is necessary for the family to "name" itself and assign a "function" or "role" to play. Each new child born into a family is given an ikon—and we mean that literally, a sacred image—by the parents, or parent-substitutes, which was decided upon before the birth of the child in most instances. The ikon is the role of the child is expected to play in the family, and it is through the ikon the false personality is formed, which is the personality available until the fourth internal monad, where true personality is manifest or false personality—that is, the family ikon— becomes fixed. That is not to say that the family ikon is not Good Work: it provides a necessary framework for the fragment to use to find its place in the world. Family ikons remain as the shared "mythos" of the family well after the fragment has transited the fourth monad and manifested true personality. In this society, the fourth monad is usually transited in the mid-to-late thirties, or about half-way through an average life-span. In some societies, of course, the monad takes place at a younger age to accommodate a shorter average life-span.

Within families, parents, as adults, create ikons for their positions, as well. This also occurs, but with less stringency, to those who do not have a family with children. In a domestic partnership, adults assume ikons reflecting the role they play in the relationship. For many families, all "communication" is done ikon-to-ikon, with no other possibility considered. We would think that in these instances, many family members have a sense of frustration and futility that makes family dealings difficult at best.

"Will Michael give some examples of family ikons?"

To begin with, we are aware of a Mature Artisan who was expected to be male and because she was female, was stuck with the ikon The Inappropriate Daughter. This caused her much difficulty in dealing with her family, for nothing she could do or say would give her access to the family in the manner she sought, and it was generally perceived by the family that she was not able to "understand" her "place" in the family. Eventually, as a result of the third internal monad, this adherence to the ikon led to a degree of estrangement between her and the rest of her family, and while she began the fourth internal monad, the process proved too "grueling" and she abdicated it at the fifth level. Her ikon as a parent is The Parent Who Does Not Criticize, a direct response to her ikon in youth. We are also aware of a mature Slave with the ikon A Constant Source of Pride and Joy, which has been a tremendous burden to him, for his family demands that he comport himself in such a way as to fulfill the ikon. As a parent, his ikon for himself is The Tolerant One Who Enables Others to Grow. His wife's adult ikon is The Sensible Decision Maker. We are also aware of a most unfortunate fragment given the ikon The Fallen Angel, by a parent so conflicted with guilt about sex that the only "punishment" sufficient to her "lapse" was bearing Lucifer himself. The son with this ikon has not had much good rapport with his mother in many years, and none with his father, who deserted the family when the boy was young, being unable to cope with his wife's constant turmoil about the "duties" of a wife to her husband.

Family ikons are predicated on familial needs, not on the fragment's actual personality, and occasionally these can be at such variance that the "trouble" of living up to the ikon is apparent early, such as a Young Priest born into a family of musicians, who is not himself musically talented, whose ikon is The Happy Prodigy. His talents and interests have already begun to reveal that the ikon is not suitable to his life, but the family has not been able to understand this, and dismiss his nonmusical interests as a "phase" he is going through. We would think that the third monad, the out-of-the-nest monad, which usually occurs in this society at about age eighteen to twenty-five, may, in fact, be transited early by this fragment as a way to lessen the pressure the ikon brings to bear in his life. We are also aware of a fragment born to a family after the mother had a series of miscarriages. The ikon for this daughter is, The Most Precious Girl in the World, and while it might sound useful and rewarding, it means a level of protectiveness and reinforcement of remaining a child that is proving, now the daughter is approaching the third monad, a very real burden. We are also aware of a fragment who has been "trapped" at the third monad for more than twenty years because of the limitations imposed by the ikon, which is The Child Who Never Makes a Mistake, and mistakes, in this case, include the break with the family implied in the third internal monad, which this fragment has obligingly abdicated. As a result, this fragment, facing the fourth internal monad, is unable to do more than "fiddle" with the perceptions of the fourth internal monad. There is also a Young Warrior fragment who was given the ikon of The Girl Who Always Depends on Her Daddy, and was then promptly—at age two—"disenfranchised" when her father left for a three-year engineering work contract in the Middle East; by the time he returned, alienation and resentment had set in and remain staunch to this day.

"How are ikons chosen?"

Ikons reflect how the family sees itself and the members within it, and sets the "tone" for the family and its actions in the world as well as among the members of the family. The choice is made as we have indicated, by the parents, to give structure to their perception of what the family is, which, in turn, provides the youngster with some "framework" for accustoming itself to living that particular life. The ikon is tied into the family "legend", that is, the story it tells of itself and the people within it, which the ikon permits to continue. In most instances the parents agree on the ikon, but occasionally this will not occur and the child will have an ikon from each parent, which can create a real problem within the family, for the role the child then has to fulfill for the father and the role to be fulfilled for the mother is not the same. Depending on the child, its role in essence, the overleaves, the life plan, and the measure of divergence inherent in the two ikons, this can be anything from "awkward" to "calamitous". Another "wrinkle" in the fabric is that the maternal side of the family will tend to reflect the mother's ikon, and the paternal side, the father's, so that a degree of "adaptation" to each side of the larger family will be "demanded" of the double-ikoned child. Double ikons occur in about one percent of children, incidentally, and for some, lead to personality disorders in later life, and for others, a difficult childhood, many times marked with an early interest in areas of endeavor that "get" the child "out of the house". Many of those children—though by no means all of them—who develop career interests in grade school are in part driven by double-ikons and a need to reach the third internal monad "ahead of schedule".

Of course, not all childhood "troubles" are ikon-spawned. We did not say that and we did not imply it. We are aware, however, that ikons, while "necessary" to growing up within a context and a culture, do not enhance life after the fourth internal monad. It is also true that ikons are often strong components in family disputes and conflicts. If, for example, a fragment has the ikon of The Patient Peace Maker, family gatherings are apt to become a terrible chore because of the constant assumption that this fragment can make everything "okay" when abrasions occur. The ikon of The Black Sheep can be assigned most arbitrarily, and we are aware of a world-renowned scientist who has this familial ikon, and has striven to "get beyond it" most of his life. It is interesting to note that he is the only academic in the family; it is also interesting to note that the ikon is stronger than his accomplishments, for he continues to hold the ikon, in spite of honors and high regard not only from the academic and scientific community, but the populace at large. In fact, his success in a field not "endorsed" by the family serves only to strengthen the ikon in family perceptions. Many fragments suffering from what is called "low self-esteem" are in actuality burdened with familial ikons that cast the fragment in an unflattering or unsupportive position, such as but not limited to: The Extra Child, The Lump, The Unwanted Burden, The Last Addition, The Unfortunate Child, The Adorable Little Baby, The Child to "Practice" On, The Child Who Is a Disappointment, The Family Curse, The Child Who Never Complains, The Child Who Will Make Up for Our Errors, The Child Who Always Supports Its Family, The Child with Nothing to Offer, The Tax Deduction, The Rival, The Child Who Endangers Mommy's Heatlh, The Unwelcome Intruder in Our Love Nest, The Child Who Promises Much and Accomplishes Little, The Child Who Will Fill the Place of the One We Lost, The Vindicator of the Family Honor, The Very Best Second-Rater, The Proof of Sin, The Child Who Might Be Worth Something Someday, The Offense Against Its Parents, The Blank Slate, and so forth. We assure you that all these ikons, and many more less "gracious" ones, are in place in the world; these, in fact, are ikons held by fragments known to fragments in our little group, although none of them are from our little group itself.

━━━━━━

"**I**t sounds like a family ikon is a real mixed blessing."

Yes, we would agree, although not in the judgmental sense of "blessing". At "best" family ikon is a "boost up" on life; at "worst," it is a "necessary evil" as the means of achieving a place and a way to "fit in". The impact on all fragments, no matter what the ikon, is mixed, as are many "necessary" things in life. Removal of tonsils prone to infection is not pleasant, but it is far less "damaging" than the staph infection that could prove deadly. Incidentally, we would wish to digress here once again on the matter of "hurt" and "harm". Most fragments fear hurt because it is painful, and this is not astonishing, although hurt, such as in the removal of tonsils, prevents harm in the form of deadly infection. Things that harm may seem pleasant, and offer no hurt at all, but the damage done, such as not removing the tonsils, is far more damaging and intrusive than hurt can be. We would therefore suggest that differentiating the hurtful from the harmful would be Good Work. And in the context of familial ikons, most—and we stress most—of them are often hurtful, but once the fourth internal monad is completed, recognized, and validated, it is not harmful. Where the fourth internal monad is abdicated or left unvalidated [by which Michael means that the monad was completed but in the negative pole, which is acquiescence, rather than the positive pole of self-realization], the familial ikon, by subsuming the true personality, that is, the function of the chosen overleaves, with the false, that is, the family ikon, it inevitably becomes harmful, for it makes self-intimacy all but impossible, and the insights sought in the life are not likely to be brought to bear, which in turn makes work on the life task "haphazard" at best. We would think that for those who have "surrendered" to the ikon, the benefits are more illusory than real, and will tend to be present when the ikon is reinforced by the presence of family. Also, those fragments abdicating the third monad will find it difficult to fulfill the adult ikon chosen when family was "broken away" from, and will tend to have an adult ikon as much like the ikon of childhood as possible.

Regarding an extended family as a tribe—which, in fact, it is—we would think that the assignment of "functions", that is, ikons, is an essential part to survival. Given that within most tribal societies remaining today the individual fragment is less "important" than the role he or she fulfills in the tribe, it is easy to perceive the significance of the ikon, and to appreciate its necessity for the youngster in "earning its keep". This is not a trivial consideration in most tribal societies, for whether stationary or nomadic, the demands of daily life are strictly proscribed, and must be fulfilled before any expression of individuality becomes either desirable or possible. The ikon, therefore, is a tool to bring about the continuity of the tribe, just as the legends of the tribe are, in fact, the direct antecedents of the familial "legends" of the "modern" world.

We would wish to say that in societies and cultures such as this one, which have gone beyond the tribal concepts and "requirements," identity is an entirely different thing for fragments, in that it must address far more than the family ikon can "handle". In complex and multi-cultural societies such as this one, the ikon is more essential than ever for the youngster confronted with the intricacies of daily life. Without an ikon to provide context—even a negative one—the entire problem is apt to prove over-whelming and threatening beyond adult comprehension, due to the lack of cumulative experience, which is the basis for what you call good judgment. A great many autistic children, who are not seriously compromised in brain func-tion or are not involved in karmic ribbon burning, are, in fact, without ikons to provide them an "entree" into the world, which, not unexpectedly, brings about retreat. The artificial creation of an ikon "after the fact", if it takes place after the second internal monad, is of little use for such children, for the "window of opportunity" has been lost, and the monad is incomplete. We would think that providing context to those autistic children who are not compromised in brain function and are not burning karmic ribbons could, at least, mitigate the terror they experience when confronted with the world. There is "good reason" for the terror, for without the structure provided by the ikon, the very young fragment has no means to choose a means to bring about life action. It is interesting to note that many of those families with one autistic child will report the greatest "uncertainty" or "ambivalence" about having the child, that is, if they are being candid. That does not mean that many autistic children are unwanted. We did not say that and we did not imply it. We are only saying that those autistic children who are autistic for having an ill-defined ikon or none at all were not perceived as having a "place" to occupy in the family structure, which led the fragments in question to seek out a "haven" where they could encounter as little confusion as possible.

━━━━

"**W**hat about the family legends Michael mentioned? Where do they come from? What are they, and what function do they fulfill?"

All families, even the most chaotic ones, have legends they tell of themselves, that is, the narrative account—we will not call it history, for facts often have little to do with it—of the family's "roots" and developments. These legends are "essential" in defining itself and presenting its aspirations to the members within it. All characters have the ikons to be their archetypes, and we would think that holiday discussions would reveal much, should you choose to listen to them in this context. There may be tales of Uncle Willy, the Wastrel, who was Charming and a bit of a Con Man but Never Hurt a Fly. His nephew, named after him, has the double burden of his own ikon and a degree of his uncle's ikon, as do all children named after older family members, which is one of the many reasons we would think more fragments would choose to give their offspring new names in order to make the process of having an identity less "arduous" than it is. Incidentally, juniors are the most burdened of all, and expectations of such children are often so contradictory that a "sense of self" is "colored" with the child's perception of the ikon of senior. To resume the family gathering scenario, and the "traditional" recitation of "the legend". There may be tales of the Saintly Aunt Sarah who spent years doing charity work—in fact as a way to avoid dealing with an abusive husband, but reported as having a "heart of gold"—who Sacrificed Everything for Others. There are also little family "parables", such as

The Time Timmy Ate a Gallon of Ice Cream, or The Valor
of John when His Neighbor's House Burned Down and He
Helped Them Escape, or the Terrible Change That Came
Over Helen after Tom Returned from Vietnam, or Why
Penny's Divorce Was Such a Mistake, or Why Harold's
Wedding Was Almost a Disaster, or How Uncle Lou Got
His First Business after Leaving Home, or Grandmother
Alice's Treasure Map, or What Became of Cousin Benja-
min in Paris, or The Silly Feud Between Aunt Sandra and
Aunt Betty. There may also be new additions to the legend,
such as Chuck, who is about to enter third monad, whose
familial ikon is The Capable Scalawag, and who is Smart as
a Whip, or Diana, at fifteen having trouble in school, whose
ikon is The Odd One Out, and who is Lacking Direction.
Perhaps one of the adults has an adult ikon of The Arbiter
or The Wise Magistrate, and will be the one to "edit"
the legend and preserve it for further use. There is also
the treasury of family ills: Why We Are Not Permitted to
Get Ahead, What We Have Never Received Credit For,
Why the System Fucks Us Over, How Our Accomplishments Get Ignored, and similar recitations of misfortunes,
real and imagined, form most of this negative family legend,
and we would think that some form of them might be
familiar to most fragments, although this is less often the
case in multi-cultural than mono-cultural families.

Families, that is, nuclear families of parents and off-
spring, usually have an ikon for the family unit, such as,
but not limited to: The Safe Adventure, The Model Citizens, The Thwarted Ones, The Indefatigables, The Misfits,
The Diverse and Talented "Gaggle", and similar designa-
tions. These family familial ikons are the result of a shared
"purpose" and are generally more easily established in
families where culture and society are common to both
parents. The more divergent the societal influences of the
parents, the less cogently defined the family familial ikon is
likely to be. However the family familial ikon is established
and maintained, it "shapes" the perceptions of the fragments in terms of approaching the world at large and has a
great deal to do with style. This is, of course, incorporated

into the familial legend and generally reinforced by the retellings of the legends.

━━━━━━━━

"**W**hat about single adults, or single-parent families, or divorced families, or families without children, or adopted children, or orphans? How does all this influence them?"

To take this in order of questions asked: Single adults under the onset of the fourth monad are "colored" by familial ikon, and may have a lingering sense of the family familial ikons, in the sense that there will be a link, not strictly defined after the third internal monad, which will still influence the manner in which the single fragment addresses the world, unless there has been a complete estrangement with the family, in which case the single adult is likely to create an adult ikon for him or herself as a means to ensure independence and a separate identity from the family in question. The "reason" for the singleness also plays a role, for if the fragment has become a nun or is a physician with UNICEF in Africa, it is different in impact than if the fragment is a "workaholic", a phrase which, incidentally, we consider misleading and inaccurate, or if the fragment has been "playing the field". If the fragment remains single after the fourth internal monad, we would think that most will have "evolved" their own adult ikons, which will tend to influence all partnerships undertaken by the fragment after that time. Single fragments who become single in late middle or old age have trouble, for generally the family familial ikon is predicated on a partnership that is no longer available. For such fragments, the sensation of "unconnectedness" or "rudderlessness" is often present. If the extended family is "intact," there is a degree of reinforcement for the widowed or divorced fragment that makes the loss of partner more "comprehensible," for context is available and an "approved" range of reactions has been presented to the fragment. But if there is no extended family to provide "ballast" it is not uncommon for such elderly fragments to take on short- or long-term behavior that might be described as mildly autistic, that is, "shell-shocked," until some new context is found and the ikon modified sufficiently to provide a sense of function to the fragment.

In single-parent families, the reason for the single parent is significant, as well as the stage the singleness is in, in that where a fragment has lost a spouse, there is an adult ikon that is no longer "accessible" and therefore can be "hallowed", which is painful but unconfused, and readily incalcated into the family legend in readily understood terms, and can be safely venerated as "memory" instead of the "messy" results when the spouse has only "departed" and not died. When the single parent is single due to divorce, the ikonographic situation is more complex, for although the absent fragment is "accessible", that is, alive, the fragment is no longer part of the familial ikonographic structure. This is very confusing to all fragments concerned, particularly for younger children, most of whom long to have the full ikonographic display at hand to reinforce their own validity. Most divorcing parents "disown" their adult familial ikons and try to establish new ones in the context of the revised family familial ikons. When either or both former partners fail to do this, serious conflicts can arise and "harm" is possible for all fragments concerned, for not only are the adult "expectations" denied, the children are not permitted to accept the change in the family, for the ikonography is still in place and as such "requires" certain responses from all those in the family. Oftentimes, the "necessary" process of mourning the breakup of a family is postponed for years due to inappropriate ikonographic "maintenance," which leads to a kind of familial ikonographic "logjam" where the ikons are given precedence over "reality", thereby blocking emotional release.

For families without children, there are still adults ikons and family familial ikons, based primarily on partnership, although the context of the partnership is, of course, myriad. These relationships have less "fixed" ikons than families with children, and we are aware that this can be both beneficial and nonbeneficial, depending on the fragments involved and the need for definition in relationships. For some childless families, the very lack of children is perceived as a "blight" and the recognition of the family as being a family by others is not generally the case, the partnership viewed as "incomplete," and the partners as pitiable or selfish for their lack of offspring: it is sometimes impossible for extended families to view any but child-producing life-partnerships as valid, and in these instances, estrangement is not uncommon. This, we would think, is a limiting perception, and for those who choose to do so, a more comprehensive definition of a family might not be amiss, not only for themselves, but for others around them, in anticipation of the day when children grow up and the family will define itself differently, no matter what the ikon. There are also couples who have lost their children prematurely, through ill health, accident, crime, or "upheavals," in which case it becomes necessary for them to "reinvent" their ikon or take on the impossible task of trying to uphold the ikon without the familial components that make it valid.

Where adoptions occur, it is a question of how old the adopted child is, and who is adopting it, and the circumstances surrounding the adoption process. If the child is being adopted or taken-care-of by family members, the parental ikon is continued with only minor modification, and an occasional "privilege" status for the child due to the adoption. If the child is a newborn adopted shortly after birth, the ikon of the adopting parents—often a very "stringent" one due to the parents' desire for children—becomes the "ikon of record", and although there may be an actual parental ikon extant, it will have little bearing on the child, although the parent may have lingering manifestations of the ikon to "contend" with. If, however, the adopted child is not a newborn but under the age of three, the new ikon will become, in fact, a double ikon; this can lead to real misunderstandings at the time of the third internal monad, for leaving the nest with an unacknowledged ikon for "baggage" can be trying for all concerned, for the unacknowledged ikon will still be "operative" for the young fragment, although others may be unaware of it. We would think that the services of someone skilled in familial negotiations might prove useful for such a fragment during the third and fourth internal monad, should the fragment choose to consult a competent negotiator.

As regards children in a "new-formed" family, such as after divorce or widowhood, again, the impact of the ikon depends on when the new familial structure is put in place. If the child or children are more than three years old, then the ikons do not much change, although, of course, the family familial ikon does, and occasional abrasions can and do result. Let us digress in this context and remind you that until a little over a century ago, marriage for life, on the average, meant twelve to fifteen years, with males outliving females by an average of six years. Due to longer and healthier lives, marriages are apt to be longer, but that does not mean they must be "endurance" contests. Most family familial ikons still suffer from "culture lag" and are not conceived of having to accommodate more than the raising of children, although this is clearly no longer the case. Since the creation of ikons is not "conscious decision," we would think it may be difficult to alter the patterns any time soon, but in regard to dealing with family familial ikons, we would think that increased accommodation might not be amiss for all concerned.

Where multiple caretakers are concerned in a young child's life, such as a succession of nursemaids, or a number of foster families, we would think the problems would be obvious—too many, and too-ill-defined ikons imposed upon a child in such a way that a sense of "how to fit in" never fully "takes", and the fragment is left to function without a well-established context. This can be far more distressing than having an "unsuitable" ikon, for the lack of definition makes it almost impossible to "shed" the expectations associated with the ikon in such a way that the fragment is able to be out of the nest at the third internal monad, in large part because the fragment was never fully in a nest in the first place.

In the case of orphans raised institutionally, again, we would think it obvious that the patterns cited already show how the ikons work, depending upon the age of the orphan and the circumstances of the loss of family members. For children who have been abused and neglected, we would think that removing them to a "safer" environment is not only advisable but "necessary" if any real sense of personality is to be preserved in the abused child. For those orphaned by illness or disaster, we would think that the nature of the shock, although different from that of an abused or neglected child, would be as severe, and the need for personality reinforcement as marked as in that of the abused child. Given the nature of orphanages, however, there is a lack of a true family familial ikon, which serves to confuse and disorient the children raised in institutions. Where the family familial ikon has been rendered invalid the children left with no substitute family familial ikon to "honor", the "stakes" for maintaining the personal familial ikon go up sharply, and can lead to many difficulties for children and caregivers alike. We would encourage those providing care to children in this context to establish a supportive and generalized ikon for their group, in a tribal sense, and have it maintained by all those providing care to the children as means of lessening the confusion such an upbringing can cause, but without making the "family" familial ikon so overwhelming that it negates all other ikons in the lives of the institutionalized children. Of course, such extended-family familial ikons are as much a matter of choice as anything else in life, and there is no overriding "reason" to choose to do this other than easing the way of the children who choose to be eased.

It may be of interest here to note that all independently mobile ensouled species have some form of ikon-structure as part of their "cultural" framework, although it is not always predicated on genetic links. In some instances, territory is the crucial factor; in some instances, it is a matter of appearance; in some instances, it is a question of what you would call "accent"; in some instances, the ikon reflects historical "precedence"; and in some instances, the commonality would be unexplainable in any context recognized by your species, although we assure you such a commonality always exists.

―――

"Would Michael describe what they perceive as the most viable family structure for our species?"

This is assuming there are no other considerations in the family choices, such as karma, agreements, external monads, or similar factors, and that all family members are healthy and functional: we would think that while children are young, at least three adult primary caregivers, two of them preferably the childrens' parents, would be the core unit. The extra adult caregiver is to act as balance and relief for the parents, as well as to broaden the child's understanding of family structure and gives a chance for the child to perceive multiple points of view within a safe context. There would also be enough of an extended family to provide the child a sense of a wider society, as well as ensuring the child a sense of having a place in that extended society, and a broad enough "spread" of cultural "types" to reflect the nature of the society where the child lives, so that "unfamiliarity" itself will not create societal fears in the child. This does not mean that all "real" families have to follow this model, only that from our perception, this arrangement is the most functional of all we have observed over time. We would also think that the opportunity for young children to spend time in their "own" company is not amiss, so that the fragment can "sort out" all the information of youth that floods into the child's world every day.

―――

"Isn't that asking a lot of parents?"

We ask nothing of anyone. We merely point out that the work of being a parent is more complex than it is generally assumed to be. We remind you it is not within our "scope" or "wish" to do so, had we the capability of doing so. You asked a question, and we provided our response as we see it, without any expectations "adhering" to the response. You may choose to "parent" in any way you wish. There is nothing in our answer that "demands" anything from you, not even your attention, for that would deny choice. But we are aware that given the nature of human society, the model for parents is varied and potentially overwhelming. Parents tend to expect many things of themselves, and we would think it would not be amiss for them to be aware of what those expectations are before undertaking the "task", although, of course, such cognition is a matter of choice, as are all things. However, let us observe that were families more willing to recognize and validate the various monadal transits of its members, there would be fewer instances of "distress" within families and significantly less "alienation" for those who have completed the fourth internal monad, for often now we perceive that family members interpret these transits as criticisms or "rejections" of the family, which, of course, they are not. In fact, when a family member completes and validates fourth monad, a family "should" be willing to give itself credit for providing the security and opportunity for the transit to occur. The one time this would not be the case would be when fragments undertake such internal monads significantly early or late, for both scenarios indicate a level of "pressure" on the fragment undertaking the transit, which is not Good Work, and which can bring about much "unnecessary" pain for the fragment transiting. Those fragments having ikons referential to other family members—Mommy's Little Angel, A Real Daddy's Girl, A Living Tribute to Grandpa, The Best Oldest Brother in the World, and so forth—are apt to experience the keenest "conflict" during monadal transits with the fragment to whom the ikon is linked, for in many families, children are "tacitly" divided up between parents in what may be a fairly arbitrary way, having more to do with family ikons than any other aspect of the life choices. We would think that all here present have perceived such family "divisions" in the past. There are also families in which the parents take on a "them-against-us" posture in regard to their offspring, and occasionally to their families as well, such as older parents and siblings.

———

"Then the competition between and among siblings can be the result of familial ikonography?"

Of course it can, although it can also reflect societal expectations and archetypes, as well as past experiences and current overleaves, as well as such things as birth order and cultural patterns of "favor" reflected in such things as appearance, gender, talent, skills, demeanor, and similar recognizable factors. We would think it would be of use to consider the "dogma" of the competition in order to understand what the source is. In older siblings, there is always the question of chief features, which are obtained at the beginning of the third internal monad, and are strongest when the third internal monad is abdicated, for then there are none of the perceptions of the transit to mitigate the fear driving the chief features. However, in youth we would agree that family ikonography often has a significant role to play in the manner in which fragments relate one to the other, and since familial ikonography tends to be reinforced by the family itself, the patterns can be well-established long before the validity of such rivalry is apt to be questioned by the participants. In many cases, the patterns linger long after the transit and validation of the fourth internal monad.

———

"When it comes to making a family work well, in Michael's view of such things, is there anything that can be helpful to do or anything that we might do well to avoid?"

You are, of course, not compelled in any way to act in accordance with what we say, but in order to answer the query, we will say, with the caveat that all is chosen, that in terms of what is most helpful to family members, we would think that those choosing to listen to other family members with as little reverence to the ikon as is possible, and with an ability to understand experiential differentiation, would be Good Work. As to what would be useful to avoid, again, if it is your choice to do so, we would think that expressions of contempt are most disruptive within families, far more than expressions of anger or upset. Most family fragments can "weather" a calamity better than they can "stand up" to a barrage of slighting comments, no matter how "well-intended". Contempt is, in our point of view, the single most fear-driven "acceptable" attitude in this or any culture, and also potentially the most "destructive". There are, of course, societies and families that "enshrine" contempt in the form of all the various "isms" of your contemporary parlance: racism, sexism, age-ism, health-ism, height-ism, looks-ism, work-ism, money-ism, celebrity-ism, and a host of others. Until recently, most of those isms within your society had general religious support and therefore could not be readily questioned without bringing about more trouble for the fragment questioning. This spills from families to societies to cultures quite readily, as any review of history and other countries will reveal. We perceive that contempt permits a degree of solipsism that reinforces the fear by making all fragments except the one having contempt, less "valid" and therefore of "less consequence". Most fragments in this and all Western societies respond to contempt with resentment. When such patterns develop within a family, their results are truly devastating, if not obviously, in covert ways.

"Then self-control is called for?"

Not by us, by your society and culture. That is not to say it is not Good Work to have some "rein" on your impulses, for demonstrably this is "encouraged" in society, and is a

valid choice for societal actions, and within families it is
equally valid. However it is not amiss to recall, should you
choose to do so, that what constitutes self-control changes
from society to society, from culture to culture, from era
to era, and from family to family. A Greek fisherman in the
tenth century, common reckoning, would evince displea-
sure with his family in a far different way than a Samoan
fisherman of the same period or a Greek fisherman at this
time in the evolution of your species. For one thing, the
societal position of the fisherman is different in all cases
cited, and what would displease a head of the family in all
these instances is dissimilar. Self-control for family members may constitute keeping within doors for a period of
time to "keep it in the family", it may consist of a few hot
remarks followed by an attempt to engage a passer-by or
casual acquaintance in combat, it may consist of using
some of the coping techniques we have suggested over the
years [and some of which are described in the last chapter],
and it may consist of religious or physical disciplines to
reinforce desired behavior. Self-control, when it comes
from inner acknowledgment of the validity of others, is
Good Work. When a fragment chooses to avail itself of
alternatives to aggression, we would think that this may be
regarded as a sign of validation of the "reality" of the other
fragment's point-of-view, without necessarily endorsing it.
When it is fueled by chief feature, it may accomplish much
the same "benefit" outwardly, but inwardly it is "lacking"
in validation. In any event, the choices are choices and as
such are valid.

―――――

"**W**hat sorts of things do children learn before age two? What
does a major family disruption at this time do to the process?"

All concepts of propriety and behavior are learned before
the process of individualization occurs. Most aesthetics,
most taste in food, most taste in environment, most standards of attractiveness, most of the relationship between

"favorable" and "unfavorable" behavior, most religious conduct, and most affinities to various peoples and groups, although in the last case, that can be significantly influenced by past lives, as can aesthetics. The rest are more or less a product of the immediate life. When a major disruption occurs during this time, which could include a serious injury or illness, the death of a parent or sibling, the drastic relocation of the family, natural disaster, war, and similar all-encompassing events, the infant may develop a deep doubt about what has been learned, and it is not unlikely that in later life the fragment will question or reject the validity of the early experience. This can become an openness of mind that might otherwise not occur, it can bring about "outlaw" behavior, it can lead to compulsions and obsessions (that you mislabel addictions), it can bring about a lifetime of "shopping" for "answers", it can bring about a disinclination to resume the familial process, and so forth for all fragments experiencing disruption.

There are fragments—statistically more often the action polarity than others, for this transpires in lives of action polarity fragments twelve percent more than is usual for others—who will occasionally have a "string" of disrupted family lives. This occasionally results in the fragment having a number of family ikons "haunting" the fragment as "carry-overs" from incomplete lives. Confusion can result from this, particularly if memories of the past lives are "near the surface". In cases of this sort, the fragment with the "left-over" ikons will tend to have more difficulty than most in "fitting in", due to remnants of other sets of familial expectations. We would think it might be "worthwhile" to introduce such children early to the art of the world, for context of the past is generally more sharply differentiated in your species through visual aesthetics than through any other readily accessible process. The same means of access to the past is available to all fragments, of course, but for children with a number of unresolved life beginnings, we would think that appreciation of what has gone before would help in establishing experiential differentiation within the fragment in question.

━━━━━━━

"**H**ow much influence do past lives have on current family life?"

That question is not possible to answer on a general basis, for it involves much more specific instances than is practicable. Every case is, of course, unique. However, we will give a few examples in order to help you to assess the range of such "aspects." [Michael thinks this is very funny.] We are aware, for example, of many instances of fragments doing the parent-child external monad, that is, each "trading off" the complementary "role" in order to assimilate the experience. This is often the most "enduring" sort of parent-child relationship, and sustains itself well past the point when it would be societally expected to change. That does not mean all "captive" spinster daughters and all "mama's" boys are locked in the parent-child external monad. We did not say that and we did not imply it. In fact, that monad is not "intended" to infantilize the child-part of the monadal pairing, but to have available the full range of experience, including shared adulthood and the parent's old age, although, of course, not all such relationships are monadal in nature. We are also aware of many fragments with several past associations with immediate family members, although we must add that not all the past associations were "favorable". That does not make the family contact valid—all experience is valid. We are also aware of a significant number of families, usually of Young souls, where all are having a first contact, and have chosen the family structure as a way to get acquainted. We would think it is as "direct" a method as any, and in a Young soul world like this one, we would think it is a "typical" Young soul approach to the "task at hand", for such things as familial ikonography fit right in with the Young soul motto of "Do It My Way". Many other possibilities exist, of course, and each is no more or less valid than any other. We assure you that the experience of family is myriad in its implications, and the expression of the experience is as diverse as the whole range of experiential differentiation.

━━━━━━

"Speaking of experiential differentiation, isn't a family one of the best ways to see it in action?"

If that is what you choose, yes, of course, in that it is possible for all fragments to have a look at the same experience "coherently" should they choose to do so. But we would have to remind you that the ikons may get in the way of assessment, if they are not recognized for what they are. Experiential differentiation is "hampered" by dogma of all kinds, including familial ikonography, which will tend to support one fragment's version as more valid than another's. Also, there is much reinforcement in family legends on the continuing validity of the family as such, which means there is pressure to regard each contact as being "the same" as any of the previous contacts, which we assure you, it is not. Each contact is, of course, unique, and a valid means of experiential differentiation, for no reason other than the clothing worn will tend to be different from one occasion to the other. In general, we would think that familial experiential differentiation, without the "bludgeon" of ikonographic dogma, would provide a number of welcome insights as well as the means to lessen habitual misunderstandings.

━━━━━━

"What about those who have lost, been rejected by, or have rejected their families?"

We would think that the perceived reasons for this would be crucial in order to provide a response to your inquiry. We would also think that this question reveals some of the basic conflicts between society-as-family and family-as-society. But in many instances, such responses are ikonoclastic [literally, ikon-breaking] in nature, either on the part of the rejecting family or on the part of the rejected fragment. That is not to say all "vagabonds", "drug drop-outs", "crazies", "cultists", and the like are all on iko-noclastic missions, for we are not saying that. We would think that knowing something of the nature of the life plan, to say nothing of the last few lives, might provide insight into these choices. We would also wish to point out that one of the lessons of the mature cycle for all fragments is honorably serving a corrupt master. Of course, most cor-rupt masters do not perceive themselves as such, but in-stead are inclined to think of themselves as "crusaders", "messiahs", "revolutionaries", and, most consistently, "heroes". So fragments setting their families and ikons aside for such an experience might well have "signed up" for it, as in the case of three of the female followers of Charles Manson who are still in prison for their devotion to his self-proclaimed heroism.

When families "throw out" children, the most "telling" factor is the age at which this takes place, and how much ikon-related pressure is functioning at the time of the "expulsion". We would think it obvious that families with children cast off before the age of five are in the throes of external demands or such internal pressure that continuing with the obligations of being parents is beyond "accept-able" limits. This is especially true in single-parent fami-lies, where the household is as "intrusive" as the immediate demands of family. If a child is separated from a family by external causes—disaster, war, etc.—then the "significance" is, of course, different from those "disown-ings" brought about by internal stresses. In most cases, we would think that some degree of parental "ineptitude" would be a factor, or an ikonographic dispute too enormous to be "adjusted-for". Where teen-age or older children are in conflict, we would think that family ikons clashing with societal expectations are involved on some level. And it is not unlikely that the child's behavior is exacerbated by recognition of the ikonographic conflict. Where parents are forced out of families, such as through divorce, criminal actions, health considerations, mental distress, geographic necessity, economic "realities", religious or political pressure, we would think it not uncommon to find that parental ikons are not sufficient to deal with the stresses added to the family structure. In all cases, we would think that a review of familial ikonography would not be amiss when turmoil erupts, should you choose to do so.

━━━━━

"Can Michael give some suggestions of how to avoid being 'suckered' by family ikons?"

If by suckered you mean "deceived", we would think that a degree of this is unavoidable, for to "deny" the ikon is to remove needed structure from the family and from the individuals within it. However, it would not be amiss to keep in mind that all perceptions of all familial members is, of course, distorted, and because of that, each individual fragment may have wholly invalid perceptions of others within the family. It is also of use to recall that although an adult fragment may acquire an adult ikon, within the family in which the fragment is/was a child, the ikon of childhood reigns preeminent and of singular, abiding position. It is also not inappropriate, should you choose to do so, to keep from ikonographic dogma by refusing to deny the perceptions of others, no matter how "out of character" they may seem. Such statements as, "You do not mean that", and/or, "How can you think such a thing" make for real "damage" in validation for the fragment doing the "unexpected". In families, there is no formula for a "right" way because, of course, the right way does not exist; and we would think that recognizing familial ikonography for what it is, not with the purpose of rejecting it, but permitting its function to keep from becoming immutable dogma would be a most commendable insight, for those choosing to undertake such a task.

When dealing with the nature of families in the immediate context of daily life, we would have to remark that we do perceive the many "necessary" uses of familial ikonography, but we also perceive its many limitations, and we would think that for fragments willing to "strike" an evolutionary "balance", there may be much worthwhile insight to be gained. However, such "dedication" is not "required", and if you do not choose to pursue the matter, there is no "error" this, or any other choice.

CHAPTER 5

Being Here

We would wish to remind all here present that the process of living on the physical plane is the focus of the "reason" for ensouled life on the physical plane. Any life where this perception is recognized and validated is one in which essence evolution is possible. On other planes of existence there is no on-going and recognizable manifestation of "time" or the aspects of choice that stem from the hazards of the physical plane. On no other plane does choice have so many forms of manifestation as it does on the physical plane, and on no other plane of existence does the nature of the plane itself impinge so relentlessly on fragments extant there. So you may consider much of your task at hand related to the process of being on the physical plane, for that is why you have chosen to be here in the first place. There is no "shortcut" out of the cycles on the physical plane, for that would deny the process of recognition and validation. There is only evolution and for each fragment, evolution is the result of choices made by that fragment. Doing evolution more quickly or less quickly than other fragments has no "value" attached to it, and it is a misunderstanding to assume that it does. The progression of days is a valid experience, and all days, no matter how many or how few, are equally valid. What you are here to do in each and every life on the physical plane is, in fact, deal with the physical plane and being ensouled in the human species. That does not mean that living is a grim endurance contest with the physical environment, although you may choose to see it that way, or that every second is so precious life must be prolonged at any cost and under any circumstances, although, again, you may choose to see it that way. We would wish to warn you that such points of view may provide much "food for thought" in the astral interval, they provide little in the way of insights, and in that sense are not conducive to growth. Life is rarely a "monolithic" experience, that is, a single slab of the same material and density throughout. No matter how dreadful or how fortunate a specific life may be, there will be times less dire and less insouciant, and interactions with other fragments that influence the perceptions of the fragments. Life, by the nature of your species and the nature of the physical plane, is subject to constant change, and for that reason, if no other, makes adjustment a "physical" "necessity". [Another one of Michael's puns.] Failure to recognize this means, among other things, never having the proper size of shoe, for feet, like noses and ears in your species, continue, albeit slowly, to grow all through life. An occasional assessment of passages of life may be undertaken, should you choose to do so, over a matter of time, and eventually compared, to enable the fragment to identify areas of growth and areas of "blockage" and, should the fragment choose to do so, there would then be an opportunity to develop methods for dealing with the blockage. Incidentally, in making an evaluation, it is of use to "reserve" judgment, which, we suspect, is almost impossible for most fragments, chief features being what they are. It is often impossible for a fragment to bring an untrammeled view to the process, which is where the insights of others may prove useful, or the comparison of insights at least five years old. This may seem arduous, and if it that is the case, we would not advise such an undertaking. If you choose to have the five-year comparison, we must point out that "peeking" will interfere with the whole purpose of the "exercise". Nonetheless, having a record of insights can be insightful itself. This is by no means "required", and we do not recommend it if the fragment is not inclined to such contemplations, for that, too, would defeat the purpose of the exercise, although we would wish to add, it is, obliquely, the driving force behind "New Year's Resolutions".

The hazards of growth, and by that we mean growth of all sorts, is not only "basic" to the physical plane, it is especially noticeable on independently mobile ensouled species, and for that reason, if no other, we would think that it is likely to be important to "factor in" growth in most assessments made, whether it involves the size of house being constructed or the amount needed for college tuition in a decade or the dishes needed to serve a feast. The planet itself is subject to the flux and stretching of evolution, and this can have ramifications for the ensouled species on it—cetaceans as well as humans. Given the nature of the planet itself, we would think that all fragments extant upon it have at some time in every life had to make abrupt adjustments to deal with the "realities" of planetary evolution, which in turn, can lead to growth on the part of the fragments dealing with the intrusions of the environment. It is not "sensible" to assume that a life will not have impositions made by hurricanes, floods, earthquakes, volcanic eruptions, and all the rest, as well as by deaths, marriages, births, divorces, business failures, and all the other "personal" developments, as well as wars, famines, plagues, and all the other inclusive catastrophes that directly or indirectly impinge on the life and "demand" an adjustment of some sort.

After the question of "real world" intrusions, one of the first lessons of being human is learning to make contact with other members of your species, beginning in most instances with members of one's own family. Obviously for infants this is done by crying. For socially adapted fragments, there are rules established for the levels of contact that may "correctly" be indulged in as a function of what we might call "social" intimacy, which is the way in which most social interactions are conducted, and each is a sort of relationship "schematic". There are, of course, seven levels: one we would describe as standard polite, in which no personal information of any sort is exchanged, but a valid "social" contact is acknowledged. For example, you say to a bank teller or grocery clerk, "How is it going?" and the teller or clerk answers, "Fine," which actually provides a validation for each of the reality of the other, an indication that you are aware you are dealing with another fragment and are willing to indicate it. Two is a minor information exchange: you say to the teller or clerk, "How is it going?" and the answer is, "Well, you know." This communicates that each recognizes the other has a context in life beyond the one immediately apparent. Three actually volunteers some "human" information. You asked the teller or clerk, "How is it going?" and the answer is, "I have a headache," and you say, "Too bad," or some expression of commiseration. This is valid information on both sides as well as "creature" sympathy. At level four, when you say "too bad" or the like, you add, "I hope you're taking something for it," which in actuality creates a parity that is lacking in the previous levels of contact. Level five, after the basic exchange recounted thus far, the teller or clerk reacts with a comment along these lines: "Oh, thank, you very much. I have an aspirin in my bag," to which you respond with something like, "Take care of yourself," which expresses an on-going process of concern. The sixth level has all the elements of the previous five plus an additional recognition of on-going concern, such as, "I'll do that; I appreciate your asking/saying that." This brings about a double validation, and a stronger sense of external context. At the seventh level, you would make an addition to that, which would indicate a willingness to do more that sympathize, with an assurance of this nature: "If you don't get better soon, get some help or call me," which completely validates the experience of the clerk or teller. We would think that the "occurrence curve" for these interactions would be the same as for the incidents of essence role distribution, with level one interactions taking place about twenty-five percent of the time, and level seven about four percent of the time. Incidentally, the "style" of such interactions changes from cycle to cycle, as the nature of the perceptions vary, but not the "social message" of the interaction, which is shaped by "training," not by evolution. Obviously, these exchanges are not only cultural in shape, but are dependent on forms of address, social expectations, and uses of language that have become "traditionalized" over time.

Certainly it is possible to express validation in nonverbal ways, but overwhelmingly among your species, speech is the preferred means of communication, which is not uncoMmon in Young-soul, independently mobile fragments, for speech, or its equivalent, not only serves the immediate purpose of habitual communication, it can be noted by others and "gauged" as appropriate or not. Speech has the capacity for multiple interpretations, as well, which makes it a more interesting "tool" than most other senses provide with the possible exception of vision. What constitutes appropriate social language, of course, changes from year to year, culture to culture, society to society, place to place, institution to institution, fad to fad, and, of course, family to family. The current trend in what is called "politically correct" speech, incidentally, while "noble" in purpose, has become so distorted in its attempt to offend no one that it is often inappropriate to the circumstances, so that the judgmental implications of the politically correct uses implies greater contempt than the more traditional word does, in that it drains the words of any meaning, such as saying visually challenged instead of blind. Such "mealy-mouthed" diminution of experience is more to provide comfort for those sighted who feel awkward around blindness than to "save the feelings" of the blind. While we think that diminishing the occasion for religious, social, ethnic, and similar "slights" we would think that current "trends" makes it difficult if not impossible to have any useful discussion on the problems confronted by such groups that are being so carefully "unoffended". Desiccating language does not, in fact, correct societal ills, but rather disguises them in ambiguous phrases that obfuscate the matter so that the societal ill is "clouded" and made less readily identifiable. Calling a man who beats women into unconsciousness an abusive partner is exculpatory for him and trivializing for the beaten women, and we would think that it serves no useful end. On the other hand, to make our point clear, racial, social, ethnic, political, economic, and/or sexual epithets of an insulting nature are and have always been demeaning—that is the purpose of such "slurs".

The development of language as language took place when your species was ensouled, and we would think its advantages far outweigh its disadvantages. Having ways to identify, extrapolate, temporize, mediate, appreciate, theorize, rhapsodize, elevate, inspire, reveal, recount, codify, quantify, qualify, persuade, inform, insult, prevaricate, et cetera, et cetera, through all the permutations of language applications more than make up for the limitations imposed by the use of language itself, for language does impose limitations, and we cannot repeat that often enough. For some fragments, learning how to "move beyond" language is an impossible task, and even what you on the physical plane call the arts are largely incomprehensible. But through "the arts" and certain aspects of mathematics, the limitations of language may be transcended, although the level at which such concepts communicate is esoteric enough to make it not readily accessible, or, often as crucial. A statue, no matter how inspired and how capable of intimacy in application cannot take the place of the warning that there are terrorists with guns waiting to board the plane. However essential language is, it is not inconceivable that as this world evolves to a mature soul world, the heavy dependence on language for all communication will lessen, and the species will be more inclined to make what you call the arts an integral part of communications of all sorts, as more "genuine" though less "specific" than language. To use speech accurately is one of the greatest accomplishments any human fragment can aspire to achieve, for it is through accurate speech that recognition and validation are brought to bear in the life. The more accurate the speech, the more coherent the perception it entails, the less accurate the speech, the less cogent the perception.

Language is the clearest and most basic "evidence" of your ensoulment, for your species and for the cetaceans as well. All ensouled species have one specific ability that differentiates them from hive-soul beings. In your case, the ability to "discuss" is the beginning of not only society, but of knowledge, history, myth, and religion. No matter how intelligent the hive-soul creature may be, the use of language as the conveyer of abstract thought is simply not possible. Let us discuss the most popular domestic animals—dogs and cats. We agree that an intelligent pet can "read" its people more quickly than most humans can, but not, for example, over the telephone. And while these creatures can come to recognize many "words", they are associated not with "concepts" but with desired results. To explicate: a clever and well-trained dog, told to "go find Betty", if he has experience in knowing who Betty is (by demeanor and smell), and he is told by a human he regards as having authority, he will be able to find Betty if she is near enough to be accessible. That does not mean that the dog understands the word "go" or "find" or the name "Betty", but that he has learned that these sounds require specific actions on his part, and accepts the authority of the human giving the order. Because of the "hardwiring" of "canine-central", following orders comes "naturally" to dogs because—with the exception of foxes—they hunt in groups. Felines come to recognize as many words, but do not respond to most orders because they are—with the exception of lions—solitary predators, and hunt alone— they are not "hard-wired" from "feline-central" for cooperation with group leaders as canines are. No matter how many words the animal may come to recognize, they will not be regarded as containing information, but as sounds demanding certain responses. Dogs being used to fitting into an "order", may be taught trained responses to words whose meanings have nothing to do with the response commanded. A dog may be trained to "heel" at the word

"spaghetti" or "werewolf" with no vocabularistic conflicts, if the human teacher selects such a word for the
response. The dog cannot differentiate between the meaning of the word and the trained command. Human beings,
on the other hand, along with cetaceans, are assessing
language from their first breath, and quickly come to recognize words for what they are. Most infant humans understand that words have meaning and specificity by the fourth
day of life, although they, of course, are not yet able to use
them. This is because human beings are "hard-wired" by
ensoulment to think in abstracts, which for your species,
means words, for all later abstractions begin with words.
Try as they will, no hive-soul animal can grasp the concept
of a metaphor, but most humans not only grasp but use
them by the time of the second internal monad; metaphors
are "essential" to the use of language in almost all cultures,
and in some, such as the Chinese culture, metaphor is the
basis for the language itself.

"Will Michael comment on the different ways in which the
various roles in essence experience the physical plane?"

We would think that the understanding of what the role in
essence sees as its purpose might lend some understanding:
Slaves serving the common good in whatever capacity they
define it; Artisans seeking structure in all things; Warriors
seeking challenges; Scholars looking for information; Sages
striving to communicate; Priests serving their individual
higher ideals; Kings mandating their kingdoms. There are
other aspects to experience that can be linked to roles in
essence, and that is the manner in which they "process"
experience: Kings, Warriors, and Scholars have one channel of input, or in other words, they are experiential fun-
nels. They do not possess a back-burner, although they can
adjust their priorities rather quickly and can concentrate in
the midst of chaos. Priests and Slaves each have two
channels of input, one having to do with the here and now,

the other having to do with the ideal they serve. They have a back-burner. The problem for them is not to confuse channel one with channel two. Sages have three channels of input, so that they can "monitor" the response they are creating as well as have a back-burner. Artisans have five channels of input and this, when not recognized, can lead to a "spaciness" due to "spinning the dial". When focused, however, an Artisan can handle a multiplicity of things more or less at once, which is the real strength of the multiple-channel input. It is "useless" to try to change this pattern of input, for it "comes with" the role in essence. Occasionally misunderstandings stemming from different sorts of input capacity can lead to serious altercations, which is a lamentable thing to occur, for the channels of input are not subject to change, and for no reason other than their immutability might be thought of as a more useful way to gain many points of view rather than "bones of contention", as we see in many cases at present.

"**W**ould Michael do the same for language, if there is a difference between the essences' use of language?"

Of course there is. Often the essence, or the thrust of the overleaves, is revealed in the use of language. Slaves use language reflective of service, addressing issues the Slave perceives to be for the common good. Slaves often "pepper" their speech with reminders of society at large or humanitarian concerns. In the Baby and early Young cycle, this can take the form of extreme positions, often of an "elitist" nature, such as but not limited to religiously Fundamentalist positions. Artisans are often not good at speech as such, but will present works of art or craft as a response to language, which for the Artisan is appropriate, although often baffling to other essences except Sages. In the Young and Mature cycle, Artisans are often attracted to professions that require less speech for communication, such as professional sports, esoteric electronics, commercial design, athletics and dance, innovative construction, and diverse forms of cooking. Warriors often use battle language for mundane situations, such as having a "strategy" for a dinner party or a "chain of command" for holiday arrangements. As a "group", Warriors tend to be direct, or plain-speaking, and are often seen as more confrontational than they actually are, due to the directness of their speech. In the Mature and Old cycles, Warriors develop language skills as a technique for going into the positive pole of their essence, which is persuasion, and can be effective negotiators, in that they rarely lose sight of the goal in negotiations. Scholars love language because it is the "home" of information. They may not be great speakers themselves, but they love eloquence when it contains insights, style, and information, and distrust it when there is no useful information in it. In the Young cycle, the information is the most important factor in language; in the Mature and Old cycles, what you on the physical plane call art becomes a significant factor in Scholar language appreciation. For Sages, language is the "heart" of the matter, for as the great communicators, they have a greater comprehension of the impact of language than any other essence, and, by that token, are more readily seduced by it. In the Baby and early Young cycles, Sages look for language that has the greatest immediate impact on the largest "audience" possible. Popularized religion, politics, and entertainment are all attractive venues for such Sages, although in later cycles, the Sages are no longer as eager to move audiences as to communicate something of "value", such as philosophy, psychology, and "art". Language for Priests is their means of communicating the higher ideal all Priests serve, and the usual Priest assumption that all understand the higher ideal and share it makes for a highly personalized and dogmatic "jargon" based on the "shared" dedication to the higher ideal. After the first half of the Mature cycle, Priests can be insightful and inspiring when they realize that the higher ideal needs to be communicated. At such times, their use of language, particularly poetry, can be as remarkable for its clarity as their work until that time can be obscure. Please note we say can—at any time in its evolution, a Priest fragment may choose overleaves that will "ground" it, making it more accessible to those around it. As regards Kings, their language tends to echo their purpose of mandating. They have the same sense of strategy as Warriors do, but with a much broader intent. Kings, by their very nature, motivate others. In fact, most Kings spend the first decade of their lives learning to mitigate the tone of their speech so that they will not become bullies. Of course, many Baby and Young Kings do become bullies, but once into the Mature cycle, that tendency quickly disappears in favor of assisting their "kingdom" to the goal. This is when Kings cease to "suffer fools gladly" because they no longer need "tools" to do their bidding and seek for respect as well as the recognition of authority. Those with Kingly overleaves [Aggression, Dominance, Realist, seventh level] take on masterful speech but rarely demonstrate the force to mandate. And while these observations we have presented are valid, they are also "simplistic" in that they do not take into account past life experiences, overleaves, casting, and the like, all of which influence the way in which a fragment manifests any life. For example, a Young Scholar in the Power mode with a goal of Acceptance and an attitude of Idealist who is fifth cast or in a fifth cadence will look and act like a Sage more than a Scholar, just as a Mature Sage with Slave overleaves and one casting will not have the initial impact of a Sage, although the natural eloquence will not be lacking in the fragment.

———

"**M**ichael has said that we can only experience matter on the physical plane, but they have also said that there is such a thing as astral matter. Would they clarify this for us?"

There is no contradiction in these statements, however, since clarification is desired, we will do what we can to provide it. Matter has validity on both the astral and the physical plane, but the nature of the matter, its uses and purposes are different on the two planes. On the physical plane most matter is not readily altered by human intention, although occasionally human action will alter it. On the physical plane the matter itself, no matter how "accommodating", cannot be made what it is not simply because a human being wishes it so. The matter itself is obdurate and specific. What is solid cannot easily become liquid, although such events as volcanic eruptions can accomplish this transformation for a relatively brief period of time. What is flesh does readily take on the characteristics of other substances. On the astral plane, there is a matter of a sort, but unlike your physical-plane physical matter, astral-plane matter is infinitely malleable, of limited duration, a kind of "soup" that adjusts to all situations and requires no tools other than the will to shape it. It is also less enduring, rarely lasting more than twenty minutes, although there have been occasions when such manifestations, "fueled" by more than one human will, have lasted for an hour or more, such as in apparitions of "holy" or "demonic" "personages". On a less ambitious level, you may conjure up an image of your dead grandmother using astral matter, but the features will be little more than a blob with eyes, and your memory will supply the actual details. The "likeness" will endure only so long as you will it to endure, at which time it will go back to astral matter, which is the astral equivalent of "Silly Putty", and much less tenable, tangible, and plastic. [Michael was very pleased with this pun.] We would have to say that in our experience, the occasional manipulations of astral matter by human will has resulted in something like slender children without real features except eyes. The same can be said for fragments in the astral interval: when they seek to make themselves "physical", they rarely achieve more than the human-like shape, not very large, and without distinguishing characteristics, those being hard to maintain, and from the astral point of view, unimportant.

"It sounds like the image of aliens many people have claimed to see."

We would think that observation is valid, for from our perspective, such encounters are far more often astral encounters rather than encounters with aliens, meaning members of a species not extant on your planet. These "events" are significant in terms of experiential differentiation as well as recognizing "anomalies" in life. Incidentally, we have said before but we will reiterate: there are a few alien species making observations of your planet, one of which has confined its studies to species living in the water, being what you would perceive as an aquatic species itself. Of those actively interested in your planet, only one is even vaguely humanoid in configuration. Most of the observation units sent to your planet are robots, for, like you humans, most species do their initial exploration with robot ships that send back "reports" for species evaluation, much the same as you have done with your planetary probes. If you think about the problem of distance and supplies, using robots is the most practical means "at hand" to get information with relatively small risk in losing a trained crew and/or endangering the planet being studied with extraterrestrial bacteria, viruses, and similar "contagions". Devastating your species with alien viruses would be irresponsible in the extreme, and would not redound to the credit of the species doing it, as would permitting a highly trained crew to expose itself to the hazards inherent on your planet, for there are viruses and bacteria on this planet that would be completely fatal to species on other planets. The concern for your well-being is not wholly altruistic, but practical as well. For a standard of evaluation, we would think that if the supposed aliens are human in appearance and behavior, they are probably astral humans, not physical-plane aliens. The incident of actual alien encounters as compared to astral encounters interpreted as aliens is astrals, seventy-seven percent; aliens, five percent (although they do not look like big-eyed human dolls); delusions, eighteen percent. That does not mean such contacts are invalid, only that they have been inaccurately identified.

━━━━━

"Michael keeps referring to experiential differentiation, which apparently has to do with individual perceptions. Could they be more specific? What is it, and how does it work?"

We would have to say regarding differentiating experiential differentiation that much Good Work is being done in this manner: to recognize that each fragment experiences everything differently from every other fragment is the first step to validation and recognition of the equality of fragments and the validity of the lessons and choices of each and every life. Nothing can be repeated for each experience is its own experience, unique and distinct from all others. This can be extended to validating the experiential differentiation of individual lives of each fragment. In other words, in one life the fragment may be allergic to milk and sneeze when roses are present; in another life the fragment may have smallpox, resulting in facial scars and dislike the taste of root vegetables; in another the fragment may love the scent of jasmine and be unable to tolerate spicy foods. These experiences, being personal truths, are just as valid for the individual as are world truths and universal truths but, being personal truths, are not necessarily valid for any other fragment. In each life, the experience is valid for that life, but it does not follow that what is true in one life of the body is true in another life of the body, even though the essence experiencing those lives is the same.

Let us further explicate: within the scope of a single life, the differentiation of experiential differentiation most usually occurs in this manner: a fragment will visit a restaurant and at that restaurant have indifferent food in the company of a couple having an argument. This does not mean that another trip to that restaurant must necessarily provide indifferent food and quarreling couples. There are those who assume after such an event that *all* restaurants will present similar experiences, and therefore will avoid them in what is assumed to be prudence and the "benefit" of learning from experience, being unwilling to experience every experience as individual. In a more favorable light, for many couples engaged in sexual activities, there is a tendency to repeat—often dogmatically—those behaviors that in the past have proven most pleasurable. That is not to say that couples "must" vary sexual behavior at all times. We did not say that and we did not imply it. We mean to say that the activities themselves are not going to provide satisfaction if turned into a ritual. Many times when the first episodes of pleasure begin to flag, the couple will renew dedication to the same behaviors instead of seeking new ones because of the superstitious certainty that there is no other way to achieve the level of pleasure they are seeking. This "perception" denies experiential differentiation as well as differentiating experiential differentiation, in that it assumes that both fragments must always find certain activities gratifying, and that the elements of individual excitation never vary from encounter to encounter. This is not to say that most fragments do not develop distinct preferences in sexual behavior, but adherence to such behavior without allowing for such things as state of mind, state of health, state of surroundings, state of concentration, et cetera, will generally prove disappointing. By extension, failure to achieve satisfaction with certain activities at one time does not absolutely guarantee that such failure must always be the result of such activities. Affectionate and playful experimentation is not amiss when it is not chosen to the exclusion of all other activities.

One of the reasons we have spoken against ritual in regard to spiritual exercise is the trouble that arises in differentiating experiential differentiation, the extension of experiential differentiation. To propose that transcendent experiences or essence contact may only be valid when certain ritualistic conditions are met is patently absurd, for it presupposes that there is only one "correct" way to have an experience, which renders choice unnecessary. This formularistic approach to experience can lead to serious emotional distress if carried to extremes. It is true for most fragments deliberately seeking spiritual enlargement that certain "rituals" can help prepare the fragment to recognize and validate the experience more fully, but not if the ritual becomes "essential" [ha, ha, ha] to the experience and therefore any spiritual insights obtained without the ritual are deemed invalid. Such things as chakra scrubs and similar routines are designed to reduce the "static", but if a fragment seizes on them as the end rather than the means, such a choice is likely to prove unrewarding, and the routines will prove disappointing for those seeking to use them as the necessary means to an end or the "correct" way to achieve "enlightenment".

We agree that there are needs for plans and a framework of activities. Most fragments would not accomplish much if they had to reinvent their lives each and every day. But plans are not expectations, and expectations are not scripts. What we would recommend, for those who choose to do so, is to hold events in a frame of mind that is at once flexible and "tolerant", that is, capable of accepting that others sharing the event do not, in fact, have the same experience as their "companions". To see the truth of this, talk to the various members of a jury regarding the events of a trial. You will quickly discover that the jury members each witnessed a different event, although they may agree on most of the particulars, their individual emphases will not be the same. For example, one juror might dislike the judge because he or she reminds the juror of his/her second-grade teacher, and therefore the juror tends to distrust the judge's rulings; one juror may develop a crush on the defendant (an event that happens more often than you might suppose) and therefore sees the entire trial as a form of persecution; one juror may be sensitive to the light of the courtroom and as a result spend the entire trial attempting to ignore a low-grade headache; one juror may decide that the "cops" are "railroading" the court, and therefore reacts negatively to all police testimony, no matter who it benefits; one juror may sympathize with the prosecution and see this as his or her star performance; one juror may not like the suits the prosecutor wears and therefore distrusts his/her judgment in all matters; one juror may have strong opinions about members of the clergy as witnesses, and therefore centers the issues of the trial around such testimony; one juror may be desperately in need of a sense of control and therefore seek to influence other jurors—for this fragment, the deliberations are the real issue of the trial, not the testimony, cross-examination, and presentation of evidence; one juror may have chronic problems at the office or at home, and for this juror the trial is a distraction, either welcome or unwelcome; one juror may be in awe of the whole proceeding and be caught up in the societal machinery so completely that the juror becomes an extension of the court itself; one juror may be recently bereaved and therefore subject to emotional responses that are not directly attributable to the trial; one juror may be prone to constant vacillation and incapable of evaluating evidence and testimony with any discretion, and therefore has no coherent assessment of the trial or the issues of the trial. Recognizing that each and every juror has a valid experience is what we mean by experiential differentiation. Realizing that each and every jury will be different from all other juries is differentiating experiential differentiation.

We would wish to digress on the matters of planning, expecting, and scripting. In planning, the state we have already remarked upon is maintained. The fragment is receptive within the convenient framework of the event. In other words, the fragment appreciates that it is socially inappropriate to wear sweats to a diplomatic reception or to insist that everyone bring German potato salad to the picnic. The fragment recognizes appropriate behavior in the circumstances and *plans* with "realistic" perceptions without imposing demands or punishing inappropriate behavior that is not distressing or aggressive. Expectations imply rewards and punishments: the fragment expecting, in effect, says, "If you do thus-and-such, I will behave. If you fail to do thus-and-such, I will not behave". Expectations demand limitations that block insights and intimacy and make experiential differentiation difficult. For those with expectations, if the fragment does not enjoy the party, no one is "supposed" to enjoy the party. Scripting, of course, takes expectations farther, to the point that the fragment has worked out in advance the entire proceeding of the event in question, and any deviation whatsoever, even a beneficial one, is seen as threatening at best, and catastrophic at worst. Scripting has many ramifications, all of which mitigate against the validity of choice. Where "serious" scripting is active, there can be no experiential differentiation, for the perceptions of other fragments are invalidated from the outset. Differentiating experiential differentiation is extremely difficult where scripting is present. Let us illustrate our point in this manner: we are aware of a fragment not part of our little group who attended an outdoor family dinner during the last month of her first pregnancy. Being a second level Young Scholar with pronounced stubbornness, this fragment is prone to script on the "best of occasions," which this was not. During the festivities, her water broke, which was not part of the script. So acute was her embarrassment at this that she has been unable to return to this relative's house since the event, although she is no longer pregnant and the event cannot possibly repeat itself. Her inability to differentiate her experiential differentiation has led her to believe that it is impossible for her to go to that house without disastrous embarrassment. She is also convinced that the breaking of her water was the most significant moment of the party for all those present, and would not believe that to most of the fragments in attendance, the incident is hardly important at all except that it led to the birth of another family member early the following morning.

Another means of differentiating experiential differentiation is to view the same performing arts demonstration several times during a life. For example, Mozart's "Jupiter" Symphony has been interpreted many times, most of them sufficiently different from one another that a reasonably informed listener may easily note the differences [ho, ho]. But there is another level of experiential differentiation here—that of a fragment at various times during the life. Let us remark that the work, no matter how much or how little liked, will evoke different responses at each hearing, as much from the perceptive state of mind of the listener as from the interpretation of the musicians playing it. By the same token, everyone hearing any performance in question will hear something slightly different, which is completely valid. Those performances where over-all experiential differentiations are within coherent bounds are generally deemed exceptionally successful. By the same token, *Hamlet* is altered by the actors, the director, the technical crew, and the audience at each and every performance. Good, bad, or indifferent, each performance has some validity, although it may not bring the lessons of the play to bear— which to our perceptions, concerns rationally versus passion—or result in essence contact. To see a bad performance is as valid an experience as seeing a good one. The "trick" is to be willing to experience either or both.

In regard to multiple experiences, just as you can only have a first day at the office once, you can also have a two hundred seventy-sixth day at the office once, on the two hundred seventy-sixth day you are at the office. All days are equally valid, and the cumulative experience is valid as well, both as individual experiences and as cumulative experiences. Although much of the experience seems repetitive, each experience is, in fact, unique, and cannot in any valid sense be repeated. Repeated experiences are the main "shoring up" of the illusion of permanence that is so essential to a Young soul world, just as the presumption of rationality is. If you are in doubt that each experience is unique, you may wish to keep a diary of daily experiences to record ways in which each day is different from all others by making note of deviations, which may be as major as "flood took out the morning commute route" to "coffeemaker on the fritz" in order to help the differentiation process. Most independently mobile species at the Young cycle place high value on however the species defines rationality, that is, they demand that "things" "make sense" within the context of their experiences. This is not necessarily not Good Work, but it denies many of the experiences of life because a great many experiences in any given life do not "make sense" and are therefore ruled out in evaluations of the life. Repetition, for Young souls, brings a kind of "built-in" rationality—if I do anything repeatedly, it must be a rational thing to do—which, upon any reflection, is ludicrous. Let us point out that one of the reasons mass murderers continue to murder is to make it a "rational" thing to do by virtue of repetition. For your species, and a great many others at the Young cycle, habit and rationality are conceptually interchangeable. The discarding of this perception is a necessary part of the early levels of the Mature cycle, and for many mature fragments currently extant as human beings, the clash of the perceptions of the Young soul cycle and the Mature leads to serious emotional distress that can only be ameliorated with "appropriate" help, such as but not limited to psychotherapy.

━━━━━━

"Does optimism and pessimism play any role in this? And if so, what role?"

What you perceive as optimism and pessimism have bearing on the nature of your insights and experiential differentiation. Let us provide an example. If a major and unwelcome political change occurs, the pessimistic fragment may perceive it as a sign of the imminent collapse of the whole of civilization, the optimistic one may see such a change as a "call to arms" against the perceived negative repercussions of the change, although occasionally optimism can be as "distorted" as pessimism, for there are those fragments, who, in the guise of optimism, will assume the unwelcome change will be all right when the unwelcome faction "comes to its senses". Neither is "right" or "wrong", although pessimism tends to support chief feature more than "sensible" optimism. The tendency to believe pain more than joy is part of the "mechanism" by which the hold of pessimism is "validated", for the immediacy of pain, as compared to the more self-intimate nature of joy, is readily identifiable and made acceptable by the experiences and apprehensions of others. Prove it for yourself, should you choose to examine the premise: say "paper cut" aloud and see how many people wince. Then say "ecstasy" and notice how many are confused or even shamed by the word. Joy is not considered trustworthy and is therefore not as readily acknowledged. You may also notice that pain is more appropriate socially than joy. Most fragments may feel awkward about admitting to pain, but they will be chagrined at admitting to joy.

This is reflected in many ways, usually presented in "rational" forms such as health. Let us explicate: in regard to the chief feature of Self-destruction, there is a constant "desire" to maintain control, and any loss of this supposed control is seen as "capitulation" and, of course, any resultant treatment would be by definition, doomed to failure. Those with a chief feature of Self-destruction will often ignore the body until it has effectively ground to a halt, at which point Self-destruction determines all is lost and often will do little or nothing to aid in the "impossible" recovery. The chief feature of Martyrdom often expresses itself in prolonged and determined suffering. Often those with Martyrdom will search out long-term debilitating physical conditions, the better to endure all things, and to excuse pessimism as a "natural" state of mind. The chief feature of Self-deprecation often strives to convince the fragment possessing it that obviously whatever is wrong with the fragment is its own fault and then insists the fragment is not up to handling whatever methodology is used to treat it, which is pessimistic in all aspects. The chief feature of Stubbornness will often insist that nothing is wrong in the first place, no matter what evidence there is to the contrary, but once illness has become manifest, it then strives to continue the pattern so that nothing so dangerous as new improvement is permitted. The bleaker the picture, the more satisfied the pessimism is. Of course, in the case of greed, the fixation of greed is crucial; however, once the habit of ill-health is acquired, it can be presented with endless theme-and-variation, enhancing the pessimism with each new "wrinkle". The chief feature of Arrogance requires a "good reason" for ill-health, and once that has been provided, uses it as an example of the failings of the fragment, and embarrassing to boot, enhancing the lure of pessimism. The more vulnerable the disease renders the fragment, the greater the failing. The chief feature of Impatience most often jumps to the worst possible scenario and relentlessly seeks out evidence to support its position and entrench its pessimism. This often appears as hypochondria, although it is not: "I have a headache. It must be a brain tumor, malignant and inoperable". All these health issues are "bolstered" by pessimism and serve to make the chief features more "credible", for there is the discomfort of the body to "prove" the pessimism, and hence the chief feature is appropriate to the situation at hand.

━━━━━

"Will Michael discuss what they see as crucial issues of being on the physical plane, especially for our species?"

We would say that beyond essence need for intimacy, for your species we would begin with shelter, which includes clothing, is the principle concern of all human beings, no matter what stage of history or evolution, for without appropriate shelter, the fragment will be unable to survive. Demonstrably, it is less difficult to obtain necessary shelter in Samoa than it is in Greenland, but that is only a question of degree. As a species, physical protection from the "elements" is "required" given the fragility of your species which has also made your high adaptability possible. Then, of course, nourishment is a close second, for once you are protected, you must have fuel for the machine or the shelter will be useless. These two issues, for your species, have the highest priority, and will take precedence over other "requirements" in times of extreme emergency. If your region has been, for example, subject to fires, once the fire is escaped, the most urgent need is for shelter of some sort, and then food. Other concerns "kick in" once those two essentials have been met. When those two needs are fulfilled, maintaining social context comes into play, which may mean being reunited with family members, or returning to whatever unit has become the central definition of livelihood, such as but not limited to occupational or religious institutions. Then concerns about future generations become paramount, not only as a means of protecting existing young, but procreation as well, and we would think these phases of development are readily identifiable should you choose to make assessments of behavior after major "disasters". We have said before but we cannot repeat enough that the urge to continue the species, while valid, has led to your current crisis in population and may well be regarded as a dangerous inclination as far as your survival goes. From the most untechnological to the most technologically "sophisticated" societal groups, these strata of "necessity" may be perceived, for they are expressed with minimal cultural "scripting". Only when the societal groups are restored do cultural imperatives come into "play", and the manner in which problems are dealt with is shaped as much by societal expectations as by the "demands" of the external circumstances. We would think that the divergence of cultural influences becomes marked from this stratum on, and for that reason, the definitions are likely to have more cultural "framework" than these more "atavistic" issues. For example, in technologically "sophisticated" societies, transportation is a major consideration, and we would think that there are many levels to the problems of transportation, which are different for goods and people. We will begin with the question of transportation of people, and the process known as "mass transit", for this is an ever-burgeoning issue for most urban fragments.

"Will Michael discuss the transportation issue more thoroughly, particularly in regard to mass transit?"

Given the current "realities" of your species' relentless "urbanization", we would think that mass transit is apt to become a major concern in many parts of "the globe". One of the most prevalent aspects of transporting individual fragments is the problem of the "average commuter", who, on a more or less daily basis, must get from a relatively distant housing area to a city working area and back again in a timely and reliable fashion. The second level in the individual transportation process is the long-distance traveler who singly or in groups is required to present themselves and their goods for journeys of some duration and significant distance. Whether dealing with ocean-going freight or foreign-shores-bound airline passengers, the problems presented are essentially the same. The third level is the interconnection of one transportation system with another, enabling passengers of one form of transportation to have reasonable and reliable access to another in such a way that it obviates the need for single-person transportation for connections or time-consuming "interfaces". The greatest number of persons using such a system will wish to travel at the "average commuter" level in most instances. The second greatest number of persons using "mass transit" will want to avail themselves of it in the long-distance context, and the third group, the connecting group, will be the least-often encountered. We would think that approaching the transportation problem from the point of view of the "average commuter" might be the most "rewarding", for it would solve the greatest number of problems first, and make for an atmosphere of approval for any enlargement of activity contemplated, so that by the time the "interfacing" is developed, the acceptance of the concept is well-established and of "proven" worth.

Some general understanding of the current time and expenses incurred by the regular commuter in outlying areas might be the most efficacious beginning for presenting a welcome solution to what so far has been an inadequate approach to a regional problem. There are other applications of this technology, which we will gladly discuss. It would seem obvious to us that the more remote the "average commuter" is from the commuting "target", the more the service must supply this commuter with dependable transportation for the use of such a system to be a reasonable choice for the commuter. Safety is another issue that enters into the "equation" for the fragment availing him or herself of the system, and not only safety from other human beings, but safety in terms of the system itself, particularly in regard to local environmental hazards, such as but not limited to floods and/or avalanches. Availability is another factor to consider. The system would need to be available "around the clock" and with sufficient frequency to make it a reasonable choice, and at enough places to make its use practical. We would have to say it would not be inappropriate for such transit systems to be flexible enough to accommodate the various demands for service, based not only on times of day, but such things as major events, which would reasonably include major sporting competitions, national celebrations, and "Christmas shopping". If preparedness were part of the system, we would think it would be more readily used by many fragments currently unwilling to improve current systems or to develop new ones.

"What about individual transportation issues? Will Michael discuss them?

We are aware that in most technological societies, the individual is generally "required" to be more mobile than those fragments in societies that are less technologically advanced, and for that reason alone, the individual is "expected" to be able to get from place to place in a speedy manner, and to be prepared to do this with some regularity. This means that travel for fragments in technologically advanced societies is more of a "fact of life" than in societies where mobility is defined by the speed at which

humans and beasts of burden walk. The amount of time a
member of a technologically advanced society is expected
to devote to travel and the distance the fragment is expected
to cover in that time is radically different than such equa-
tions are in non-technologically advanced societies. This
means that much skill in traveling is part of the life of those
in technologically advanced societies. For those in such
societies, the ability to drive an automobile is a "standard"
skill, and one that many occupations require. The ability to
fly airplanes is less often required, although there are
businesses where such an accomplishment is not only
prudent but recommended, and we would think that in time
this will more often be part of an employer's expectations
for those in his employ. What is the most "troublesome"
from our point of view, is that these skills, while "reasonable" given the nature of technologically advanced societies, do not, in fact, demand a more "responsible" conduct
in regard to the environment. We do not mean by this that
all fragments "should" commute on bicycles. We did not
say that and we did not imply it. But we do think it short-
sighted not to develop automobile and airplane fuels based
on methane rather than the currently popular hydrocar-
bons. Not only is methane less toxic, it is readily available
and relatively inexhaustible. We have said this before on
other occasions, but we would wish to repeat it. So long as
technologically sophisticated societies make fast individual
travel "necessary" we would think that switching to methane fuels would have major environmental advantages, and
not be so impossible to develop as to be impractical. We do
not propose that the individual automobile be "banished"
for that is not a practical notion, given the current state of
work and housing, but that a less-intrusive fuel be considered. The internal combustion engine may readily be
adapted to methane fuels, and that alone makes the transfer
not only "easy" but useful for all concerned. Also, in
matters of public health, many environmentally triggered
illnesses would be reduced both in frequency and severity
if methane were the popular fuel of choice.

"Would Michael expand on that, please?"

Many chronic diseases, particularly those of mid-life onset have a link to the state of the environment. Some development sites of cancer are directly affected by environmental conditions, as are such syndromes as Chronic Fatigue, Systemic Lupus, Chronic Sinusitis, and many allergic conditions, including adult-onset asthma. We would have to say that particles in the atmosphere and water contribute to the presence of such diseases, and while not all fragments "must" contract them, given that well over ninety percent of all bodies are genetically imperfect, the stress imposed by environmental contaminants can tend to "overload" the system and result in chronic illnesses. The impact of environmental "ills" cannot be overstated, for we would have to say that out of every fragment with a chronic health impairment, seventy-eight percent of them have an environmental component. Although the current medical "fashion" does not deal much with anything but the most severe forms of environmental elements in health compromise, we would think that closer examinations would prove of interest in this regard. We agree it is frustrating to deal with health issues that are at once ubiquitous and ephemeral, but without any careful analysis the problems are apt to increase and compound. Tackling the matter now is likely to be more successfully "defined" than if such studies are delayed until the synergetic impact is so complex that getting a grasp on the problem becomes the most difficult aspect of the "program". In other words, the problems will tend to become more complex over time, and harder to assess because of that complexity.

There is also the matter of immunizations, for while we do not mean to discourage immunization, we would have to remark that infecting infants protectively can contribute to various illnesses occurring in later life. That does not mean that it is "recommended" to avoid immunization, for that is not the case. It is a commendable effort to minimize the events of disease in the life and to diminish the severity of disease. Immunization does far more to preserve life than the lack of it does, but we do wish to advise you that you cannot escape repercussions from such therapies as immunization. Many fragments develop low-level chronic conditions as a result of the immunizations administered in early childhood. We do not think that it is advisable to postpone or limit immunizations, for that is far from the case, especially at a time of such population density, but we would think that a reassessment of many chronic health conditions in the light of the immunization history might reveal much of interest. We would think that if immunizations were given at lower dosages over a longer period of time that the protection desired would not significantly be reduced and the stress to the infant's body would not have the damage potential it now does.

There are many public health problems that are not being dealt with in a "sensible" manner, not the least of which is the treatment of cancer, which is, as we have said many times before, a collagen disease, which is why it spreads in the way it does. To poison the body to the point that the compromised cells die with the hope that the healthy ones do not is typical of medical thinking six hundred years ago, as is burning the tumors with radiation. We would think that reassessing the disease as a failure of collagen and striving to "recondition" the collagen might lead to more efficacious treatment than anything currently available in standard Western treatment. There are some medical practices in China that have proven to have a better impact on the patient with cancer, both in reducing the presence of the disease and maintaining a reasonable "quality of life", and although Western medical practices regard such treatment as heresy, there are many benefits to be had from the Chinese perceptions. Aside from cancer, systemic conditions such as clogged arteries and damaged nerves have been approached with the same perspective as they were approached a century ago. The means of detecting and measuring impairment has improved significantly, but the assessment of the nature of such conditions is largely unaltered, even though much genetic research has shown components of many diseases that are genetic in origin.

Since the current methods of the culture of the United States of America is to view health as a product and the provision of health care as an industry, we would think that there are many sound commercial reasons for the way in which such care is made available, and as long as the concept of "health-as-product" remains the standard, we would think that progress on certain chronic diseases will not be too pronounced because the long-term investment in treating chronic diseases might be jeopardized by a too-comprehensive "cure" or other treatment. This does not mean that individual health professionals do not seek to end diseases, only that the current perspective on the nature and goals of health care are such that the industry is inclined to continue to want to earn as much as possible from a predictable source, that is, chronic conditions, which are the "cash cows" of the medical industry. Only when and if the perceptions of the culture in general come to view the availability of health care a matter of public service would this "state of affairs" be likely to change. And, of course, encouraging the birth of more children makes the business of medicine flourish.

▭

"Will Michael discuss the whole issue of procreation? Is it instinctual or cultural or a bit of both?"

As primates, you have a "need" to have off-spring, for it comes with the "hard-wiring" of your species. And while there are many cultural structures in place to promote enlarging population, in fact, most mammals, as you may observe in other mammalian creatures, have quite legitimate and very strong programming from their species-central, which is what you would call instinct, to give birth to and nurture their young. This is not limited to mammals, but is more readily identifiable in them because of shared behavior patterns. Primates as a group generally bear no more than two young at a time, and these off-spring generally require a period of intensive care and training; witness the behavior of gorillas, chimpanzees, and orangutans. So yes, there is validly a maternal and paternal instinct and there are equally valid but distinct sexual drives. However, and we must stress this, few, if any, creatures of hive-reason associate the sexual drive with the parental urges. Wolves, being a species that mates for life, will essentially turn off all sexual drives if something happens to the mate, but will, in fact, nurture the young of other wolves. And it is well-known to farmers that nursing sows and ewes will accept any number of unlikely "off-spring" and care for them even if they are members of a species ordinarily hostile or even predatory to pigs and sheep. This most often occurs due to human intervention and with some degree of supervision. It has also been noted on many occasions that most mammals will tolerate behavior from the young of other animals they would not tolerate in the "adult" version.

What has made the biggest difference for your species is the discovery and recognition of paternity, accompanied by legalized pride, otherwise known as the law of primogeniture, which in most cultures applies only to males. This has done much to distort the simple mammalian perceptions inherent in your incarnate species. This is also what has allowed your various legal systems to evolve so that they essentially define females and off-spring as property of males: as long as these legal suppositions are in place, "rational" decisions regarding fertility, reproduction, and sexuality are not likely to occur except on an individual basis. Most cultures are structured to continue what is regarded as a "natural" order, based on male-dominance, which is a remnant of your species' hard-wiring, and reinforced by religious assumptions that for the most part are based on social paradigms more than four thousand years old. It is, of course, possible for you to choose not to uphold the decisions based on the sexual behavior of your nearest species relatives, and we would think that once the mature soul cycle is the average for your species, you as a species will be less likely to respond to the sexual territoriality of your fellow-primates, and culture will change to accommodate the shift in perceptions.

━━━━━━

"**W**hat if we make the earth so polluted we cannot survive here as a species? What happens then?"

Then you will incarnate in another independently mobile species on another planet and continue your evolution. There is no short-cut to evolution, and many species cease to be viable before the evolution of the fragments ensouled in those species have completed their physical plane cycles. At such time, a new species is selected and ensouled. Often, when a species has been in a species-form capable of manipulating its environment—as you are—the next species chosen to incarnate will be one that cannot manipulate its environment, and the experiences of that phase of evolution will therefore be markedly different from those experienced in this species. That is not, incidentally, a matter of "punishment", only of experiential differentiation. You do not choose any species for the purpose of self-punishment, but for quality of experience. When a species is incarnated with fragments of entities, that species becomes capable of choice. How the choice is manifest is determined by the nature of the species in which the fragment is incarnate. For example, you might choose to sprout wings and fly, but that is not a possibility for your species. So you may choose instead to invent airplanes for the same purpose, which is something your species is capable of doing. The nature of evolution is such that duplicating species experience from one species to the next would tend to interfere with experiential differentiation, and we would "expect" that whatever limitations a new ensoulment species would have would create new realms of choice for you, within the limits of the physical plane. And we assure you, that progress is possible on many levels no matter what the characteristics of the ensouled species may be.

CHAPTER 6

Evolution, Extinction, and Reincarnation

If there is one experience to be experienced on the physical plane, it is the ability to experience the passage of time, and the visible manifestations brought about over "time", in each ensouled fragment, in the artifacts of the species, in geographical "reality", and in astronomical events. This is by far the most "unique" experience possible on the physical plane—linear time. We cannot say this with sufficient impact, for just as we are not part of physical-plane time, so you, being extant upon it, cannot divorce yourselves from it, nor would it be appropriate to your experience, even if it were possible. From the development of galaxies to the most perishable bacterium, we would think that the "cycle" of life would be considered revealing of the validity of the experience of the physical plane.

"Michael, that all sounds a little elliptical. Could you be more specific?"

We perceive time in a manner we have already described, based on possibilities and choices. From our perspective, all available choices are equally valid, and only on the physical plane can evaluation be made as to which is most "appropriate" for the fragment in question. We would think that this is the "value" of lives on the physical plane, having possibilities that are chosen and bring about consequences in the context of linear development. We would think that by assessing choice in terms of "what comes next", a valuable tool of insight is made accessible to all fragments on the physical plane. To be able to see events "unfold" is an experience that can only be fully realized in linear time and in the context of an on-going life. The recognition and validation of experience in a chronological context provides many opportunities for dealing with personal and world truths and their evolution within the particular life being led. For example, being able to place in time the process of learning to read enables the fragment to understand the personal truth of evolution, from the personal truth of "I cannot read" to the personal truth of "I can read". The world truth involved here is that it is possible for a human being to read. Without a concept of time and its passage, such identification is less readily made, and as a result the lesson of the process is not as well discerned as it is within a comprehension of time.

Evolution occurs on many levels, not all of them related to hive-soul species. The human species is in the process of evolution, and each fragment ensouled in the human—or any other species throughout the physical plane—is evolving. It is the nature of all energy, no matter how expressed, to evolve. Since matter is, as we have said before, coagulated energy, it, too, evolves in ways readily perceived by the evolution and extinction of species over long eons, well before mammals, let alone primates, entered "the picture". We would have to remark that the various species that have evolved over time were, of course, suited to their environment. When they were no longer suited to their environment, they died out, leaving a "vacuum" to be filled by other species, which, of course, evolved to fill the vacated "niche" more effectively, as the "niche", as well as the species, was evolving, too. We say this in order to remind you that you are not the glorious fulfillment of the evolutionary process, but only one of its manifestations, and when your species ceases to be viable, it does not mean that your sun will go nova and the galaxy implode. If that happened every time an ensouled species went extinct, there would be a constant eruption of novae all over the physical plane, and ensoulment would shift from species to species with dizzying speed. That does not mean that the departure of ensouled species from one planet is without impact. We did not say that and we did not imply it. The presence of any species, plant or animal, ensouled or hive-souled, is "significant" and its absence impacts the planet and the environment of the planet. We do wish to remark here, however, that planetary existence does not depend on the presence of ensouled species for planetary viability. In fact, the presence of ensouled species can be more a hazard than a benefit to many planets, yours, of course, among them. Ensouled species impact environments to the degree that their choices can alter the environments, and their presence or absence is significant to the degree that their choices lead to environmental impact. All species, no matter how "insignificant" have impact on the environment to a greater or lesser degree, and we would have to say that where the species has the option of manipulating the environment, it will, by the nature of its "hard-wiring" or instinct, for that manipulation is the result of evolution. For example, the *Tyrannosaurus Rex* would not have evolved had there not been a plethora of other dinosaurs to serve as prey, and having evolved for that purpose, the species could not survive without sufficient prey to sustain it. As the environment of the dinosaurs evolved, so, of course, did the dinosaurs. Those that did not went extinct.

━━━━━

"Speaking of dinosaurs, did they die off or evolve into birds?"

Yes. Many of the species died off long before the cataclysmic disruption that altered the environment so drastically that survival for most was impossible. However, yes, those species with the greatest adaptability were able to survive the major extinctions and evolved, as is apparent, into birds. Remember, should you choose to do so, that when the environment changed suddenly, many other species that had been marginal suddenly became more active in an environment that supported them more readily than the well-established species. Many forms of bacteria and viruses flourished in the new environment, and insects adapted to feeding on decaying flesh thrived in this period. So, of course, many other species succumbed to disease that they had not had to deal with before. Changes in the environment always cause an increased activity in diseases and their vectors, because the evolutionary cycle of diseases "requires" a weakened host or vector population in order for the disease to become virulent, and this has been true since the first paramecia entered the earliest seas. In physics this is expressed in the following way: "For every action there is an equal and opposite reaction." Where many fragments become confused is the assumption that equal is a quantity measurement, not a quality measurement, which is misleading. The principle of action and reaction is, to use another "old saw", "Nature abhors a vacuum". This is true in terms of evolution as much as in biology, and can be repeatedly demonstrated. There are, as has long been established, many species of mammals that have also gone extinct, from the time of the dinosaurs to the present day. Their remains do not excite the general enthusiasm and interest in the way dinosaurs do, but study of them can be as revealing as study of the ancient reptiles, which were, we assure you, not simply overgrown lizards, but another evolutionary branch on the lizard tree. More of dinosaur central is now incorporated into bird central than is currently in reptile central.

———

"Is 'survival of the fittest' valid? If not, what is?"

We would have to say that "survival of the most adaptable" is the rule. Fitness implies that the species is appropriate for its "niche", which is not the case with species surviving. Most of the species that survive and evolve do so because they were not ultimately suited to their "niche", and therefore subject to extinction, as the most fit are, when the "niche" disappeared. You may see this in terms of cultures—those that can adapt survive, those that cannot either mutate or are subsumed by a more adaptable culture. One of the hallmarks of cultural survival as well as species survival is tolerance, the word to be interpreted in the broadest possible scope. If a species can only survive on certain species of plants, if those plants are mutated by a plant virus or they die off for other reasons, the chance for the species surviving or those plants being able to survive is slim. But if a species has a wider dietary tolerance, even though its main source of food disappears, the species has a better chance of surviving and evolving along with its food source. By the same token, a culture that has become so rigid that change cannot be accommodated is "doomed" to extinction, for change will occur, change being the nature of the physical plane. Those cultures that have only one "frame of reference" in which to operate are in the same predicament as the species with a single food source or a very limited habitat. Of course, choice does enter the picture where cultures are concerned, and in cases where cultural rigidity leads to danger, we would think that it is likely that the members of the culture would be able to choose to alter their culture rather than loose it, although history is littered with examples of cultures that failed to do so and have gone extinct.

———

"Is there karma associated with species extinction?"

Generally there is not, although the "files" kept by species-central on each fragment with which the species of the central interacts, might put you in an unfavorable position with the other members of the species surviving. In other words, where you are dealing with hive-soul creatures, karma is not operative the same way it is if you interfere with the life choices of other human beings or of cetaceans. For example, if you deliberately killed the last Great Auk for sport, bird-central might not have a favorable "report" on you, and your relationship with birds for the next dozen or so incarnations might be "chancy" at best. The same is true with animals of other species. For another example, if you set out to wipe out the last white rhino with the idea of having a unique trophy, we would think that related species, including equines, might not respond well to you for many ensuing incarnations. We would think that in a few lives after such a choice, you would choose to make amends by beneficent actions toward the species in question, such as, but not limited to, founding and supporting a major bird sanctuary in the former case, or establishing major research facilities into extinct mammals and ways to protect currently endangered species in the latter. That does not mean that all fragments working to support various animal and wildlife projects are making amends to some species-central, or that all those who wish to make amends will choose such ways to do it, but it does mean that when someone devotes his or her life to such a pursuit, making amends may be a component in the choice. Please note that we say "may", not "is". For many fragments, caring for animals is the means of escaping their own animosity about other human beings, and by this "sideways" concern, seek to avoid dealing with people. This is not an error, for as we have said many times, there are no errors, there is only choice and the consequences of choice. But we would think that those fragments who use hive-soul animals as a substitute for interaction with other human beings might want to examine the underlying focus of this choice, if evolution in the life is desired. We would wish to point out that human intervention has preserved a great many species that might otherwise have gone extinct, and not just in the last century, but over the last ten millennia. As soon as human beings started farming, that is, raising plants and animals for food and other sustenance, they took "a hand" [Michael thinks this is very funny.] in preserving and adapting species to human benefit, which has meant that the species "domesticated" have been bred for diversity and adaptability, which in turn has increased the species' chances of survival. We would think that the adaptations of "domesticated" species have been most successful when undertaken with herd animals, so that the human could "take the place" of the senior animal of the herd. Less success has resulted when solitary animals have been brought into the "domestic fold". And while we would agree human beings have caused species to go extinct, this is not limited to human action, for so have other hive-soul species. Many carnivorous dinosaurs "wiped out" herbivorous species, and certain more adaptable herbivores encroaching on territory and food of other, less adaptable herbivorous dinosaurs, caused the less adaptable ones to die out. This had nothing to do with karma or destiny, only with the nature of the species in question and its adaptability to changed environment, for certainly the presence of competition or predators changes the environment, as much as such "natural" disasters as floods, plagues, famines, droughts, and all the rest of the catalogue of physical-plane "misfortunes". With the coming of mammalian diversity, which was possible due to the lack of dinosaurs in the environment, many species have been unable to survive because of the greater adaptability of other mammals. This is part of evolution, and appropriate to its manifestation on the physical plane.

Let us remark here that from our point of view, the single most significant theory in human thought is the theory of extinction, for it was only after that theory was propounded and accepted by those exploring the nature of life that it was possible to develop the theories and schematics of evolution. For while geological change had been somewhat understood and chronicled since the sixth century before Common Reckoning [meaning sixth century B.C.], the relation of such "earthly" changes to species development had not been made and recognized until much later. We say somewhat because without the understanding of extinction, much of the assessment of geological information was "incomplete". That is not to say that no exploring had been done or discoveries made. Bones dug up before the first explorations into extinction, and hence evolution, were considered to be "proof" of the existence of giants—which in fact they were, but not of the human species. The reevaluation of these bones and the cognitive process that brought about shifted the whole of human perception, although very few, including Cuvier himself, realized the extent of its impact at the time. Without the theory of extinctions, many biological studies would have languished due to lack of a "frame of reference". The past, until that theory came about, was largely a religious and political record, stopping at the founding of the religious or political system, either in documented time or in mythic origins. Realizing the past went far beyond the "human" past was a shocking innovation in the early nineteenth century, Common Reckoning, and the repercussions were felt throughout the scientific world for more than half a century, and are still causing problems in many religious centers. When Old Scholar Georges Cuvier presented his theories on extinction, he brought a new definition of the past along with his attempts to account for the fossils he had analyzed critically and—in this case the second part of his "discovery" is the more significant aspect of his theory—placed in temporal context. That such creatures had existed was startling enough, but that they had ceased to exist called for an enormity of thought not many at that time could grasp; and few, even now, have an accurate perspective on the matter. Given the fact that the theory of extinction has had to "swim upstream" against a powerful cultural and religious current, it is remarkable that it has, in fact, survived. Had Cuvier introduced the theory two centuries earlier, he might have found a dramatically different reception to his ideas, and far less "intellectual curiosity" about his thoughts. In fact, an accomplished mathematician in what is now Jordan proposed a theory of similar nature, based on his astronomical calculations and extrapolations, in the eleventh century, Common Reckoning, and was blinded and his tongue cut out for such blasphemy. We would have to say that Cuvier chose a more appropriate time to introduce his "discovery", for although the reception he received was far from universally favorable, the cultural climate was such that innovative thought was tolerated by most members of the academic community of the time, and his discoveries were given respect by his peers, and his theory not only discussed but advanced in intellectual institutions. Now that his theory has led to scientific verification, we would have to say that the subsequent development of evolutionary studies has made it possible for many fragments to understand the validity of a past that does not directly bear on them, but is related to the planet, not the human species. The nature of evolution does not focus on any one species at any time, but the viability of the environment all the species of the planetary environment, without any "favoritism" for those species ensouled as compared to those hive-souled. Let us also comment that the current resistance to the theory of evolution by those preferring the "comfort" of religious dogma to the "perils" of evolution is the manifestation of the fear of loss of power on the part of those espousing the religious interpretation of the past, thus making human beings the glorious end-product of evolution occupying a favored position with the "powers that be", whether that power is called Jehovah, God, Allah, or Krisna. And while their beliefs are not accurate, they demonstrate the problems of those who confuse religious myth with actual past events, and we would think that adhering to dogma in the face of factual evidence will tend to lead the religious dogma to the same fate as the dinosaur, and for the same reason.

━━━━━

"Will Michael discuss how reincarnation works in terms of human evolution?"

That is all we ever discuss, but we will do so in specific terms. Each fragment, from first incarnation to last, is experiencing a unique life, with overleaves chosen to enable the fragment to accomplish the task chosen for the life. The lives led are all equally valid and contribute to the evolution of the fragment as well as the species the fragment en- souled. There are no "wasted" lives. Let us offer some examples, one of each essence, the fragments chosen now living their final lives on the physical plane, and follow them from first incarnation to this last one. Incidentally, those lives where the transition from level three to level four "overlap" in function are, in fact, mid-cycle lives, although we will not usually identify them as such.

To begin at the beginning with a first cast Slave who is now a final level Old Slave in his forties, living in Switzer- land and working in a medical facility for the dying. This is his one hundred ninth life, with the added reminder that Slaves come into their own from their first incarnation, and are adaptable in ways other fragments are not, which in terms of evolution, is a real advantage. This particular Slave fragment began its evolution 5,233 years ago, being born male for its first life into a family of brick-makers in what is now Afghanistan. That life lasted twenty-two years, and the fragment learned to make bricks. The second life, still at the first level of the Infant cycle, lasted only four years in what is now Burma. The fragment succumbed to food poisoning. The third life, still first level Infant, took place in a settlement on the Danube. In this life the frag- ment was female, and the fragment lived for thirty-one years, had four children, and learned how to paint pottery. The fourth life, the fragment was at second level Infant, and was male, living in western China, as a farmer. He had six children with his wife and two of them survived to adulthood. The life lasted twenty-nine years and ended as the result of pneumonia. The fifth life began in what became Persia, where the fragment was born into a slave family and was sold to a smith, who made him a eunuch and put him in charge of his family. The fragment died in a flood, aged nineteen. The sixth life, at second level Infant was begun in early Egypt, where the fragment was employed in preparing paints. He lived thirty-four years, had one child, and died of complications resulting from an infected gallbladder. The seventh life was as a weaver in India, the fragment was female, and considered unmarriageable due to partial deafness. The fragment was still at second level Infant. That life ended when the fragment was unable to escape a fire in her village. She was twenty-eight. The eighth life moved the Slave to third level Infant, and the fragment, male again, served as a kind of game warden on a holding in northern Greece. That life ended as the result of fever contracted from wood ticks, at the age of thirty-one. The ninth life, again at third level Infant was brief, the fragment being offered as a sacrifice to regional gods at age six months. The tenth life, at third level Infant was spent in what is now Brazil, where this fragment, now female, served as village cook for more than a dozen years, had seven children, and died at twenty-nine as the result of a fall that injured her liver and spleen. The eleventh life brought the fragment to fourth level Infant, when the fragment lived in north Africa, a female who was part of a nomadic "tribe", and busied herself having children and weaving tents. She died at thirty-two from complications during delivery of her ninth child, who also did not survive. The Slave's twelfth life was lived for fifteen years in a fishing village in what is now northern Spain. The fragment was male, and drowned. The thirteenth life this Slave was at the fourth level of the Infant cycle, and the fragment lived in Crete, dying at age eight, killed by marauders. The fourteenth life of this fragment, again at fourth level Infant, was in Sri Lanka, where, as a female, the child was given to the local temple at age ten and served there until age twenty when she died of snakebite. The fifteenth life of this Slave took place in what is now Venezuela, where this fragment, male, spent most of his life as the "right-hand" man of the local priest, of whom he was homosexually enamored. He died of cholera at age twenty-six. The sixteenth life, again at fourth level infant, was lived aboard a ship at the mouth of the Nile, where she, then female, was alternately a fisherwoman and prostitute, murdered by a cousin at age nineteen for her boat, which she had inherited from her brother. In the seventeenth life, this fragment was at the fifth level Infant, male, and apprenticed as a woodworker in what is now Cambodia, lived for seventeen years, and died of parasite infestation. In the eighteenth life, this Slave was born female in what is now Normandy, and died of exposure at age two. In the nineteenth life, this fragment was once again in China, male, now occupied building houses, at which he prospered. He married twice, had seven surviving children, and died at age forty when a half-built wall collapsed on him. In the twentieth life this fragment was still at the fifth level Infant, born female in eastern Africa, made baskets, which she sold from her youth to her death at the hands of her husband at age twenty-two, killed for her failure to have children. At the twenty-first life this fragment was at the sixth level Infant, female, and was sold in childhood to a traveler, who sold her to an innkeeper near the Black Sea where she was a maid-of-all-work and concubine to the innkeeper, but was not used as a prostitute for travelers because of a birthmark on her face, which was considered a bad omen. She died at age thirty-four of general exhaustion. In the twenty-second life this Slave was sixth level infant, male, a spear-maker in central Europe, who froze to death at age twenty-seven. In the twenty-third life, this fragment was crippled, an orphan, female, and born in what is now southern France. The village elders put her in the care of the local herb woman, who cared for her until her death at age nineteen, thus burning the karmic ribbon from the Slave's sixteenth life, with the herb woman, who had been her murderous cousin. In the twenty-fourth life this Slave became a seventh level Infant, and was born in what is now western Canada, into a family of skinners and "tanners", that is, hide-preservers. Now male, he married and had five children, four of whom survived to adulthood. The fragment died of heart failure at age forty-three, having become a respected elder of the community. The twenty-fifth life of this fragment was in what is now Turkey, where the fragment was a metal worker, male, being a youngest son, he was too poor to afford a wife, and died as a result of infection from a partial amputation of his foot by a cartwheel, at age twenty-five.

At the twenty-sixth life this Slave entered the Baby cycle,

the first life being lived in what is now Korea, where she made jugs and other large pottery vessels, and was very "proper". She married "late", at age eighteen, had two children, and died giving birth to twins at age twenty-three. The Slave was reborn in what is now Poland, was female again, and died of starvation at age five. The twenty-eighth life began in eastern China on the Yellow River, where this fragment, male, was a carter, lived forty-four years and died of fever, having two wives and eleven children. At the twenty-ninth life, this Slave "advanced" to second level Baby, was once again female, sold to a brothel at age six, and lived in the brothel for another twenty-two years, was turned off, became a beggar and died of malnutrition at age thirty-two. In the thirtieth life, this fragment was female again, a "servant" in a peasant village in what is now Hungary. She was killed by soldiers at age twenty-four. In the thirty-first life, the fragment was third level Baby, male, an initiate priest in a minor temple during the reign of Sesostris I, lived an uneventful life of ritual and writing, and died at age fifty-one of cancer, the senior priest of his temple. The thirty-second life of this Slave was brief, ending at age three, when this male child was killed by political rivals of his father, in northern India. The thirty-third life was at the third level Baby, when this fragment, female, became a "nurse" and "midwife" for the people of her village in what is now Croatia. Widowed at eighteen, she lived forty-six years, and died of appendicitis. The thirty-fourth life of this Slave entered the fourth level of the Baby cycle, and in this life earned some reputation as a teacher of "numbers" in what is now Syria, where teaching reputations at that time were "jealously" sought. The fragment was male, homosexual, and rigid in his thinking. He died at age thirty-eight, poisoned by "academic" rivals. The thirty-fifth life of this Slave was spent on the west coast of Africa, farming and making up songs about local legends, some of which endured for more than five hundred years. He died at thirty-nine, the father of twelve children, and husband of three wives. At the thirty-sixth life, the Slave moved on to fifth level of the Baby cycle and being male again in Egypt, became something of a reactionary figure, opposing the recent "reforms" and contributing to the social unrest that plagued the country for the greater part of a century. He died at forty-one, stoned to death by those who opposed him. The thirty-seventh life was spent as a female in central China, the wife of a farmer, dying at age twenty-four of gangrene, leaving two living children. The thirty-eighth life ended at age two, from sunstroke, in central Asia. The thirty-ninth life was spent as a female in eastern Greece, the wife and partner of a weaver, who was also her Task Companion. She lived thirty-five years and died of malaria, as did six of her eight children. At this point, the fragment had spent more than one thousand years incarnate on the physical plane, and approximately one thousand eight hundred years had gone by. The fortieth life was also at the fifth level Baby cycle. The Slave was again female, born in what is now Mexico, became a skilled basket-maker, married twice, had nine children, four of whom lived to adulthood, and died, aged forty-one, from medical treatment administered following a miscarriage. Life forty-one ended at age ten when this male child suffered a fatal concussion. The forty-second life began the sixth level of the Baby cycle, when the Slave, now male, was born in Tyre to a Phoenician family of boatwrights. He became skilled in the trade, and his business went well. He married, had a family of seven children, all of whom drowned, along with him, on a voyage to Egypt. He was thirty-eight when the ship went down. In the forty-third life, this fragment perished in what is now Java at age six, in the wake of a volcanic eruption. The forty-fourth life was lived in what is now Alaska, hunting elk, bear, otters, and other fur-bearing animals for trade with other "tribes". He lived to age fifty-six and died of a stroke, leaving five children and sixteen grandchildren to carry on the family tradition. The forty-fifth life took the Slave to the seventh level of the Baby cycle, and put her into a "harem", and the position of Second Wife, which she maintained by a program of discreet murders of rivals. She bore five children, all but one male, making her highly valued. She died of slow poison at age thirty-seven. The forty-sixth life was one of traveling, this time in northern Spain, with a family of "tinkers". She was female and lived nineteen years, dying of "neglect", and burned two karmic ribbons in the process, one from the fortieth life, one from the forty-third.

Life forty-seven brought the Slave to the first level of the Young cycle. He was born into a military family in Egypt in the twentieth Dynasty. At this point, the fragment maneuvered and bribed his way into a favored position, serving as one of the personal guards of Pharaoh, and making a point of avoiding any direct fighting. He married three times and had fourteen children, and was executed for treason (of which he was not guilty) at age thirty-nine. The fragment then incarnated in Sparta, female, ended up again in a temple, advanced to a senior position where she exercised a fair amount of civic authority and used her position to advance her nephews in the power structure. She died at age forty-six by suicide. The next life, number forty-nine, brought the Slave to the second level of the Young cycle, in which life the fragment, male, was framed for debasing coins, had his hands struck off, and ended up an outcast after the triumph of the Philistines, dying at age thirty-one. The fragment then incarnated in Japan and became a carpenter, working long hours on ambitious projects and becoming well-known for the speed at which he and his men could build. He had four children, all girls, and died of frostbite at age forty-two. In the Slave's fifty-first life, she was trained as a midwife in rural China, and practiced that profession until a male physician took over much of her business when she was thirty-eight. She died five years later from starvation. At life fifty-two, the fragment became third level Young, and died of fever at age four months in what is now Belize. Life fifty-three began in Corinth, shortly after the Dorian conquest, when this fragment, female, was a literal slave, tending to farming chores and weaving, and incidentally paying karma from life number fifty until she died at age thirty-one. Life fifty-four saw the Slave female again, and the youngest daughter of an important land-owner in what is now Germany. She was kept "at home" to take her mother's place and to run the household. Since she preferred her own sex, she did not mind the arrangement as much as many others might. Upon the death of her parents, she was imprisoned by her oldest brother to prevent any argument about inheritance. She died of a multitude of ills at age forty-seven. Life fifty-five brought the Slave to fourth level Young cycle, and to prominence as a merchant in brass and ceramics. He spent time in many of the Mediterranean ports, consolidating a considerable fortune as well as six different families before his death from kidney failure at age fifty. Life fifty-six saw many changes for this fragment, who was born to slavery in Greece, ran away to what is now Italy, where he set himself up in business, after a little literal highway robbery, as a stonemason. His success was moderate in large part due to his ferocious temper, and he died of infection after being partly crushed by one of the loads of stones he was delivering. He was thirty. Life fifty-seven ended at age eleven when infection developed after the youth was made a eunuch. Life fifty-eight was lived as a female who lived and died in Carthage. She was noted as a skilled weaver and an ambitious wife who served her merchant-husband's interests for more than a dozen years, paid two karmic "debts" and finally died of cancer at age thirty-nine. The Slave then moved to the fifth level Young and incarnated as female in India, to a high-caste family which she took full advantage of, aided and abetted by a chief feature of greed. She had four miscarriages and nine children before her death at age forty-four from systemic parasites. The Slave's sixtieth incarnation was as a male in Sparta during the war with Athens, supplied arms and ships to the Spartan forces, was accused (fairly) of treason, and was tortured to death, aged forty-nine, his family exiled, and all his goods seized by the state. The next incarnation, number sixty-one, began in the Etruscan city of Veii, and upon its defeat by Romans, she was made a slave and carried off to Rome where she died of fever at age twenty-eight. Life number sixty-two lasted fourteen years and was lived on the east coast of what is now Mexico. The Slave was female, and was killed on her wedding night by her new husband for failing to gratify him. The Slave's sixty-third life was spent as male, with a "city" of pirates on an island just off the southern coast of China. He was bloodthirsty, but no more so than the rest of his society. He had two wives, nine concubines, thirty-four children, and took great pride in dying in battle against the Chinese at age forty-three. Life sixty-four, and the sixth level of the Young cycle began in what is now western Panama and involved coastal trading. The fragment was female, of very low caste, and worked primarily as a cook and deck hand, burning three karmic ribbons when she went down with the ship after saving most of her shipmates. She was twenty-one. The fragment was then reborn in what is now Switzerland to a family of herders. Due to a club-foot, the fragment had little "value," but as he was the only son, he was permitted to live and eventually became a kind of regional magistrate for the hamlet where he lived and a number of neighboring hamlets. Because of his deformity he was not allowed to marry. He died at thirty-nine of food poisoning. The Slave then reincarnated in what is now Iraq, in an area of salt marshes, and devoted his life to building boats. He married, had six children, all of whom died of the same fever that killed him at age thirty-four. In the next life, this Slave moved to the seventh level of the Young cycle, was female, the daughter of a family of boatwrights in Carthage, who supplied boats to the military in Spain. She was married at fifteen to what might be called a naval officer who took her to Spain and deserted her and their three children. She starved to death in an attempt to save her children at the age of twenty-nine. In life sixty-eight, this fragment was again female, this time living and working in Rome in the lupanar [red-light district] as a prostitute, which, we remind you, was an honorable occupation at that time. She achieved an enviable reputation, treated her customers fairly, enjoyed her success and fame, married her two children well, and retired to the country with a small fortune and died of typhus at the age of fifty-four, after providing all her slaves writs of manumission and small grants to get themselves started in the world as freemen.

At the sixty-ninth life the Slave entered the Mature cycle, the first life being spent in China, making brass instruments for scientific use. He married three times, had ten children, and finally withdrew from society and his family at age forty-nine, dying of pneumonia at age fifty-one. The Slave at this point had just over two thousand years of life experience on the physical plane and three thousand two hundred seventeen years had passed since the fragment first incarnated. The Slave then incarnated in Egypt, was female, lived two years and died of a fungal infection of the lungs. The Slave was born for the seventy-first time in what is now France to a family of wine-makers. As the youngest son, he stood to inherit little, and so he allied himself with Roman merchants and became a wine-broker. He had four children from three different women, one of whom he married. He died of epidemic disease at age forty-one. Life seventy-two was lived in a remote region of the South Pacific where the Slave, now female, tended goats and younger siblings, dying at age nineteen of shock after having her shoulder broken by an angry goat. The Slave was again born female, this time in Greece to a merchant family. She ran away from home when her family attempted to arrange a marriage for her, and eventually arrived in Alexandria where she went to work with a "charitable" organization dedicated to raising orphans. She died there, aged twenty-seven, from osteomyelitis. At life seventy-four, the Slave went to the second level Mature, and was born male in Sumatra, became a priest of the local god and oversaw the construction of a new temple. He contracted leprosy, was exiled and died at age forty-four. Life number seventy-five was lived in Siberia, where the Slave was the oldest daughter of the most successful reindeer herder in the region. She was abducted, ransomed, and set to run the herding for her family, since her abduction made her unmarriageable. She died of advanced frostbite at age fifty-nine. The next life, number seventy-six, began the third level of the Mature cycle, and was lived in Britain, where this fragment supervised the building of enclosed settlements. His reputation made him so much in demand that he was murdered by rivals at age thirty-eight. The Slave was born for the seventy-seventh time in what is now Florida, was female, became skilled in working with wood in the making of body-armor, hence married well, had five children, and died of yellow fever at age thirty-six. The seventy-eighth life brought the Slave to the Hindu Kush and the beginning of the fourth level of the Mature cycle. The fragment was male, raised horses, and fought off bandits, who eventually slaughtered his family. He died while attempting to exact vengeance at the age of twenty-nine. In his next life, this Slave became a monk who served Pope Innocent I, dying in the same year his pope did, at the age of sixty-one. The Slave was born into the eightieth life, female, just in time to be killed at age three when Attila sacked Worms. The eighty-first life was in a Mayan city, where as a simple laborer, this fragment lived in a semi-slave state for twenty-two years, dying as a sacrifice before battle. The eighty-second life began the fifth level of the Mature cycle, when the Slave was born male in Japan and devoted his life to making "Shinto" shrines, dying of leukemia at age thirty-seven. The eighty-third life began near Constantinople, where this fragment, again male, rose to prominence as an administrator of a hospital noted for the high recovery rate of the patients. The fragment burned over ten karmic ribbons in that life, and succumbed to viral infection at age forty-one. In the eighty-fourth life, this fragment was female, in northern Europe, married at age sixteen to an ironworker who, in an uncontrollable rage, beat her to death at age twenty-four. The next life, number eighty-five brought the Slave to the sixth level of the Mature cycle, and the life of a female. She entered the convent of Saint Cesaire the year the Emperor Tiberius II died, and spent most of her sixty-seven years as a gardener and farmer. In the eighty-sixth life, this Slave was born into a family of dyers in Antioch, was female, married at fifteen, had seven children, and died of heat exhaustion at age thirty-four. In the next life, this Slave was male, born in the reign of Charles Martel, whose father sought glory and riches at Martel's side, and enlisted his son as a page at the court. The boy died at age sixteen, the result of homosexual rape. The eighty-eighth life of this Slave was lived in what is now Belgium. The fragment inherited the family business and spent his life repairing water wheels all over his immediate region. He was married once, had three surviving children, and died of a broken neck at age forty. The Slave began his eighty-ninth life as a farmer, but advanced in the world when he purchased the right to run a horse-changing post for royal messengers in central France. He was killed by ''spies'' at age thirty-two.

In the next life, the Slave entered the Old cycle, was born male near Baghdad, and became a copyist at the university there, specializing in transcribing old texts on astronomy. He died of cancer at age thirty-five. The ninety-first life of this Slave was spent trading on what you call the Saint Laurence River, assisting her husband and raising four children to marriageable age. She died at age twenty-nine. In the next life, this fragment served as a regional judge in northern China. He was noted for his civic concerns. He had one wife and two concubines, and six surviving children. He was murdered at age thirty-eight, along with most of his household. In the ninety-third life, this fragment came to the second level of the Old cycle. The fragment was born in Bombay to a family of instrument-makers, was female, and showed skill at the work, and so was married to a cousin who inherited the business and ran it into the ground. She died in poverty at age twenty-five. The Slave was then born in the south of England, again female, and was sold to traders to be a servant and cook. She died at age eleven when the traders' cart ''accidentally'' ran over her. The ninety-fifth life was spent as a female in Constantinople, where as a nun this fragment dedicated her life to prayer and service to the poor. She starved herself to death during an Easter fast at age twenty-eight. The ninety-sixth life was spent as a male in Italy

where he served as a scribe and copyist for Guido d'Are-
zzo, dying two years before his master at age thirty-six.
The Slave's ninety-seventh life began in France, where the
boy studied architecture. He was soon called to London to
help supervise construction of the Tower of London. He
married an English girl, had no children, and he died of
smoke inhalation at age forty-four. In the ninety-eighth
life, this fragment, again male, contributed to the treatise
"Antidotarium Niclai", and worked as an apothecary for
the latter part of his life. He died at fifty-seven. In the
Slave's ninety-ninth life, the fourth level of the Old cycle
was entered. The Slave, then female, lived in Tibet, raising
her own four children and the children of her brothers as
well, making the total thirteen. She eventually died of liver
parasites at the age of forty-seven. In the one hundredth
life, this Slave, again female, was born in Spain, the illegitimate daughter of one of the founding instructors of Sala-
manca University. She was given a settlement of enough
money to find a suitable husband, to whom she bore five
children and died at age fifty-three, outliving her husband
by a decade. In the next life this fragment was again
female, but the life was brief, ending in the aftermath of the
massacre known as Sicilian Vespers at age six. Life one
hundred two put the Slave at the fifth level Old, and once
again in Japan where he helped in the development of No
drama. The life lasted fifty-nine years and was generally
"happy". The fragment now had more than three thousand
years of physical incarnation, and approximately four thousand five hundred seventy years had passed. The Slave's
one hundred third life was spent as a female nurse at the
newly established Bethlehem Hospital in London where
she cared for the inmates with as much compassion as
anyone working there at that time, until her death at age
forty-two. One of the inmates was her sister, and would be
diagnosed as schizophrenic by most health professionals
today. Life number one hundred four was spent as a ship's
cook, male, which included voyages along the African
coast for Portugal. The man died at sea at age forty-nine.
The fragment was born once again in Mexico, of Creole

parents, became a nun at age seventeen, and remained in her Order until her death at eighty-six. The Slave lived in what is now Turkey for a total of fifteen years in the one hundred sixth life at the time of Kara Mustafa. The one hundred seventh life, which also started the seventh level of the Old cycle, began in the year 1710, Common Reckoning, in eastern Russia, where this female lived for one hundred nine years, tending her family's flocks and raising eight children, twenty-nine grandchildren, and sixty-two great-grandchildren. Long life was not uncommon to the people of the region. The one hundred eighth life began in England in 1864 Common Reckoning, and the fragment was male. At age twenty he went to India to "seek his fortune", "went native" and died there, at age sixty-nine, in 1933. This Slave's current life began approximately twenty years after the last, is the third life at the seventh level of the Old cycle, and a final life for this fragment. In the course of these lives, the Slave burned four-hundred-seventy-six karmic ribbons, the figure somewhat lower than "average", even factoring in the Slave's general tendency to earn less karma than other fragments. The Slave has had twenty-one contacts with the Essence Twin and twenty-eight contacts with the Task Companion, and has had contact with the six other members of the cadence a total of one thousand two hundred seventeen times.

For the Artisans, we will follow the lives of a second cast Artisan who first incarnated five-thousand-three-hundred-sixty-eight years ago in what you call Australia. The fragment was female and died at age five of a broken leg infection. The second life was again at the first level of the Infant cycle, when the fragment was born male in eastern Mongolia, spent his nineteen years as a shepherd, and died of dysentery. The third life was as a female, lived in central Africa and lasting two years, until she was abandoned during a period of famine. The Artisan reincarnated in South America where he lived for twenty-six years and became a weaver of reeds. In the fifth life, the Artisan moved to second level Infant, living a restricted life in what is now Nepal as a female. The sixth life lasted seven years in what is now northern Canada, when she froze to death. The seventh life for this Artisan was spent as a female in eastern India. She married, had five children, made beautiful wooden beads and was killed by her in-laws at age thirty after two miscarriages. Life number eight was spent in a South American marsh where this Artisan, now male, trapped birds and died of parasite infestation at age sixteen. At life number nine the Artisan entered the third level of the Infant cycle and was born female in central Africa, became the concubine of the area's leader and was poisoned at age twenty-one. The tenth life, this fragment was a wood gatherer in what is now Bulgaria. Male and slightly "retarded", the fragment was not allowed to marry and died age twenty-nine from fever contracted from mites. The eleventh life of this Artisan lasted ten years and was spent on the shores of what is now called the Adriatic Sea. The Artisan was the son of a net-maker and would have followed his father's trade if raiders had not sacked the village and killed all the males. The twelfth life brought the Artisan to the fourth level of the Infant cycle. The fragment was born female in what you call Canada, in the eastern part of the country, the female child of the village "scribe"/"recorder"/"historian". She married, had six children, and died of bacterial infection at age twenty-five. In the thirteenth life, the fragment was again female, living in the south-eastern part of Africa. She had two "husbands" and ten children, and died at the fairly advanced age of thirty-three. The Artisan then incarnated as a female in what is now central France, was provided a place to live by the man who claimed her and by whom she had two children. He arranged a better "marriage", threw the Artisan out and she died of exposure at the age of seventeen. The Artisan's next life was again female, this time in what is now Pakistan, where the Artisan was sacrificed at a religious festival at the age of eight. In the sixteenth life, the Artisan entered the fifth level of the Infant cycle, living as a male, practicing the fishing trade in western Africa. He had two "wives" during his twenty-eight years, and five children. He died of illness during a year of famine. The seventeenth life of this Artisan was spent as a female in what is now called Ukraine. She was part of a large farming family, approximately married to a cousin, had three surviving children, and died of abscessed boils at age twenty-seven. The eighteenth life of this Artisan was spent as a female in western China. She was crippled at age nine, and over the years her condition deteriorated until her death at age twenty. The Artisan lived a brief nineteenth life that began the sixth level of the Infant cycle as a female in what is now central Mexico, and died in a fire at age three. The twentieth life of this Artisan was spent as a male in the upper reaches of the Nile. The fragment was "accidentally" killed in ritual combat at age thirteen. This fragment's twenty-first life was spent in Babylon as a beggar where he died of dental infections at age thirty-one. The Artisan reincarnated in central Europe, female, who tended the farm for her husband, who traveled and traded. She proved more successful than he, raised their five children, and died at age thirty-three. Born female in her twenty-third life, this Artisan was a slave in what you call Central America, and died at sixteen as the result of severe punishment. In the Artisan's twenty-fourth life, the fragment was born in what is now Iraq, female, became a ritual dancer, and died at the age of thirty-five as a religious suicide. The twenty-fifth life of this Artisan took place in what is now north-eastern Spain. The fragment was male, and as the result of a bad fall, blinded at age six. He was abandoned and died shortly after that. For the twenty-sixth life, the fragment was female once again, and lived a fairly uneventful life in the Sinai, having two children before her death at age twenty.

This Artisan entered the first level of the Baby cycle at life twenty-seven, lived as a female in what is now Burma. Considered sacred because of the time of her birth, she was taught to make wooden chimes. She had no children and died of anaemia at age thirty-six. The twenty-eighth life was spent in eastern Europe where this Artisan, now male, raised grain, fathered seventeen children, and practiced his religion with extremist zeal. He died at age twenty-three. The twenty-ninth life was spent in eastern Russia. The Artisan was female and died at age seven after being mauled by dogs. The thirtieth life of this Artisan was lived in central China, the daughter of a brass-worker, who died of epidemic disease at twelve. In the thirty-first life, this fragment incarnated in what is now Guatemala, was male, of "slave" status and was given the work of tending and slaughtering livestock. The thirty-second life moved this Artisan to the second level of the Baby cycle, when the fragment was born female in the Philippines, was married at thirteen, had three children before dying in childbirth at age eighteen. The next incarnation was in southern India as a female in a family of leather-workers. She was one of two surviving daughters and was reluctantly taught "the business" by her father and worked at it diligently for all her adult life. She died at forty-four of a stroke. The thirty-fourth life of this Artisan was spent as a male slave, building roads and bridges. He died of a broken back at age twenty-nine. Life thirty-five began the third level of the Baby cycle and was spent as boatmaker in Egypt near the First Cataract. The fragment was male and died of amoebic dysentery at age thirty-one. In the next life, the Artisan was born female in northern Europe and became an adept treater of hides first for her father and then for her "husband", both of whom were trappers. She had no surviving children and died at age twenty. The thirty-seventh life was lived in northern China, where the fragment, female, was killed at age six during an attack on her family's camp by feuding warlords. The thirty-eighth life was lived in what is now Pakistan. The fragment, female, was taught to use herbs by her mother and aunt, was sold into slavery out of financial necessity, and died of abuse at age seventeen. This fragment then moved to the fourth level of the Baby cycle, was born in what is now Denmark, was female, "married" three times, became known for her carving on bone, and died of hemorrhage at age forty-two, leaving four children and eleven grandchildren behind. The fortieth life of this Artisan was lived as a female in Ethiopia, where she died of infected skin ulcers at age three. In the forty-first life, this fragment was in what is now Algeria, was training to be a market-scribe when he was bitten by a rabid dog and died at age fifteen. The next life was spent as a female in north-eastern America. Her relatives starved her to death when she refused the "marriage" they had arranged for her at the advanced age of twenty-four. At the forty-third life, this Artisan entered the Fifth level of the baby cycle, born male in Egypt, became a stone carver and died of skin cancer at the truly advanced age of fifty-eight. Some of his work is still extant. In the forty-fourth life, the Artisan was born male in China, became a juggler in China and died of fever at age twenty-seven. The forty-fifth life was lived for ten years in what is now the Czech Republic. The fragment was female, and succumbed to shock after being struck in the leg by an axe. The Artisan was then reincarnated in the Greek islands and was taught the principles of mosaic work. He died of scorpion stings at age sixteen. At the forty-seventh life, this Artisan entered the Sixth level of the Baby cycle. Born female in what is now Austria, she became the wife of a leather-worker, and, in fact, labored with him when not bearing or tending their seven children. She died of heart failure at age thirty-four. The forty-eighth life was spent as a male in the South Pacific, where the Artisan made boats and drowned at the age of eighteen. At this point, the Artisan had lived more than one thousand years incarnate on the physical plane, and more than one thousand seven hundred years had passed. The forty-ninth life of this Artisan began in northern Europe, and gradually drifted south as the hunting "village" moved to more promising areas. The Artisan was female had six children, four of whom died in infancy, made many wooden utensils, and died of bacterial infection from tainted meat at age twenty-nine. At the beginning of the seventh level of the Baby cycle, this Artisan lived in Japan, was male, and died of fever shortly before his fourth birthday. The fifty-first life of this Artisan took place in the region now called Prussia. The fragment was part of a fishing family, female, and died of hypothermia at age twenty-one. In the next life this Artisan was a male slave in

Laos, given the task of cutting trees and assisting in building huts. A load of logs crushed him to death at age twenty-
two. The fifty-third life of this Artisan was spent in what is
now Sierra Leone, a female child with a skill at making
shell jewelry. She died of bone disease at age eleven.

The Young cycle began for this Artisan at life fifty-four.
He lived for thirty years, was a sculptor in eastern India for
ten years, and then was exiled for religious reasons. His
family was not allowed to go with him. He died at age
thirty. The fifty-fifth life of this Artisan was spent in Ireland, the second male child of a farming family. He died at
age eight of acute bronchitis. The fifty-sixth life of this
fragment was lived in northern Spain, where she was a
dancer of some repute, although of slave status. She died
at age seventeen. The fifty-seventh life of this fragment was
lived in the region of the Great Lakes where she had five
children and was renowned for her basketry, which served
to support the family when her "husband" was crippled in
an accident. She died at age twenty from fatigue. The fifty-
eighth life brought the Artisan to the second level of the
Young cycle, where the fragment was female and the survivor of a horrendous epidemic. She had fled the region and
eventually became the "bonded servant" of a merchant.
She bore him four children before she died at age twenty-
six. The fifty-ninth life of this fragment was lived on the
Chinese-Mongolian border, where she was part of a saddle-
and-harness making family for fifty-three years. Her husband married into the family and the business, and they
prospered until the husband's death some five years before
hers. They had four surviving children and three surviving
grandchildren. The next incarnation, the sixtieth life for the
Artisan, was lived in what is now Turkey, where this
fragment was male, enslaved while young, and set to building roads at which task he died, aged twenty-nine. The
Artisan then moved on to the third level of the Young cycle,
being born female in what is now Indonesia to a family that
made puppets for religious plays and festivals. She was
deaf and never married, though she continued to make
puppets until her death at age thirty-six. The Artisan's

sixty-second life was spent as a prostitute in Greece. She was murdered at age twenty-five by her employer. The sixty-third life marked the beginning of the fourth level of the Young cycle. It was spent in Nubia, where the Artisan, female, had nine children before dying of thirst at age thirty-two. In the next life, the fragment was male, in southern Africa, and starved to death at age five. The sixty-fifth life was spent as a female in what is now western France, where the fragment was the daughter of an impoverished farmer. She was sold to the local strongman after the father abandoned the family. She died at age thirteen of complications following rape. The Artisan's next life was in Java where she was the daughter of a minor priest, married at age seven to the senior priest to be part of his "harem", and died at sixteen from poison. Life number sixty-seven was lived in Tyre, where the girl was blinded and maimed at age four and sold to a professional beggar, who beat her to death at twenty-two. The Artisan spent life sixty-eight as a female child of a drum maker in what is now the state of Maine. The Artisan and all her siblings in that life died in a raid. She was ten. The sixty-ninth life began the fifth level of the Young cycle for this Artisan. As a female in southern Spain, she was taught to make furniture and continued to do so through two marriages and eight surviving children. She was forty-seven when she died of appendicitis. The seventieth life of this Artisan was lived as a female in Japan. She was considered mad, and the attempts to "cure" her resulted in her death at age twelve. The seventy-first life of this Artisan brought the fragment to the sixth level of the Young cycle. The fragment was born male in what is now Morocco where he became famous for his superior wood-inlay work. He died at age twenty-three from injuries sustained in a fall. Life seventy-two was spent in eastern Europe where this Artisan, female, was taken into a rope-making family and finally "earned her keep" in that capacity. She died from chronic sinus infections at age eighteen. In the next life, this Artisan was female, a slave in Greece, trained as a cook, she invented two useful kitchen utensils, one a workable garlic press, the other a simple kind of whisk. She died at thirty-one of uterine cancer. The seventy-fourth life of this fragment lasted less than two years. The Artisan, then female, was drowned as part of a religious observance. The seventy-fifth life was lived in Central America, where the fragment contracted a parasitical infestation that killed her at age nine. The seventy-sixth life of this fragment started the seventh level Young cycle. The Artisan incarnated as female in a chariot-making family near the Black Sea. She committed suicide at age fourteen. The seventy-seventh life was lived as a female in Greece as a cloth merchant's slave. She learned to weave and died of typhus at age nineteen. In the seventy-eighth life, this fragment was a Japanese female who married into a potter's family and gained prestige through her skill in firing pieces. She died at twenty-eight from postpartum infection. Life seventy-nine was spent in Greece, although the fragment was from the region around Antioch. He was a slave and an athlete who performed feats of strength for his master and the general populace. He died at twenty from a ruptured hernia.

The Mature soul cycle began for his Artisan in Rome where she trained dancers for theatrical entertainments. She was sexually attracted to women and never married. She died by her own hand at thirty-two. The eighty-first life of this Artisan was spent as a ship's carpenter in the Indian Ocean. He drowned at age seventeen. The eighty-second life of this fragment was spent as a female in eastern Europe. Abandoned at age ten by an incestuous family, she managed to survive in the forest, where she continued to live in isolation until her death at thirty-eight. The second level of the Mature cycle began with a very brief life of less than a year when the female infant was smothered accidentally by an older sibling. The eighty-fourth life lasted twenty-three years in Alexandria, where the fragment was a recognized sculptor in wood. The eighty-fifth life, the Artisan was female in what you call New Zealand, lived for eleven years, dying in an earthquake-triggered mudslide. The eighty-sixth life was lived in the city of Byzantium where the Artisan made harnesses and chariots of superior quality. The fragment had a wife and seven surviving children, and died at age thirty-six from heart disease. Life eighty-seven initiated the third level of the mature cycle, at which time the Artisan was a male in a "clan" of sheep-and-goat herders, and were therefore leather-workers and weavers, in the area near the Caspian Sea. This fragment married three times, had nineteen children and forty-two grandchildren before he died at age eighty-one. The eighty-eighth life was spent in what you call Alaska. The fragment was female and noted for her cooking skills. She had five children, one of whom survived, before her death at twenty-eight from chronic breathing problems. The eighty-ninth life was as a female in what is now Nigeria. She was the first wife of the senior male in the village, the mother of four sons. She was murdered by political enemies of her family at age thirty-nine. The ninetieth life was lived on what is now the border of Russia and Poland. The Artisan was female, and had just delivered one child when marauders sacked and burned the village and she and her daughter died in an attempt to escape. She was fifteen. The ninety-first life began the fourth level of the Mature cycle for this fragment. The Artisan was female in southern Africa where for reasons of ritual and karma, she was murdered at age eight. As her death supposedly ended the drought, she became a hero of her village and eventually a lesser deity of the region. Life ninety-two, the Artisan chose to be female in what is now Sweden, was a leather-worker's wife, and died in childbirth at age seventeen. The next life was lived in the hills of Albania as a cenobite monk. He died of malnutrition at age twenty-one. Life ninety-four marked the beginning of the Fifth level of the Mature cycle and was lived as a merchant's wife in India. The family fortunes fluctuated greatly, and three of her five sons failed at business. She died of cancer at age sixty-three. At this point, the fragment had lived more than two thousand years incarnate and approximately three thousand four hundred years had gone by on the physical plane. Life number ninety-five was spent as a female in what is now Latvia. She was orphaned at

nine and starved to death at twelve. The ninety-sixth life
was lived in northern Spain where the Artisan became a
very successful stone-cutter whose work may be found in
early Christian structures to this day. He died of epidemic
disease at age twenty-eight, leaving three mistresses and
four illegitimate children to fend for themselves. Life
ninety-seven was spent in China, where the fragment was a
carpenter and builder of fortified houses. He made a fortune, which he gambled away, and died by accident at age
forty-two. Life ninety-eight began the sixth level of the
Mature cycle. The fragment was female in what is now
known as Colorado. She died when she was thrown out by
her husband. She was seventeen and "apparently" sterile.
The next life the Artisan was female in Scotland, married
to a shepherd, had five children, all female, and became a
recognized fine weaver in the district. She died at age
thirty-six. In the next life, this Artisan was Greek, of a
noble family, and regarded as a great beauty. She married
very well, commissioned jewelry and art, had two surviving
children, and died at forty-nine of self-administered poison
after her husband was accused of treason. Life one hundred
one began the seventh level of the Mature cycle for this
Artisan, who was born male in Persia, learned to paint in
the prevailing miniature style, married once, had three
children, and died of a heart attack at age fifty-one. The
one hundred second life was spent as a female in a religious
community in south-central France, one still much influenced by Saint John Cassian. She died at age forty from
complications of influenza. The one hundred third life was
lived in a Mayan city, where this Artisan was a female
servant, given the task of cook. She died at age twenty-six
of an infected foot. Life one hundred four was spent as a
priest in Germany, where he died a martyr's death at age
thirty-eight during a regional upheaval. Life one hundred
five the fragment was born female in what has been called
Flanders. She was the youngest daughter of five daughters
and three sons and therefore remained "at home" to take
care of her aging parents. She and they died of smallpox
when she was twenty-five.

The Old cycle began for this Artisan at life one hundred six in what is called the Azores. She was killed in a severe storm at age seven. Life one hundred seven was lived for the most part in the German city of Bremen where he was a shoe-maker, married and had three children before being killed by robbers at age twenty-nine. Life one hundred eight was lived as a female in Ireland. She was regarded as a cursed child because of her parent's "mysterious" deaths, and therefore remained single, supporting herself by weaving. She died at age thirty-four. The hundred ninth life of this Artisan was lived in the mountains of South America where she was the daughter of a miner. She fell to her death at age eleven. The one hundred tenth life began the second level of the Old cycle, where this female fragment lived in central China in a Christian community. She made the ritual drums and cymbals for almost forty years, was one of three wives to her husband, had no surviving children and died at age fifty-three. The one hundred eleventh life was spent as a female in North America among the people known to you as the Mandan. This Artisan was female, made beads and served as midwife. She died at age twenty-two of exposure. Life number one hundred twelve was lived in the north-eastern part of Italy near the town of Udine, where the Artisan, male, was a stonemason and bridge builder. He was unhappily married, drank to excess, and died when a load of stone collapsed and crushed him at age thirty-five. The one hundred thirteenth life was lived in Roman "ruins" in north Africa, where she was a cook for a family running a kind of caravan campground. She died at twenty-one from gang rape. Life one hundred fourteen brought the Artisan to level three of the Old cycle. The Artisan was born female in Tahiti, had seven children by three different men, was a noted song-maker and poet. She died at age thirty-seven. Life one hundred fifteen was lived in Hungary, where the Artisan, now male, was part of a family of well-known carriage makers. He died in a cholera epidemic at age thirty-two. The fragment began the fourth level of the Old cycle in northern Europe, where he was a vagabond and beggar for most of his twenty-eight

years. Life number one hundred seventeen this fragment,
female, came to America from England at fourteen as an
indentured servant. She was turned off when she bore her
employer's child out of wedlock and died of starvation and
exposure at age eighteen. The one hundred eighteenth life
of this Artisan was lived in Goa, where as the widow of a
textile designer, she ran the business on behalf of her five
children, dying of plague at age thirty-six. The Artisan then
began the fifth level of the Old cycle, incarnating in what
you call Algeria where he was a stable groom until he was
dragged at age fourteen. The one hundred twentieth life
was lived in Japan, where this Artisan became a master
calligrapher, living to age sixty-eight. The next life was a
female in southern Russia, killed at age six when the
Cossacks rode through her town spitting dogs, pigs, and
children on their lances. The sixth level of the Old cycle
began with a life in eastern Italy where this fragment, male,
was a fresco painter. He died at twenty-one in a brawl. Life
number one hundred twenty-three was spent as a female in
Samoa, where she was a dancer. She died in the aftermath
of a typhoon, age seventeen. The next life was lived in
Germany, where the Artisan white-washed houses, and
died of cancer at age thirty-three. The one hundred twenty-
fifth life was lived in Russia, where she became an Orthodox run at age ten, dying at age twenty-four from tuberculo-
sis. The seventh level of the Old cycle commenced with life
number one hundred twenty-six, where the Artisan was
born female in Madagascar, and died of a virulent virus at
age two. Life one hundred twenty-seven was spent as a
female in western China where she was part of a group of
itinerant musicians. She had four children along the way
and died at age fifty-one of exhaustion. Life one hundred
twenty-eight was lived in England where this Artisan became a noted gardener and spinster. She was killed in
what you call the Second World War, age thirty-eight. The
fragment at this point has now lived three thousand years
incarnate on the physical plane, and more than five thousand three hundred years have gone by. The fragment
is now twenty-two, a horticultural assistant in Australia,

female, not interested in higher education, but "good with plants". The fragment burned five hundred twenty-one karmic ribbons in the course of the lives, had twenty contacts with the Essence Twin and nineteen contacts with the Task Companion as well as one thousand eight hundred thirty-six contacts with the six members of the cadence.

The Warrior we will use to demonstrate a full cycle of lives is the third cast in the cadence, and was first incarnated 5,203 years ago in what is now Thailand. He died making a bamboo bridge at age seventeen. The second life was spent as a female in Sumatra. She died, age eight, in an epidemic. The third life was spent in the mountains of Spain where this Warrior, the "wife" of a hunter was mauled to death by a bear at age twenty-two. The fourth life was lived in central India, the fragment was "wife" to a river boatman, and died of exhaustion at thirty, leaving five children behind. The second level of the Infant cycle began in China where the fragment was an apprentice to an armorer and died of burns at age fifteen. The sixth life was spent in north Africa where the Warrior was a goatherd and died fighting off thieves at age twenty-three. The seventh life was spent in what is now Kiev. The Warrior was female and was killed defending her nine children from slavers. She was twenty-seven. The eighth life began the third level of Infant cycle. This Warrior was born in what is now called Indonesia, was a sea fisherman, married, one child. He drowned during a dangerous crossing at age nineteen. The ninth life was lived in Australia, the fragment was female and starved to death after wandering away from her family, at age ten. The tenth life this fragment was born into slavery in what is now Syria, was trained as a children's companion and was killed at sixteen when she got too old for the job. The eleventh life was spent in northern Greece. The Warrior was male, a slave trained to handle large livestock. He died of complications following a shoulder separation at age thirty-three. The twelfth life began the Warrior's fourth level of the Infant cycle. The fragment was male in north-western China, a horse-wrangler, trampled at twenty-five. Life thirteen was lived in Egypt, where the Warrior, female, was married to a farmer, had six children and died of amoebic dysentery at age twenty-six. The fourteenth life was spent in Russia as a miner. He was buried in a cave-in at age twenty-one. The fifteenth life was in northern India, as a metal worker, who died following an amputation of his arm at age twenty-eight. The fifth level of the Infant cycle began in what is now Canada, the western mountains, where the Warrior was the "wife" of a tracker, widowed early, and died at age thirty-one. Life seventeen was spent in Italy, the slave of a farmer, male who died at twenty in a fire. The brief eighteenth life was spent in Java, where this female child was sacrificed at a religious festival at age one. The nineteenth life began the sixth level of the Infant cycle for this Warrior, who was born on the north-east coast of South America, was male, a fisherman, had a woman and three children, and was killed at sea, age twenty-six, by raiders after his boat. The twentieth life was lived in western Africa. The Warrior was female, part of a "clan" of nomads. She had five children and died at eighteen of genital infection. The twenty-first life was lived in Central Asia, the Warrior was female, a slave sold three times in her life, died in childbirth at age fifteen. The twenty-second life was in China, where the fragment, now male, bred donkeys on a farm he shared with his brother. He died of a punctured lung at age twenty-nine. The seventh level of the Infant cycle took the Warrior to Spain, where as a female, she was married at twelve to an orchard keeper, and died at twenty, the victim of her husband's wrath. The twenty-fourth life was lived in what is now Korea. The fragment was a guard and torturer for the local warlord. He was flayed alive at twenty-four. The twenty-fifth life was on the Arabian peninsula. The fragment was female and killed by bandits at age eleven.

The Baby cycle began at life twenty-six for this Warrior. The life was in the southern part of South America, the fragment was female, married to the village shaman. She had nine children, two of whom survived, and died at age thirty. The twenty-seventh life took place on an island off China, where the fragment was one of a contingent squad guarding the island's priests. He was killed in that capacity at age twenty-seven. In the next life, the Warrior was born on the Danish peninsula, was male, a whale-and-seal hunter, had a "wife" and four children. He drowned age thirty-two, a respectable age for the time and the occupation. The second level of the Baby cycle began in India where the Warrior was a male slave, taken captive by rivals of his master and butchered, age nineteen. The thirtieth life was spent on the Hungarian plains, where the fragment was female, had three children and died at forty-three, the oldest woman in the hamlet. The thirty-first life was spent in Russia, where the Warrior was male, a woodcutter by trade, who killed his wife, thus burning a karmic ribbon, and was exiled. He died of exposure at age twenty-six. The thirty-second life began the third level of the Baby cycle when this Warrior was born in north Africa, a slave, male, who tended camels, and died of abuse at twenty-one. The thirty-third life was spent in western France. The fragment, female, died at age four after becoming lost in the woods. The thirty-fourth life was in Mongolia, where the fragment, guard for the camp, was killed at age twenty-five. In life number thirty-five, the fragment was born in what is now Portugal, female, "wife" of a farmer, five children. She was taken captive by raiders and committed suicide two years after her capture, age twenty-nine. The next life began the fourth level of the Baby cycle. The Warrior was born female in the Mississippi valley, had five children, became an herb woman, and died at age thirty-eight. The thirty-seventh life was in the South Seas, where the fragment was female, had eight kids of her own and "adopted" six more. She drowned at thirty-three, during a move from one island to another. The thirty-eighth life was spent in Siberia. The Warrior was male, a scout for regional hunters, who died, the victim of the very animals he tracked (tigers), at age twenty-six. The thirty-ninth life was in Egypt, the fragment was male, a military underling who built chariots and trained asses to pull them. He was dragged to death at age thirty-one. The fortieth life began the fifth level of the Baby cycle for this Warrior. The fragment was a Hittite female, blinded and crippled in order to be a professional beggar. She died at age fifteen, having burned a karmic ribbon. Life forty-one was Persian, the fragment male and a sword-maker died at fifty-one. He had been married four times and had seven surviving children. Life forty-two was lived in Tyre, the fragment was male, a kind of "hired gun" for merchants on their travels. He died at sea at age thirty-two. The Warrior had now been incarnate for a total of just over one thousand years and just over sixteen hundred years had gone by on the physical plane. Life forty-three began the sixth level of the Baby cycle for this fragment. The Warrior was born male in eastern India and was killed by the elephants he tended at age seven. The forty-fourth life was lived in southern Africa where the fragment, a slave and concubine, died of poison at age twenty-three. The forty-fifth life was spent in Greece where the Warrior was a mercenary soldier who died in battle at age twenty-four. The forty-sixth life was in central China, the fragment was female, of "good' family, and the first wife of a lesser noble who she ruthlessly pushed to a position of political advantage. She had four children and died at age fifty-two of heart disease. Life forty-seven began the seventh level of the Baby cycle for this Warrior. Born in France, this fragment was a regional warlord who was betrayed by his own cousins and tortured to death at age forty, leaving six children to scramble for his power. Life forty-eight was in the Middle East, where this fragment, female, became a noted "oracle" who traveled extensively to answer the questions of various civic leaders. She died at forty-seven of sunstroke. Life forty-nine was lived in Central America, the fragment was male, and sacrificed to "rival" gods upon his capture by people from the next region. Life fifty was lived in the Philippines. The Warrior was male, one of a group of bandits, hacked to death at age twenty-nine.

The Young cycle began for this Warrior in the fifty-first life on the Dalmatian Coast. He was a soldier for the first half of his life, but upon losing a hand, he retired to raise horses. He died age forty-three. Life fifty-two was in the

Pacific Northwest, the fragment was the shaman's daughter
and a local scout. She died of fungal infestation at twenty-
eight. Life fifty-three was lived in what is now called
Morocco. The fragment was male, the leader of a political
guard group. He died at age thirty-four from stress-related
health problems. The fifty-fourth life was in Japan, where
the Warrior became a famous fighting instructor whose
epilepsy kept him from being a military leader. He died,
much honored, at age thirty-nine. Life fifty-five brought the
Warrior to the second level of the Young cycle. The fragment was born in Egypt, a military leader of formidable
reputation, he married politically and strove to advance his
family in the world. He died at thirty-three, the victim of a
"convenient" accident. Life fifty-six was on the shores of
the Black Sea where the fragment, female, was born poor
and through a series of lovers, died rich at forty-one,
leaving no surviving children. Life fifty-seven was in
Greece. The Warrior was a regional "general", married
twice, had five children in spite of his homosexual preferences, and died in battle at age thirty-eight. Life fifty-eight
began the third level of the Young cycle for this Warrior.
The fragment was born female in Burma, became an acrobatic dancer, and died at age twenty-six. The fifty-ninth life
was spent in Turkey, where the Warrior was a musician and
prostitute, and died at age seventeen. Life sixty was lived
on the east coast of Africa where the Warrior was a leader
of a group of pirates and died of the result of wounds
sustained in battle at age thirty. The next life the fragment
was born female in what is now Thailand. She married, was
deserted by her husband to raise their four children, which
she did, in spite of being crippled. She died at twenty-nine
when the oldest child was able to go to work. The sixty-
second life was spent in Rome, where the Warrior was
active in the Punic Wars and twice promoted for valor. He
died in battle at age thirty-two. The sixty-third life began
the fourth level of the Young cycle for this Warrior, who
incarnated as a female in China. She was of high-rank, very
unhappily married to a debauched nobleman. They had
three children, two of whom were murdered. She died at

age forty-seven of cancer. Life sixty-four was spent in Carthage as a military leader who committed suicide for honor at age thirty-six after failing to achieve the victory he had promised. Life sixty-five was lived in what is now Germany. The fragment was male, of a "disgraced" family, for which this fragment was hamstrung at age twelve. He became a beggar and died at age twenty-one. Life sixty-six was spent in what is now Serbia. The Warrior was female, had eight children, cared for them and her invalid husband until her death at age thirty-nine. The sixty-seventh life began the fifth level of the Young cycle for this Warrior who incarnated in Mongolia as a horse-thief. He died rich at thirty-five, the "hero" of the region with three wives and fourteen children. And seven hundred thirty-eight horses. Life sixty-eight was started in Hippo Reggia as a male ship's boy who was thrown overboard for refusing to accommodate the sexual demands of the senior officer on board. He was fourteen. Life sixty-nine was in Sardinia, where the Warrior was female, a bandit's wife, killed in a "gang feud" at age thirty-one along with four of her seven children. Life seventy took place in Laos, where the Warrior, the youngest sibling of a large family, took care of the farm and family of her oldest sibling. She died at forty. Level six of the Young cycle began at life seventy-one, when the Warrior lived in Ostia, was female, an innkeeper and a smuggler. She was good at both kinds of work and died comfortably well-off at fifty-two. She remained single, although she had a number of lovers. Her property went to a nephew. Life seventy-two was in Judea. She was female, a relatively early Christian convert who withdrew from society while still a teenager. She died at forty-nine from a number of cumulative health compromises. At this point, the Warrior had two thousand years of physical incarnation behind him, and the physical plane had gone along for approximately three thousand four hundred years from the time the Warrior was first cast. Life seventy-three was lived along the Old Silk Road. The Warrior was male, a guide and guard. He died of exposure at thirty-three. Life seventy-four took place in South America, the fragment was male and technically insane. As such, he was an outcast and died at twenty-five. Life seventy-five started the seventh level of the Young cycle for this fragment. The incarnation was female. She was a merchant's daughter who died at nine from epidemic disease. Life seventy-six was in Australia. The Warrior, a male child, died at two. The seventy-seventh life was in Britain, the fragment was male, a fisherman, who, in an effort (successful) to save eight others drowned at age sixteen, burning seven karmic ribbons in the process.

The Mature cycle for this Warrior began in India where the fragment was a beggar and a thief. He died at age twenty-two. Life seventy-nine was lived in Sicily where the fragment was female, born to slavery, earned her freedom after nursing her master's children through a serious illness. She died at twenty-nine. Life eighty was spent in Mexico where the Warrior was male, a priest and architect who died of fever at age thirty-three. The second level of the Mature cycle was spent in Sweden. The Warrior was female, born into a ship-building family, and died at age sixteen from undiagnosed diabetes. Life eighty-two was in central Greece where the fragment, female, survived an epidemic in youth, withdrew to a nunnery and spent the rest of her days there, dying at age twenty-four. Life eighty-three was spent in Indonesia where the fragment was given the dangerous job of mapping the major roads for the military elite. Upon completion of this task, he was killed in order to preserve secrecy. Life eighty-four brought the Warrior to Baghdad as an armorer, who died of parasite-related disease at age twenty-five. The eighty-fifth life was the only one lived at the third level of the Mature cycle. The Warrior was born on the Hungarian plain, was a warlord who united the region to repel invaders. He achieved this goal but was killed in the "final" battle at age thirty-six. The fragment went on to the fourth level of the Mature cycle, living life eighty-six in Denmark as a male "navigator" who at twenty-seven was lost at sea. Life eighty-seven was lived in Paris where the Warrior led a political protest, for which he was imprisoned and killed at age thirty-eight, leaving his family to flee or starve, or both. Life eighty-eight was very short. The Warrior incarnated in southern Poland, one of a pair of twins, female, and died at one month of age. Life eighty-nine was spent on the Yellow River in China, where this Warrior was a boat-girl who died at eighteen in a flood. The fifth level of the Mature cycle began when the Warrior incarnated as a "legal" student in Arles. He died during an epidemic of smallpox at age twenty-one. Life ninety-one was in Benares, India, where the fragment, female, married for karma and died at twenty-six, leaving no living children. Life ninety-two was in London, where the fragment served as a kind of messenger for various officials. Crippled at birth, he was reliable, literate, and unobvious. He died at fifty, his work uncompromised. The sixth level of the Mature cycle began for this Warrior in Persia where he was an architect, married twice and died of exhaustion at twenty-eight. Life ninety-four was lived in Brazil. The fragment was female and considered a witch. She was killed by her own family at age nineteen. Life ninety-five was on the German-Danish border, where the Warrior was born the oldest son of a horse-breeder. He showed much promise but died of tetanus at seven. Life ninety-six was in southern China, where the Warrior lived as a training officer for naval fighters and explorers. He died of an "accident" at twenty-nine. The seventh level of the Mature cycle began at life ninety-seven when the Warrior was in Egypt, male, an explorer and opportunist. He married five wives, accumulated much wealth and distinguished himself and his family before his death at age thirty-two. The next life was in Iceland as a female. She had two children before her husband died. She herself became adept at metal repairs, and died in a fire at age twenty-two. Life ninety-nine was spent in Russia as a male fur-trader. He was waylaid and beaten to death by robbers at age twenty-eight. The one hundredth life was lived in Peru where the Warrior was a male bird-catcher who died of viral infections at age fifteen.

The Old cycle began with life one hundred one for this Warrior in Canada as a female. She had nine children and thirty-one grandchildren by the time of her death at age forty-one. The next life was in Korea where this Warrior, male, designed buildings. He died of unknown causes at age twenty-nine. The one hundred third life began the second level of the Old cycle for this Warrior. He was born in the Sudan and became a Coptic monk, and died at twenty-five. Life one hundred four was lived in Spain, where the Warrior, female, inherited the regional control from her father, having no male siblings to inherit. She proved a capable administrator and died at her desk at thirty-four. Life one hundred five was spent in southern India as a nurse to a Chinese-trained physician tending to the chronically ill. Chronic illness killed him at age eighteen. Life one hundred six was in western Russia where the Warrior, now female, supported herself as a seamstress and died of smoke inhalation at age twenty-seven. Life number one hundred seven began the third level of the Old cycle for this Warrior. He was a copyist in Italy, wandered from city to city and starved to death at thirty-three while on his way from Pisa to Genoa. Life number one hundred eight was lived in north Africa where the Warrior bred horses and mules, had two wives and nine children, and committed suicide at twenty-nine. The one hundred ninth life was in what was then Bohemia. The fragment was male, a younger son of a poor family who abandoned him and two other children. He died at age ten. Life one hundred ten was lived in Greece. The Warrior was female and killed in an earthquake at age four. The fourth level of the Old cycle began at life one hundred eleven. The fragment was born in what is now Afghanistan, male, who saved his wife and six children by willingly surrendering to family rivals and being tortured to death. This burned three karmic ribbons. The fragment was twenty-five. At life one hundred twelve, the fragment was born to a poor family in Venice and died of Plague at age fourteen. The fifth level of the Old cycle began for this Warrior at life one hundred thirteen in Latin America, female, who died in childbirth at seventeen. Life number one hundred fourteen lived in France as a high-ranking churchman and diplomat who was killed in the execution of his duties at age thirty-eight. Life one hundred fifteen was lived in China as a female of the merchant class. She had six children twenty-three grandchildren. She died of cholera at age sixty-three. At life one hundred sixteen this fragment entered the sixth level of the Old cycle, being born in central Europe as a male. He became a mustering boy, and was killed in battle at age eleven. Life one hundred seventeen was spent in Malta as a male. He worked on the streets, and died of epidemic disease at twenty-eight. The next life was lived in the Caribbean as a male. He was a fisherman, had a dozen children with various women, all of whom he supported cheerfully. He succumbed to fever at age thirty-eight. The one hundred nineteenth life, the Warrior was Karelian and female, and having become severely injured, was killed by the physician attempting to treat her at age twenty-two. She had three surviving children. Life number one hundred twenty began the seventh level of the Old cycle for this Warrior, who was born in Algeria, and male. Blind from birth, this fragment became a religious poet who was supported by the local mosque. He was twenty-seven when he died of complications following an infection of the spleen. Life one hundred twenty-one was spent in Bulgaria, as a male who dedicated his life to authenticating and restoring old manuscripts. He was married, had two children, and died himself at age thirty-one. Life one hundred twenty-two was fairly short, only nineteen years. The fragment was Austrian and froze to death in Russia during what you call the Second World War. Currently this fragment is a thirty-nine-year-old horse-trainer in Argentina, male, unmarried and without expectations or prospects. This fragment has lived three thousand one hundred fifty-five years incarnate, burned one thousand nine hundred thirty-two karmic ribbons. The Warrior has had sixteen contacts with the Essence Twin, and twenty-nine with the Task Companion. There have been a total of two thousand one hundred fifty-four contacts with the other six members of the Warrior's cadence.

The Scholar we will use for illustration is, of course, fourth cast. The fragment first incarnated 5,429 years ago in what is now northern Iraq, in a settlement so minor as to have no record of it remain today. The fragment was made a slave who worked in the fields and in storing grain. He died of botulism at age twenty. The second life was spent as a female plant-gatherer in the Amazon jungle. She had two children and drowned at age eighteen. The third life was in what is now southern Germany. The Scholar was female, and died at age seven in a year of famine. The fourth life began the second level of the Infant cycle. The fragment was born in what you call Sudan, was male and a market tally-keeper. He kept four "wives", had three surviving children and died at the "respectable" age of thirty-one. The fifth life was spent in what is now Pakistan. The fragment was male, crippled by an accident in childhood, who made his living by copying inscriptions onto the local temple walls. He died at twenty-eight of general physical collapse. The sixth life was spent in what is now Norway. The fragment was female and was sacrificed at age eight to ensure a good catch. The seventh life was spent in Eridu, as a male. The fragment was a record-keeper who died by mis-chance at the conclusion of his wedding ceremony, age twenty-two. The eighth life began the third level of the Infant cycle. The fragment was born in eastern China, was male, and earned his living as a market inspector. He was stabbed to death at age twenty-six, leaving two wives and five children to fend for themselves. The ninth life was spent in southern Africa. The Scholar was female, the fourth "wife" of one of the village leaders. She died of parasite infestation at age twenty-one, leaving three children, all of whom were killed to "keep her company" in the "afterlife". The tenth life was lived near the town of Nal in the Indus Valley. The fragment was female, had five children by a wall-builder and died at age twenty-four of viral infection. Life eleven was the beginning of the fourth level, or, more accurately, given the nature of the perceptions, mid-cycle, of the Infant cycle for this Scholar, who was born male in what you call Manchuria. He became a messenger and assistant "clerk". He was waylaid and killed for the messages he carried at age nineteen. The next life took place in north Africa. The Scholar was a male slave whose task was laying building foundations. He was immured in the temple foundation to make it more sacred at age twenty. The thirteenth life was spent in the South China Sea. The Scholar was male, was part of a family trading off the coast, which he did very methodically. He drowned at age eighteen. The fourteenth life was lived in western Europe, near what is now the French-Spanish border. The fragment was female, had three children when she was sold to pay a debt. She died of abuse at age twenty-two. The fifth level of the Infant cycle began with life number fifteen. The fragment was born male in the eastern Mediterranean, was a farmer, had three children who survived infancy. He died at age twenty-five as the result of toxic reactions to insect bites. The sixteenth life was spent in the Indus Valley. The Scholar was female, had two children by the region's most extreme religious leader. She was beaten to death for disobedience at age seventeen. Life seventeen was in southern Spain. The fragment was male and a roofer. He had one surviving child, two wives and supported four younger siblings. He died from a fall, age twenty-three. Life eighteen was lived in north-western South America. The Scholar was female, made flutes and died at age thirteen. The nineteenth life began the sixth level of the Infant cycle and was lived in Greece. The fragment was male and served as "accountant" for the treasury of the regional "king" or warlord. He died at age twenty-six, executed along with his master. Life number twenty was spent in what is now eastern Canada. The fragment was male, one of a family of seal-hunters. He died of hypothermia at age fifteen. Life twenty-one was in what is now Australia. The fragment was male, served as "clan astronomer". He had two women, five surviving children, and died at age thirty-two. The seventh level of the Infant cycle began in the western part of what is currently Russia. The fragment was male, the last living member of his "clan" and perennial captive of the neighboring "city". He managed to commit suicide at age twenty-nine. Life twenty-three was spent in the city of Ur as a male. He supervised building projects, had three women and four surviving children at the time of his death at age twenty-five. The fragment was then born in the southern part of what is now France, was female, had twin daughters before dying in childbirth at age fourteen.

The first level of the Baby cycle began for this Scholar at life number twenty-five. The fragment was male, born in China, became a registry clerk, had four children by one wife and died of insect-borne fever at age twenty-seven. The twenty-sixth life was in South America. The male fragment worked as a river guide and died at age twenty. The next life was lived in the western part of China. The fragment was female, had two children by "patrons" and died of sexually transmitted disease at age nineteen. The twenty-eighth life was spent in the Mediterranean and Aegean Seas, where the scholar, male, was a trader working the waters from Egypt to what is now Turkey. He had nine unknown children by different women, and died at the hands of pirates at age twenty-four. The second level of the Baby cycle began at life twenty-nine. The fragment was born male in Egypt, was a temple scribe, had one child and died of dysentery at age twenty-one. The Scholar then incarnated in what is now Iran, as a female. She was married to her shoe-maker cousin and died at age sixteen. The thirty-first life was spent in what is now Arizona. The fragment was female and fell to her death at age nine. The thirty-second life was spent in the western part of what is now Italy. The fragment was a male, in slavery, and ran a farm for his owner. He suffocated to death at age twenty-eight. The thirty-third life began the third level of the Baby cycle for this Scholar. The fragment was born to a herding family in Africa and died under the hooves of cattle at age twelve. Life thirty-four was lived in Babylon as a male, the keeper of religious and sacrificial records. The fragment was homosexual and remained unmarried. He died at age twenty-nine from pneumonia. Life thirty-five was lived in the Caucasus Mountains as a female, one of several wives of the local bandit-chief. She died during a raid at age twenty. She had no surviving children. The thirty-sixth life began the fourth level of the Baby cycle for this Scholar. It was lived in Siberia near where Irkutsk is presently located. The fragment was a guide for the various nomadic herders and traders in the area. He died of intestinal parasites at age twenty-three. The thirty-seventh life was spent in what is now Spain, as a female, auctioned in marriage to a distant relative, the Scholar had four children before being killed by her husband's other wives at age twenty-six. The fragment was then born in what is now western Germany, was male, and a kind of traveling "physician". He was killed by the family of one of his patients when the patient did not recover. The thirty-ninth life was spent in southern Mexico, as a female. She suffered from birth defects and so lived "on the fringes" of the community, becoming adept with herbs and potions. She died at twenty-two from eating the wrong mushroom. The fortieth life began the fifth level of the Baby cycle for this Scholar. The fragment was born in Sri Lanka, was raised to be a courier, and in that capacity was murdered at age sixteen. Life forty-one was spent in what you call Normandy. The fragment was male, a farmer's son, who died of influenza at age five. The next life was in the city of Susa. The Scholar was male, served as a priest and judge for the city. He had two wives, a dozen concubines and six legitimate children by the time of his death at age thirty-five. The forty-third life was in what you now call Virginia. The Scholar was female, the "wife" of a trader. She was kidnapped by her husband's rivals from the next "clan". She was killed during an escape attempt at age twenty-two. Life forty-four was in Carchemish. The Scholar was male, the festival-keeper and festival-songwriter, an intensely political position. The life ended at age thirty-three. Life forty-five began the sixth level of the Baby cycle for this Scholar, who was born in Burma, was male, made his living by preserving meat in spices. He had six surviving children at the time of his death at age twenty-seven. Life number forty-six was in Latin America, the fragment was male, a powerful shaman and healer. He had two wives, seven surviving children at the time of his death from a stroke at age thirty-four. At this point, the fragment had lived over one thousand years incarnate in a body, and approximately fifteen hundred years of physical-plane time had gone by. The forty-seventh life was in central Canada, the fragment was male and died of starvation, the result of a broken jaw at age ten. The forty-eighth life was in Crete, the fragment was female, an athlete and teacher. She had two children and was killed in competition at age twenty-two. The forty-ninth life was in central Mongolia, the fragment was male, the "genealogist" for his "clan." He died during an epidemic at age thirty-six. The fiftieth life began the seventh level of the Baby cycle for this Scholar. It took place in northern Europe. The fragment was female and drowned in a freak accident at age eight. The fifty-first life took place in eastern China. The fragment was male, a business advocate and politician with ambitions to be at "court". He had three wives and seventeen children when he was assassinated at age thirty-three. The fifty-second life took place at Jericho. The fragment was male, a musician and minor prophet, some of whose work is fragmentarily [another Michael pun] extant to this day. He and his wife had five children, all of whom perished in religious riots when the Scholar was twenty-one. Life fifty-three was in what is now Morocco. The fragment was male, a "bard" of sorts, had a wife and two living children when he died of an ulcerated liver at age twenty-nine.

The Young cycle for this Scholar began with life fifty-four as a male in Egypt where he was a priest and "dentist". He had two wives and ten children at the time of his death from bone cancer at age thirty-one. The fifty-fifth life was spent in Britain, as a male, the "singer" for the "clan", keeping records through poetry. He died, unmarried, at twenty-eight. The fifty-sixth life was in what is now Lithuania, the fragment was female, a good musician which made her popular with village children. She had six children of her own by the time her husband killed her at age twenty-four. Life fifty-seven took place in Indonesia. The Scholar was male and a tax collector. He had three wives and twelve surviving children when he was tortured to death at age twenty-two for suspected "skimming". The second level of the Young cycle began for this Scholar at life fifty-eight in the western part of what is now Turkey. The fragment was male, an "architect" of walled "cities". He had seventeen children before his second wife killed him out of jealousy at age twenty-five. Life fifty-nine was on the southern tip of the Arabian peninsula. The fragment was female and died of deliverate exposure at age one. The sixtieth life was in what is now Colombia. The fragment was female, a midwife and almanac keeper. She died without having any children of her own at age thirty. The sixty-first life began the third level of the Young cycle for this Scholar. It took place in northern Greece. The fragment was female, a household slave, and died of eating damaged grain at age nineteen. The sixty-second life took place in China. The Scholar was male, a musician and dancer of great regional repute. He died during the most acrobatic part of his dancing at age twenty-six. The sixty-third life in Sais in Egypt. The fragment was a priest who functioned as regional magistrate. He had one wife, three concubines, and eight children by the time someone dropped a poisonous snake in his bed when he was thirty-three. The sixty-fourth life was in Burma, as a female. She sang religious texts and had three children by the time of her death by "ordeal" at age twenty-one. The Scholar's next life was the start of the fourth level of the Young cycle. The life was in Cyprus, and the Scholar was male. He was sentenced to slavery for squandering his father's fortune, and died, age twenty-four, of heat prostration. Life sixty-six was in what is now New Guinea. The Scholar was male and murdered his way to leadership of the village, and is remembered in legend to this day as an ikon of ambition and ruthlessness whose sufferings in later life were well-earned punishment for all he had done earlier. He died of elephantiasis at age thirty. The next life was in Chilles in France. The fragment was female, the daughter of a regional "politician". She married well for her family, had three children and died under suspicious circumstances at age seventeen. The sixty-eighth life took place east of the Caspian Sea in the town of Anau. The Scholar was male and served as a kind of customs officer for caravans and other traders passing through the region. He had nine children when he died of a heart attack at age forty-two. The sixty-ninth life was spent in the Phoenician part of Spain. The Scholar was female, mildly brain-damaged, had eight children, before being killed for the "safety" of the community when she was twenty-eight. The seventieth life marked the beginning of the fifth level of the Young cycle for this Scholar. The life was in the central part of what you call the Midwest. The fragment was male, an administrative leader of his "clan", and not above accepting the occasional bribe. He fell to his death at age thirty-seven, leaving nine children behind. The seventy-first life was in Parthia. The fragment was female, had five children and raised an additional thirteen orphans. She died, worn out, at thirty-one. The sixth level of the Young cycle began with life seventy-two. The Scholar was born male in Japan and died in the wake of a volcanic eruption at age six. Life seventy-three was lived on the Dnieper River. The Scholar was female, a merchant's daughter who had a cast in one eye. She killed herself in chagrin at age twenty-two. The next life was in Africa. The fragment was male, a slave used to maintain roads. He died of infections resulting from ruptured tendons at age twenty-six. The seventy-fifth life began the seventh level of the Young cycle for this Scholar. Born in southern China, this male was a deck-hand on a merchant vessel. He was killed by a shark at age twenty. Life seventy-six was in the mountains of South America. The fragment was female, made musical instruments, had nine children and two husbands and was killed by rowdy young men at age twenty-four. Life seventy-seven was in Malta. The fragment was male, a worshipper of Mithras who made a pest of himself on the subject and died in prison at age twenty-seven, and was for the next two hundred years revered as a martyr to his faith. Life seventy-eight was spent in Manchuria and Mongolia as a scout and "spy" for various regional authorities. He "vanished" fatally at age thirty-two.

The Mature cycle for this fragment began in Herculaneum. He was male, the son of a tavern-keeper. He died at age seventeen, on the twenty-fourth day of August, in what you call seventy-nine Common Reckoning. Life eighty was lived as a female in Britain. Considered "sensible for a woman", she made a place for herself in the village, speaking Latin as well as the regional dialect. She had five children and was a widow when she died at age thirty-nine of tetanus. The eighty-first life was in southern Africa, male. The Scholar spent his days as a cattle drover and his nights drinking. He died of peritonitis at age twenty-three. The second level of the Mature cycle was spent in eastern Greece. The Scholar was male and spent most of his comparatively short life studying plants, particularly poisonous ones. He died of the cumulative effects of toxins in his blood at age twenty-two. Life eighty-three was spent in the Basque region of Spain where this fragment served as teacher and judge in a village, and was noted for the fairness of his decisions. He married three times, had seven surviving children and eleven grandchildren at the time of his death at age sixty-one. Life eighty-four was spent in Indonesia as a female, the daughter of pig-farmers. She was killed and eaten by the pigs at age thirteen. The eighty-fifth life began in Albania, where the Scholar showed early inquisitiveness that was deemed inappropriate for females. She ran away, trying to disguise herself as a boy with the hope of becoming educated. This worked until she was fourteen, at which time she was coerced into prostitution and died at age twenty-eight, the year after the Roman Empire split east and west. She was more successful than she had thought possible at the beginning of her life. The Scholar had now more than two thousand years in incarnation on the physical plane, and more than thirty-seven hundred years had gone by on the physical plane. The next life began in the year 359, Common Reckoning, beginning the third level of the Mature cycle. The fragment was male, lived in southern China, was apprenticed to an architect but died of fever at age nineteen. Life eighty-seven was spent female, in what is now Belgium. The fragment was renowned for her beautiful voice and for this talent was able to marry considerably above her family. She became the wife of the regional military leader, who eventually had to give her up to his superior. She had five children and was killed by her husband at age thirty-nine, after her voice had begun to "fade". Life eighty-eight was also spent in Gaul, but the German part. The fragment was male, a scout for whomever paid the most, and died in an ambush at age twenty-two. Life eighty-nine was lived in a religious community in Spain, a female, noted for her piety. She died of reinfected eczema, brought on by not bathing to show her lack of the sin of vanity, at age thirty-one. Life ninety began the fourth level of the Mature cycle for this Scholar. In that life the fragment was female, a slave attached to a caravan for drudgery and sexual purposes. She covered more than twenty-six thousand miles in her relatively short life, dying of dysentery at age eighteen. The ninety-first life was lived in Persia where the Scholar, male, earned something of a reputation as a poet, had twelve children by two wives, all of whom starved when he fell from favor. He was forty. The next life was spent as a merchant traveler from Kiev. He ventured as far as Kazan in Russia, Byzantium in the south, and Paris in the west. He was killed for his goods in Hungary. He had nine children with eight women in as many cities. Life ninety-three was lived in a monastery in Germany where the Scholar rose to the position of abbot and supervised the brewing of beer, for which the monastery was famous. At fifty-four he succumbed to diabetic complications. The ninety-fourth life was spent as a female in Denmark, the wife of an ironworker. She had eleven children before dying in childbirth at age thirty-one. The next life began the fifth level of the Mature cycle for this Scholar. He was male, a military engineer from Rome employed by the Byzantines to help fend off the rising tide of various barbarian groups that had weakened the city's fortifications. He was executed for treason, largely because he was a foreigner, at age twenty. The ninety-sixth life was spent as a female in China, part of a "circus" where she maintained the costumes and repaired the musical instruments and kept the books for her extended family. She died, unmarried, after twenty

years with the same female lover, at thirty-six, from anemia. The ninety-seventh life of this Scholar was in Indonesia, where he died in an on-going family battle at age
eleven. The ninety-eighth life for this fragment was in what
is now Arizona. The fragment was female, made flutes
and baskets and pottery, had three children, and died of
bronchial "collapse" from cumulative allergies. The sixth
level of the Mature cycle began for this fragment in central
France. The fragment was male, a monk and the recording
clerk to the town's "customs officers". He died at age
forty-two of chronic intestinal inflammation. The one hundredth life was spent as a female in the general area of
Byzantium. She was an accomplished musician and was
killed by her cousin, who was her greatest rival, when she
was nineteen. Life one hundred one was lived in England
and the North Sea where the Scholar, now male, served as
navigator for twenty of his thirty-three years. He had two
surviving children, one of whom was severely retarded.
The Scholar died of internal injuries after a bad fall. The
next life was as a male, in Guatemala, a regional "holy
man" noted for his wisdom and guidance. He died of
snakebite at age twenty-eight, leaving six children to "carry
on" his work. The one hundred third life began the seventh
level of the Mature cycle for this fragment. He was born
male in what is now Algeria, was made a eunuch at nine
and died at age fifteen from poison. The one hundred fourth
life was lived in Russia, a female, married, known for her
skill at gardening. She had two children and died at age
twenty-one when her husband "accidentally" broke her
neck. Life one hundred five was in western Africa. The
fragment was male, the fifth son of a regional trader. He
was sold into slavery and died soon after of malnutrition
and depression.

The Old cycle for this Scholar began at life one hundred
six, as a female in northern China. She died in a sandstorm,
age eleven. Life one hundred seven was lived in Armenia,
where this male was a soldier engaged in fighting off various
warring groups for the protection of the governmental center of the "country". He died in battle at age thirty-two,
leaving a family of nine to become wandering beggars. Life

number one hundred eight began the second level of the Old cycle for this Scholar. The life lasted thirty-seven years, the fragment was female, the places were Norway and England. The Scholar was considered to be something of a "witch" for the ability she had to "sense" the coast ahead, which was in actuality memories of former lives in the region. She died at sea. The one hundred ninth life was in the European sector of Tyre, and the fragment was the second son of a Genonese merchant who made a fortune in textiles. The Scholar widened the business to include dyes, and the fortune grew larger. He had a wife in Genoa and a wife in Tyre, a total of eleven children, and died at the hands of pirates at sea at age twenty-nine. The next life was in Mongolia, the fragment was female, the daughter of a live-stock "broker". She married reasonably well, had five children, and devoted her life to preparing them to "get on" in the world. She died of cancer at age thirty-one. The one hundred eleventh life began the third level of the Old cycle. It was in the Pacific Northwest, the fragment was male. When Chinese traders arrived with goods, this fragment asked to return with them to find out about China for the people of his "tribe". This was agreed to. The junk went down in a storm on its way back. The Scholar was seventeen. The next life was in southern India. The Scholar was female, of a lower caste, and died after being badly burned at age six. Life one hundred thirteen was lived as a male in the city of Bologna in Italy. He worked in a large pottery, firing vases, bowls, plates, and jars. He died of emphysema brought on by inhaling the lead fumes in the glazes, at age twenty-two. Life number one hundred fourteen was in southern France, and the Scholar was once again male. This time his death, at age nine, was due to what was called the Black Plague. In his region, fatality from this disease at this outbreak was more than eighty percent. The one hundred fifteenth life began the fourth level of the Old cycle for this Scholar. The fragment was male, homosexual, and an adherent to the Islamic discipline of rapturous dancing. He died at age thirty-six of heart disease. Life one hundred sixteen was lived as a female in eastern Europe. She was a camp follower, taking care of a minor infantry officer. She bore him four children, and when their camp was under attack, she saved thirty-eight children and forty-four wounded men before being killed herself in the engagement. She was twenty-seven. The next life was spent as a male in what is now Iran. The Scholar was one of a family of innovative instrument-makers. He showed much promise but died of cholera at age eighteen. The one hundred eighteenth life was brief, ending at age two when the Scholar's village was razed by religious zealots. Life one hundred nineteen began the fifth level of the Old cycle for this Scholar. Born in Japan, the fragment was male and became a prestigious teacher of decorative calligraphy. He died at age forty-one from a heart attack. The one hundred twentieth life took place in South America. The Scholar was male and died at sixteen from measles contracted from Europeans. The one hundred twenty-first life began the sixth level of the Old cycle for this Scholar. Born in southern Italy, the Scholar was male, a justice of the courts. He had seven children, two of them illegitimate. He died at age fifty from an aortal aneurism. The next life was in Poland—then part of Bohemia—where the fragment was male, an advocate for businessmen, and a part-time composer. Widowed early in his marriage, he raised his three children with the help of his spinster sister. He died of a stroke at age forty-five. Life one hundred twenty-three was lived male in central Africa. Taken captive at a young age by ethnic rivals, he was finally tortured to death at age thirteen to make an example for his people. The seventh level of the Old cycle began at life one hundred twenty-four in Australia. The fragment was the wife of an innkeeper, the daughter of "career" criminals. She had five children and ran away from the demanding and "unrewarding" life at thirty-two. She died in London at age thirty-six. At this point, the fragment had been incarnated for more than three thousand years and more than five thousand years on the physical plane had passed. Life one hundred twenty-five began in Leeds in England. The fragment, female, trained as a teacher and went out to India to serve as a tutor and librarian to English families there. She was killed in a train wreck at age thirty-four. Life one hundred twenty-six was lived in The Netherlands and Italy. The Scholar, male, was an orchestral musician. He married an Italian girl, had two children, then separated as amicably as possible. He died at fifty-one following a performance of the *Farewell Symphony* of bleeding ulcers. The Scholar is currently forty-two, a tapestry maker and restorer in Liège. The Scholar has had twenty-two contacts with the Essence Twin, and thirty-one with the Task Companion. The fragment has burned one thousand three hundred eighty-seven karmic ribbons, and has had contact with the other six members in the Scholar's cadence a total of two thousand four hundred twenty-nine times.

———

"**M**ichael, we noticed more specificity than usual in giving information on the Scholar. Is there some reason for that?"

Of course. The Scholar is noted for the pursuit of information, and as a result, the specificity you have observed can be regarded as "natural".

On to Sages. The Sage we will consider is fifth cast in the cadence, and was cast onto the physical plane 5,317 years ago, beginning the first life in what is now Turkey where the fragment, then male, carved doors and lintels. He died of injuries received from chisels at age twenty-four. Life number two was in Indonesia, the fragment was female, had three children and drowned at age twenty-one. The third life took place in north-west China, the Sage was the son of a weaver who died of eating tainted meat at age eight. The fourth life was lived in central India. The Sage was female, considered very beautiful and was executed at age sixteen to end the dissention between two of her suitors. The fifth life was also female, lived in the southeastern part of South America. The Sage was female, and sacrificed at her first menstrual period, age twelve. The sixth life began the second level of the Infant cycle.

The fragment was male, a herder in Africa, and died of a fractured skull at age twenty. The seventh life was lived along the Rhine, the Sage was male and killed in a blizzard at age twelve. The eighth life was lived in what is now Ecuador, the Sage was female, "married", had two children and died at age nineteen of malnutrition. The ninth life began the third level of the Infant cycle for this Sage. The fragment was born in the south of France, had eight children by the regional story-teller and "guru", and died at age twenty-six of anemia. The tenth life was spent in what is now Canada, as a male, a maker of masks and ritual "props". He froze to death at age twenty-six. Life eleven was spent in what is now Pakistan. The fragment was a slave, male, given the task of instructing and guarding the children of the local "despot". He did not live up to his master's expectations, and was killed at age twenty-five. The twelfth life was in Korea, where the Sage, in that life a fragile child, went into a decline very early in life and was dead at ten. Life thirteen was lived in Britain, the daughter of a forester and hunter. She developed a talent for recounting his adventures, some of which are still extant in the folklore of the region. She died at age fifteen, the result of taking a fall. The fourteenth life was lived in southern China, where the Sage was a male, a scribe, had one child and died of a ruptured bladder at age twenty-eight. The fifteenth life was lived in what is now Iran. The Sage was the son of a regional courier and was trampled by live-stock at age four when attempting to follow his father on his duties. The next life was spent as a female in western Africa where she died as the result of over-zealous puberty rites at age twelve. The seventeenth life began the fifth level of the Infant cycle. The fragment was male, lived in northern Europe and improved the selling practices at the local market. He died at age twenty-three after attempting to climb the highest peak in the region. He was caught in a rainstorm and fell to his death. Life eighteen took place in southern India. The fragment was female, a slave who specialized in massage. She died in childbirth at age thirty. Life number nineteen took place on the Russian Pacific

Coast. The fragment was male, born to a fishing and whaling community and died at age seven from frostbite. The next life was lived in Malaysia, the fragment was female and although born poor, "improved her lot" by becoming an auctioneer for household slaves. She died at age twenty-four of skin cancer. The twenty-first life began the sixth level of the Infant cycle for this Sage. In this life the Sage was born female in central Asia, and was smothered at age two by her older siblings for being "too noisy". The twenty-second life took place in a river village in what is now Argentina. The fragment was female, adept at tattoos and was killed by insects at age sixteen. The twenty-third life was spent as a male in Madagascar as the leader of a group of "break-away" villagers. The group was hunted down and exterminated when the Sage was twenty-two. The twenty-fourth life was lived as a female in western Spain. The fragment was married three times, each time to more important men. The third husband suspected her of "designs" on him and "beat her to the punch" by killing her when she was twenty-five. She had four children, one of whom—her third husband's—survived. The twenty-fifth life began the seventh level of the Infant cycle for this fragment, who was born male in Egypt, showed a flair for languages and became a translator for foreign merchants in Egypt. He had two wives and nine children when he was killed at age twenty-nine. The twenty-sixth life was spent as a female in Mongolia. The fragment was an unwelcome part of the household when her mother remarried and so was abandoned. She died at age twelve, the victim of exhaustion and hungry animals. The twenty-seventh life was spent in western Africa with a family of canoe makers. The female Sage enjoyed traveling on the river and continued to do so after being sold to her husband at age fourteen. He returned her to her family when she did not become pregnant after two years, and the family had to leave the area in disgrace. The Sage contracted a parasite-carried infection and died at age seventeen.

The twenty-eighth life began the first level of the Baby cycle for this Sage, who was born male in Egypt and

became a temple "crier", announcing processions, festivals, rites, decisions, and other news. The fragment had
one wife and four children when he died of intestinal cancer
at age thirty-two. The twenty-ninth life was spent on the
upper part of the Missouri River where, as the oldest son
of the "clan's" judicial leader he was murdered as revenge
on his family at age fourteen. The thirtieth life was lived in
Crete as a female. The fragment gained a reputation as a
"seer" which brought her much notoriety. She strove to
improve her visions with starvation, and died of it at age
twenty-five. Life thirty-one was lived in what is now Nepal.
The fragment was the daughter of the "tax collector", and
was abducted and killed at age eleven. The thirty-second
life began the second level of the Baby cycle. The fragment
was born male in central Europe. He was thrown out of his
village for refusing to work in the local mines. He became
a vagabond and died at age twenty-three. Life thirty-three
was spent in what is now Cambodia, the youngest daughter
of the sail-maker. She married a man the family thought
would "quiet her down", and ended up confining her to a
small room for being "ungovernable". She managed to kill
herself at age twenty-six. The thirty-fourth life was spent
as a male in what is now Slovenia. The fragment made the
rounds of the local hamlets and villages, carrying news,
information, and other similar things. He died at age
twenty-two, killed in a village brawl. The thirty-fifth life
began the third level of this Sage's Baby cycle. It was spent
in China, the fragment was male, a religious "singer" and
reciter of sacred texts. He was crushed to death in an
earthquake at age nineteen. Life thirty-six was spent training to be a potter in South America. The apprentice was
killed in an avalanche at age fifteen. Life thirty-seven was
spent as a female in Egypt where she was a very successful
prostitute for high-ranking clients. She was killed by rivals
at age twenty-five. She left no surviving children. Life
thirty-eight was spent on islands off the east coast of what
is now the United States of America. The fragment was
female, the second wife of one of the island's richer men.
She died at age twenty in the aftermath of a hurricane. She

left five children and two burned karmic ribbons behind. The thirty-ninth life began the fourth level of the Baby cycle for this Sage who was born female in south Africa. She excelled at ritual dancing and was given to the village shaman to help his magic for women. She died as the result of compound fractures of the left arm and leg. She was twenty-four and had five living children. The fortieth life was lived in Greece, the Sage was male and an athlete known for his prankishness. He had an accident in a chariot that left him partially paralyzed, and he died at age twenty-nine after four years of intense depression. The forty-first life was lived as a female in what is now Oregon, the one surviving daughter of a hunter and his wife. The fragment was known for her skill with porcupine quills in adornment. She had two children and died of virus-induced exhaustion at age sixteen. The next life began the fifth level of the Baby cycle for this Sage, who was born male in Nineveh, a priest whose ambitions might have taken him high in the ranks if he had not become enamored of a noblewoman. He was executed for this temerity at age twenty-five. The next life, the fragment was in Corsica, was male and died at age six from infected injuries on his legs and feet. The forty-fourth life was spent in Armenia, the fragment was female, married to her cousin by whom she had nine children, two of whom were noticeably retarded. She died at age thirty of a liver abscess. The forty-fifth life was spent in China as a flower-boat girl. She was shoved over-board by her "pimp" when one of her customers offered to buy her. She was seventeen. The forty-sixth life was spent as a male in Egypt where he had been sent to the temple of the crocodile god to be a priest. He succumbed to fever at age twelve and given to his god as an offering. The forty-seventh life began the sixth level of the Baby cycle for this Sage. The life was lived in Ireland, the fragment was considered "fey" from an early age, and so she never married, but spent most of her time telling stories and wandering about the countryside. She had and abandoned four children, and finally died of exposure at the age of forty-three. The forty-eighth life was spent as the "promoting mother" of three talented sons in China. Her husband, a gambler, deserted the family early. She saw two of her children become recognized "circus" entertainers, and the other an accomplished acrobat before the age of ten. She died at age twenty-four from a stroke. The next life lasted not quite two years. The fragment was male, taken captive and made a slave with the rest of his family, and died of starvation and "neglect". The fiftieth life the fragment was male in Greece, a reciter in religious festivals and writer of declamatory verse shortly before the time of Alcaeus. He died of alcoholism at age thirty-two. The fifty-first life began the seventh level of the Baby cycle for this Sage. It was lived in what is now Morocco. The Sage was the oldest daughter in a family of professional thieves. She was apprehended plying the family trade, had her hands struck off and died a beggar at age ten. At this point, the Sage had been extant upon the physical plane for just over one thousand years and more than sixteen hundred years had gone by on the physical plane. The fifty-second life was lived as a male in western India where he, a eunuch slave, was put in charge of twenty-nine women. He was diligent in his duties, and devoted to the women in question, protecting the women from invading foreigners with his life, which ended in a lance-thrust at age thirty-six.

The Young cycle for this fragment began at life fifty-three, when the fragment was born female in western Greece. Married to her parents' choice of suitors, this fragment became disenchanted with marriage and when her husband publicly mocked her, she retaliated by killing her two children and herself. She was twenty-two. The fifty-fourth life was spent as a "drudge" in southern France, as a slave-of-all-work, female. She died of malnutrition at age seventeen. Life fifty-five was lived in Tibet where this Sage was a religious dancer for the Bon religion. He never had children and died at age thirty from bacterial infection. The fifty-sixth life was lived in eastern Russia, the fragment was female, a farmer's wife and noted singer. She died at age twenty-six, leaving seven children and a devastated husband to mourn her. The fifty-seventh life began the second level of the Young cycle for this Sage. The fragment was female in Carthage and was sacrificed to strengthen the city at age four. The fifty-eighth life was spent in Cyprus as a male. He became "minister of state ceremonies" and was killed when the platform he had ordered erected collapsed under him. The fifty-ninth life was spent in Egypt as a courtesan. She lived twenty-two years and inscriptions to her abilities still remain. The sixtieth life was spent in the South Seas as the wife of an inter-island trader. She and he, and their two children perished in a storm when she was eighteen. The sixty-first life began the third level of the Young cycle for this Sage. The fragment was born male in what is now Austria. The fragment became a trader, plying the hamlets, villages and towns up and down the Danube. He was known as a very entertaining fellow and was able to find unusual items to trade, which make him rich before his death from drowning at age thirty-four. Life sixty-two was spent on the west coast of Africa. The fragment was male, "cute" and died from injuries of aggressive sexual assault at age sixteen. Life sixty-three was lived as a female in Indonesia. The fragment painted designs on fabric and took care of her five children, before dying of a wasting bone disease at age twenty-one. The fragment then moved to the fourth level of the Young Cycle. The sage was born male in Tahiti, was a fisherman and dancer, had six children and raised his wife's three from her first marriage as well. He died at age twenty-eight. The sixty-fifth life was spent in northern Italy, the daughter and then wife of a stone-cutter. Known for her charm and her temper, she managed to advance her four sons in the world before her death at age twenty-five from a spontaneous vein collapse. The sixty-sixth life also began the fifth level of the Young cycle for this Sage. The life took place in what is now Switzerland. The fragment was female, the oldest step-child in a combined family of eleven. She was given the task of caring for and teaching the younger children, which she did very well until her death in a fire at the age of fifteen. The sixty-seventh life took place along the Silk Road, which this Sage undertook to explore from one end to the other. The whole task required nine years and made him very famous at home in China when he returned. His reports, while generally accurate as to distance and geography were somewhat embroidered as to people encountered. He died at age thirty-one, happily married and well-reputed. The sixty-eighth life took place in northern Gaul. The fragment was female, her job, other than raising her five children, was to keep track of all family events. She excelled at both and died, much missed, at age twenty-six. The next life began in Mexico. The Sage was born to a Mayan family of farmers. He was badly deformed and so was given to the priests for sacrifice at age three. The seventieth life was spent as a performer in Rome. Known as a great comedian, the Sage performed for more than fifteen years before dying of typhus at age thirty. The sixth level of the Young cycle took place in Japan, the fragment was female, the daughter of a famous musician. She learned from him, and made a better marriage because of her abilities. She died giving birth to her first child at age sixteen. The seventy-second life took place in Greece, where the fragment was a noted competitor in poetry contests. The son of a rich wine-grower, he had the opportunity to make the most of his talents, and to do this, he traveled widely before dying of immunity exhaustation at the age of twenty-seven. The seventy-third life was spent in the mountains of Latin America, where the fragment developed a new method for feather embroidery, which brought riches to her family and a second husband to her. She died of shock at age twenty-four. The seventy-fourth life began the seventh level of the Young cycle for this Sage, who was born in what is now Virginia, a male, who proved to be a disappointment to his bellicose relatives and was therefore forbidden to marry. He died at nineteen, not quite a suicide. The seventy-fifth life was spent in China, the fragment was female, the wife of a magistrate, known to be working for his benefit at all times. She promoted his well-fare at every opportunity, gave him two sons, killed the three daughters she had, and was gratified when he was praised officially by the Emperor. She died at twenty-eight of peritonitis. The seventy-sixth life was spent as a male in northern India. He was one of twelve children, and he died with all of his family when their village was struck by smallpox. He was eleven years old.

The Mature cycle began for this Sage at life seventy-seven. The fragment was born male in Egypt, and made his living performing various tricks in the market squares of many towns and cities. He had an extensive following and a fairly regular schedule he kept to. He died of epidemic fever at age twenty-six. The seventy-eighth life, the Sage again was male, living this time in Britain, the son of a village leader who had died before he was born. Raised by relatives, the boy wandered off at age nine and died of exposure. The seventy-ninth life was lived as a female in a major Chinese city. The fragment married a wealthy merchant and cared for his children. She became expert in identifying fine antiques and eventually became a near-partner to her husband. She was thirty-four when she died of anemia. The eightieth life also began the second level of the Mature cycle for this Sage. The life took place in Borneo, the Sage was female, and a kind of "civic" courtesan, being given as a "reward" to those who actually pleased the "powers that be". She died in a civil uprising at the age of twenty-one. The eighty-first life was spent in what is now Peru, the son of a well-known "scholar" who advised on planting times and kept track of weather phenomena. The son died in an unexpected fire at age eighteen. Life eighty-two was spent in Korea, in a large family, as the fifth son of eight. He died of general neglect at age six. The eighty-third life was once again centered around a large family, this time in what is now the Flemish region of Europe. The fragment was female, married to a widower with four children. She bore him seven more, and died of post-delivery complications at age twenty-eight. The eighty-fourth life began the third level of the mature cycle for this fragment, who was born female in southwestern India, and perished of insect infestations at age five. The eighty-fifth life was spent in northern Canada as a fur trader and storyteller. The fragment was male, had five

children before his death at age thirty-three from exsangui-
nation. The eighty-sixth life was spent in central Italy as a
female. The fragment was taken into slavery at age ten, and
she spent the rest of her life in the northern part of Africa
in a bath tending to the wants of the patrons there. She
died at age twenty-nine, having had two children, and
burned six karmic ribbons. The next life began the fourth
level of the Mature cycle, the fragment was male, lived in
what is now Poland, and died in a logging accident at age
twelve. In that life the fragment had intended to become a
song-writer, but the life ended before the life-plan could be
put into practice. The eighty-eighth life was lived as a male
in western France fulfilling the plans of the last life. The
fragment was the son of a priest, for at that time priests of
the Catholic Church were still permitted to marry, and
learned to read and write while a child. He then set about
going from town to town, singing and telling stories. He
"cut a swath" through the women of the region and had
more than thirteen illegitimate children when he died in
prison at age twenty-nine, the result of offending the warlord of the region in song. Life eighty-nine was spent as a
female in what is now eastern Russia, the daughter of an
instrument-maker and performer who taught her well. She
died in a accident when the wagon in which she was riding
fell off the narrow road into a gorge. The ninetieth life
began the fifth level of the Mature cycle for this Sage, and
was lived in Central America. The fragment was a lesser
"diplomat" charged with negotiating a peace between rival
"cities". He was almost successful, but was assassinated
for his efforts at age twenty-five, leaving his wives and
children to depend on the "mercy" of his superior. The
ninety-first life was spent in what is now the Czech Republic. The fragment was female, of minor nobility, and became "known" in certain circles for her poetry. She was
unhappily married, had six children and died of uterine
cancer at age forty-nine. The ninety-second life was lived,
female, in China, the daughter of a professional gambler.
She died at age thirteen, unwilling to become a concubine
for her uncle. The fragment was then born in New Guinea,

the son of a prostitute and a sailor. He had a rough few years, signed on a ship to get away from his situation, and died with the rest of the crew when the ship sank in a typhoon. The ninety-fourth life began the sixth level of the Mature cycle for this fragment, who was born male in what is now Norway. The fragment worked with traders from many parts of the north, and managed to accumulate a small fortune before being killed by robbers at age forty-two. He was survived by his wife and seven children. The ninety-fifth life was lived in the area of what is now Florida. The son of the shaman for a small "clan", the fragment became famous for his feats of memory. He was bitten by a coral snake at age thirteen. The ninety-sixth life was spent in Sicily, the wife of a successful fisherman. She had three children and fought with her in-laws until her death at age twenty from food poisoning. At this point, the Sage had been incarnate on the physical plane for more than two thousand years and almost four thousand years had passed. The ninety-seventh life began the seventh level of the Mature cycle, and the Sage spent it in northern Europe, serving as a kind of herald for the nobility of the period. He died of a heart attack at age fifty-four, much honored for his dedication. He never married, preferring men to women, but was discreet enough that this was not known by any but a very few. The ninety-eighth life was spent in what is now Surinam, the wife of a cloth-maker. She had to "run the business" for her husband, who was somewhat mentally disturbed and could not cope with any external demands. She was killed by her husband at age thirty, leaving four children and a flourishing business behind. The ninety-ninth life was spent in the English Midlands. The fragment was female, wife of an itinerant cobbler. She deserted him and their two children for a more stable life with a farmer. She died of complications following the amputation of her left foot at age twenty-eight.

For this Sage, the Old cycle began at life one hundred. The Sage was in central Italy, for most of her life a religious recluse. She died of malnutrition at age twenty-three. The next life was spent traveling in China, one of the acrobats in a "circus", who eventually became the owner of the "show". He was mauled to death by a dancing bear at age sixty-two, leaving the circus to three of this grandsons. The one hundred second life lasted three years along the Mississippi. The fragment died of Yellow Fever. The one hundred third life as spent as a female in what is now Uruguay. The fragment, of slave status, ended up becoming the house-runner for a major regional leader before her death from parasite infestation at age fifteen. The one hundred fourth life was lived in eastern Africa. The Sage was male and considered a servant of the gods because of his behavior before his death at twenty-three from a brain tumor. The one hundred fifth life began the second level of the Old cycle for this fragment, who was born female in what is now Nepal. The fragment was a semi-invalid and so did not marry. She became a beggar upon the death of her parents and died herself at age twenty-six. The one hundred sixth life was spent in the Adriatic region, part of a troupe of musicians who also were adept thieves. The fragment was apprehended and died of starvation in prison at the age of thirty-seven. The next life began the third level of the Old cycle for this Sage. Born male in Kiev, the fragment was apprenticed to a smith and died as the result of a blow to the head at age twelve. The one hundred eighth life began near Constantinople. The fragment, female, became a dancer, then "converted" and retired to a religious community where she died in the "odor of sanctity" at the age of thirty-one. The one hundred ninth life was spent in the Solomon Islands, being something of a "lay-about" until his death at seventeen. The one hundred tenth life began the fourth level of the Old cycle for this Sage. It took place in Sweden, the fragment was born deaf and therefore became the village clown. He was regarded fondly by all those around him, and his death at age twenty-nine was sincerely mourned. The one hundred eleventh life was lived in western China as a kind of "innkeeper" on the Old Silk Road. The fragment offered entertainment and respite at his hospice. He had three wives and fifteen children at the time of his death at age thirty-four from a severe intestinal infection. The one hundred twelfth life was spent in eastern Mexico in a fishing community. The fragment was female, "married", with two children, when she died at age twenty-two from pneumonia. The one hundred thirteenth life was lived as the illegitimate son of a monk in Russia. He starved at age fourteen. The one hundred fourteenth life began the fifth level of the Old cycle for this Sage. The fragment was female, in India, and died as the result of a raid on the town where the family lived. She was six. The next life, number one hundred fifteen was spent in the Church in Spain, a supposed castrato religious singer, actually a female seeking to avoid marriage. The scandal of her actual sex marred the occasion of her death at age twenty-nine. The one hundred sixteenth life was spent in central China. The fragment was female, married quite young, had eight children and twenty-nine grandchildren as well as seven great-grandchildren at the time of her death from heart disease at age seventy-three. The one hundred seventeenth life was spent on the Amazon River, working with his family who sold goods up and down the river. He died of a poisoned blow-gun dart at age ten. Life one hundred eighteen began in what is now Bulgaria. The fragment, then male, learned a number of languages at his parents' tavern. He used this to become a business translator. He was stabbed to death at age twenty-two, leaving three semi-legitimate children behind. The one hundred nineteenth life began the sixth level of the Old cycle for this Sage. He was born in Malaysia, the son of a master carpenter. He clashed with his family, and finally ran away at age twelve. At age fifteen he died of venereal disease. The one hundred twentieth life was lived in Russia. The fragment was born the bastard daughter of a Prince, and supported by him until his death. She became a courtesan and died of a heart attack at age fifty-two. She had no living children. The one hundred twenty-first life was lived in Europe. The fragment, female, was one of the first true "divas", singing in various courts until her death of septic bronchitis at age thirty-two. The next life began the seventh level of the Old cycle for this Sage. The fragment was born male in the United States of

America, was an adept con-man who made the most of the
Civil War until he was killed by outlaws in 1862, Common
Reckoning. The one hundred twenty-third life began in
New Zealand. The fragment was female and wanted to
study art. She died at age nineteen and infantile paralysis.
The one hundred twenty-fourth life was spent in Algeria.
The fragment was male and died in a riot at age six. The
fragment is now thirty-nine, female, living in Hong Kong,
where she devotes her inherited fortune to collecting art.
This fragment has had twenty-six contacts with the Essence
Twin, thirty-three with the Task Companion. The number
of karmic ribbons burned is two thousand sixteen, and
contact with one of the six members of the cadence now
stands at two thousand eight hundred thirty.

The sixth-cast Priest considered for this review was first
incarnated 5,492 years ago in Sumaria, was male and died
as a sacrifice at age eighteen. The second life was lived in
the Old Kingdom of Egypt in a boatwright's family. The
Priest died at age twenty, the victim of sunstroke. The third
life this Priest was a temple slave in Nuzi, was female, and
died at twenty-four of hemorrhagic fever. The fourth life
was spent in a settlement on the Rhone River. The fragment
was male, a skinner who died at age sixteen from blood
poisoning. Life number five was spent in Burma. The
fragment was female and her family abandoned her at age
three. The sixth life began the second level of the Infant
cycle for this Priest. The life took place on the Greek
island of Rhodes. The fragment was female, married to a
quarryman. She died of viral disease at age twenty-one.
The seventh life was spent in what is now British Columbia.
The fragment was female and died at eleven from exacerbated allergies. The eighth life was spent in central Asia.
The fragment was male, partially blind and considered a
shaman. The fragment died of accidental poisoning at age
twenty-five. The ninth life was spent in southern Africa.
The fragment was male, the youngest son of the leader's
first wife. He was killed by his step-brothers at age fourteen. The tenth life was spent in South America in the
region of what is now Bolivia. The fragment as female, a

virtual slave, had four children before dying of fever at age seventeen. The eleventh life began the third level of the Infant cycle. The fragment was born male in what is now Iraq, was a slave assigned to guard duty of the city. He became fascinated with the movement of the stars and neglected his "job" for which dereliction of duty he was executed at age thirty-two, his knowledge dismissed. The twelfth life was spent in northern Greece, the fragment was female and prone to "spells". She was married three times and returned to her family in all instances. She had four children, two of whom did not survive infancy. She died of exposure at age twenty-six. The Priest's next life was spent in the South Seas, the daughter of a spear-maker. She was married at thirteen, had two children and died having the third at age nineteen. The fourteenth life began the fourth level of the Infant cycle for this Priest. The fragment was born male in what is now Normandy, became a hamlet shaman, and died of ritual strangulation in order to demonstrate—unsuccessfully—his immortality. The next life was female in Indonesia, the only survivor of an epidemic that struck her village when she was nine. She died at ten of malnutrition and shock. The sixteenth life was in China, the fragment was female and sold to a "brothel" where she died of malnutrition at age twenty-three. The seventeenth life began the fifth level of the Infant cycle. The Priest was born in what is now Spain, ran away from home and died of exposure at age six. The eighteenth life was spent in what is now Syria. The Priest became a male "concubine", and was murdered for jealousy at age thirty, five years after he had "retired". The nineteenth life was spent in southern Russia. She was given to the local warlord and died during a battle when the warlord's camp was over-run. She was thirteen at the time. The twentieth life began the sixth level of the Infant cycle for the Priest. The life was spent as the daughter of a farmer who managed to accumulate some land and get a little regional power in what is now Ohio. The fragment died at nineteen of a beating which she was given for refusing to marry. The twenty-first life was as a male in central Asia, where the Priest was trampled to death at age two. The twenty-second life took place in what is now Jordan. The Priest was female, had seven children by the farming brothers who bought her. She died at age twenty-eight from malaria, leaving nine surviving children. The twenty-third life was spent female, in the Indus Valley. The Priest broke an arm while young and because it healed badly and the arm useless, she was not wanted as a spouse, so was sold for very little money as a slave. She died at age sixteen, ostensibly from fever but actually from neglect. The next life was spent in Judea. Born male into a religious family, the Priest died of infection at the age of twenty-two, shortly after becoming the leader of his religious group. The twenty-fifth life began the seventh level of the Infant cycle for this Priest, who was born male in north-eastern South America, was of "slave" status, and killed by irate "clansmen" at age twenty-three. The twenty-sixth life was spent male. The Priest was born in Burma, was the son of a disgraced temple woman. They were exiled from their village and died of animal attack when he was five. The twenty-seventh life was spent male in the Caucasus Mountains. The fragment was male, the third son of a tanner. He eliminated his oldest brother in the hopes of sharing the inheritance with his older brother. The older brother killed him when the Priest was seventeen. The twenty-eighth life was spent female in Greece, as a slave in a temple compound where she was burned to death, thanks to the efforts of the priests of a rival deity, at age twenty-two.

The twenty-ninth life began the Baby cycle for this Priest. The place was western China, the fragment was male, the son of a merchant with ambitions for his family. The Priest was expected to excel, and when the demands grew too extreme, he committed suicide out of shame at age fifteen. The thirtieth life was spent in Egypt. The Priest was female, married to a town "magistrate" who relied on her judgment. She out-lived him by a decade, raised her five children and died of intestinal abscesses at age thirty-three. The thirty-first life was spent female in northern Mexico. The fragment was "married" at twelve, had nine children and died of post-partum complications at age twenty-one.

The next life was spent male in northern Italy. The fragment showed a capacity for calculations and was enlisted
to help those supervising the building of fortifications. He
died under one of those walls when it collapsed. He was
twenty-two. The thirty-third life began the second level of
the Baby cycle for this Priest, who reincarnated as a male
in northern Africa. The Priest distinguished himself as a
spiritual and military leader at a young age, and continued
in that capacity until his death at the hands of one of his
wives at age thirty-nine. The thirty-fourth life was spent in
Indonesia, the daughter of an abandoned mother. The two
struggled together as beggars but finally starved when the
Priest was eight. The next life was lived along the Danube.
The fragment was female, and found disfavor in the eyes of
the local deity. She was ritually drowned at age eleven. The
thirty-sixth life was lived as a female in southern South
America, as a healer. She died at age twenty-six of fever.
The thirty-seventh life was spent in Crete. The Priest was
the supervisor of a religious "brothel", had fifteen children
himself by the temple women. He died of self-administered
poison at age twenty-six. The thirty-eighth life began the
third level of the Baby cycle for this fragment. Born male
in central Canada, the fragment became a teacher and
shaman, lived to age twenty-four, and died of exposure.
The thirty-ninth life was spent near Ur, where the Priest
established a cult of his very own, very strict and ritualistic.
He died of botulism at age twenty-seven, which was seen
as a bad omen by his followers, and the cult disbanded.
The fortieth life was spent in a Mayan community. The
fragment was married, had two children and died of injury
infections at age sixteen. The forty-first life took place in
what is now Thailand. The fragment, male, was put in
charge of a facility for the insane. He died during a town
panic which resulted in the burning of the facility and
everyone in it, including the Priest's two wives and ten
children. He was thirty-six. The fourth level of the Baby
cycle began at life forty-two. The fragment was female,
born blind, and lived in a semi-feral state for nineteen
years. The forty-third life was spent female in northern

China, the wife of a "tax collector" with whom she never agreed. He killed her for her disobedience when she was thirty-five, leaving seven children to be raised by his concubines. The forty-fourth life began the fifth level of the Baby cycle for this fragment. The Priest was female, lived in northern France, the wife of a hunter and trapper. She died at age twenty-one, leaving two sets of twins to disgrace her family. The forty-fifth life began in western Africa, the Priest was the son of a herder. He was brought up with cattle and was considered to be a "good fellow". He died at sixteen during an athletic competition. The forty-sixth life was spend in south-east Asia. The fragment was male, one of a "clan" of roving thieves. He had captured three women and had four living children when he and most of his relatives were killed when he was twenty-five. The forty-seventh life began the sixth level of the Baby cycle for this Priest, who was born female in Burma, orphaned at birth. She was given to a temple as a slave, and died there of malnutrition at age thirteen. The forty-eighth life took place in what is now Denmark where the Priest was the step-daughter of a logger, and when her mother died, was abandoned. She died at age six. The forty-ninth life was spent male in Greece where he served as the "minister of justice" for a minor Greek "kingdom". He died of bronchial failure at age twenty-three. The Priest's fiftieth life was as a male in Latin America. He was offered in sacrifice on his first birthday. The fifty-first life took place in northern Mongolia. The fragment was female, had nine children by two husbands and died at age twenty-eight of abdominal infection. The fifty-second life began the seventh level of the Baby cycle for this Priest who incarnated in a male body in Greece, became a renowned and dogmatic mathematician and geometer. He had a wife to whom he gave six living children, but did not remarry when she died, devoting himself to study instead. He succumbed to heart disease at age forty-nine. At this point, the Priest had more than one thousand years of incarnation behind him, and more than fourteen hundred years had gone by on the physical plane. The fifty-third life was spent in northern India, the slave of a wealthy family. She died at age twenty-two of snakebite. The fifty-fourth life was lived as a female in central Africa. She died at age thirteen, stoned when she failed to menstruate "on time". The fifty-fifth life was spent in China, the debauched son of a government official. He was waylaid by street gangs and killed at age twenty-nine.

The Young cycle began for this Priest at life fifty-six. The fragment was born male in Australia, became known as a prophet. He died of heat exhaustion at age twenty-six. The fifty-seventh life was spent as a female in the Pacific Northwest. The fragment had four children and a "magical link" to bears. She died of blood poisoning at age eighteen. The fifty-eighth life was lived in what is now Turkey. The fragment was female, a woman of the upper class, married for political reasons to a regional ruler. She had seven children and died at age twenty-three. Her likeness still exists at various sites around her husband's territory. The fifty-ninth life began the second level of the Young cycle for this Priest, who was born in what is now Japan, the sister of a regional religious leader to whom she devoted her life, even to remaining single for his sake. She died at age thirty-five, still certain of the holiness of her brother. The sixtieth life was spent in central Europe as a male, the illegitimate son of a landowner who was his father's favorite and was killed at age twenty-two by his legitimate brother. The sixty-first life was spent in southern Mexico, the initiate priest of an established temple. He was twenty-nine when he died of a stroke. The sixty-second life began the third level of the Young cycle for this Priest, as the son of a ruler in western China. He was brought up to defend the family, and defend it he did, and died in battle at age eighteen. The sixty-third life was spent in south Africa, the daughter of a shaman, who, being his only child, was taught the "trade", at which she excelled. She died of stomach cancer at age twenty-six. The sixty-fourth life was spent in western Europe, where the Priest was female and froze to death age nine. The sixty-fifth life was spent in eastern India, the son of a brass-worker who expanded the business with fervor until he was crippled in an accident. He lingered for two years, dying at age twenty-one. The sixty-sixth life began the fourth level of the Young cycle for this Priest. The life took place in Upper Egypt. The fragment became a powerful leader in the religious and commercial life of the community. He established a kind of civic tax as well as a religious one, and died, equally honored and hated at age forty. The sixty-seventh life was spent in the South Pacific, as one of a group of "merchants" plying their inter-island trade. He went down with his ship at age twenty-two. The next life was spent in Greece, the fragment was female and became a courtesan to avoid becoming a wife. She died at age eighteen at the hands of a customer. The sixty-ninth life was spent in England, the wife of a messenger, and later his widow, supported by the military leader for whom her husband worked. She had eleven children, three of whom lived to adulthood. She died of a chronic gallbladder infection at age thirty. The seventieth life began the fifth level of the young cycle for this Priest. The life took place in Malaysia, the third daughter of an outcast. She and her eight siblings died at the hands of marauders at the age of seven. The seventy-first life was spent on the plains of North America with a nomadic people. He was known for his skill as an astronomer. He died of a fall at age twenty-nine. The seventy-second life was spent in Korea, the Priest was male, a student of mathematics and died of epidemic disease at age sixteen. The seventy-third life began in Persia. The fragment was female, a courtesan, who died of parasite infestation at age twenty-four. The sixth level of the Young cycle began for this Priest at life number seventy-four in southern China. The fragment was female, one of a high-ranking family who was known to be "strange". She married the man her parents arranged for her, bore him nine children, then killed him at age twenty-nine, asserting that an evil spirit has possessed him. She died under torture at age thirty-one. The seventh-fifth life was spent in what is now Russia. The fragment, then female, was devoured by wild animals for the amusement of the village at age five. The seventy-sixth life was male, the son of a trader from Tyre. The fragment was stoned to death in Egypt for kicking a cat. He was twenty-four. The seventy-seventh life was spent in Rome, where as the son of a civil servant, he was expected to go far. He died of cholera at the age of thirteen. The seventy-eighth life was spent in what is now Sweden, the oldest daughter of a boatwright. She died of exposure at age eleven. The seventy-ninth life was spent in Australia, one of a large "clan" living in the region of what is now Sidney. The fragment was female, had four children, before dying of starvation at age twenty-eight. The eightieth life began the seventh level of the Young cycle for this Priest. The life took place in what is now the Montenegran region of what used to be Jugoslavia. The fragment was male, a judicial leader of the area devoted to maintaining their regional way of life. He died while on a voyage to Athens at age thirty-three, leaving three wives and fourteen children behind. The eighty-first life took place in southern France, the fragment was male, the son of a road-keeper. The Priest died of infected tonsils at age nine. The eighty-second life was female, spent in Rome as one of the Vestal Virgins at the time of the Republic. The Priest took her duty seriously and died at her post at age twenty-two. The eighty-third life of this Priest lasted twenty-five years and was spent from age eight on in prison for the crime of being the legitimate heir to a now-Turkish throne. The fragment died of malnutrition, parasite infestations, and neglect.

The Mature cycle began for this Priest at life eighty-four. The fragment was born in what is now Illinois, became the religious leader of the region and set up a system of religious courts to redress wrongs. He had five children, two of whom lived to be adults. The fragment died of heart disease at age thirty. The eighty-fifth life began in what is now Zaire. The fragment, male, was the off-spring of incest and therefore a "clan" outcast. The fragment died at age eleven, having suffered from increasing debility brought about by a dislocated shoulder. The next life was spent in the mountains between what are now France and Italy. The fragment was female, given to occasional trace-states. She cared for infirm parents and accepted no offers of marriage. The life ended at twenty-four when the Priest decided to make an example of virtue and starved herself to death. The eighty-seventh life was spent in western China, in a small village where the Priest, female, was orphaned and was left with the task of caring for her six younger siblings. She died of malnutrition and fever at age seventeen. The eighty-eighth life began the second level of the Mature cycle for this Priest, who was born female in Norway to a family of house-builders, and died during a blizzard at age nine. The eighty-ninth life began in Greece where the Priest, born female to a distinguished family, established a hospital for lepers and devoted most of her twenty-seven years of life to the care of those who came for help. The ninetieth life was spent in north-western India as a "minister of state" to the ruler, and an advisor to the court. He ordered the execution of sixty-eight "conspirators" in order to show the depth of his dedication to the ruler. He had four wives, twenty-eight children, and fifteen grandchildren at the time of his death at age eighty-one. The next life was spent in South America, as a female. The fragment was married, had four living children and spent much of her time instructing the children of her village on the traditions and history of their people. She died of injuries incurred during a clash with "neighbors" when she was thirty. The ninety-second life was spent in western Russia. The fragment was female, born to a family of brick-makers and died at two from an infection. The ninety-third life began the third level of the Mature cycle for this Priest, who incarnated in Syria, was male, a mathematician of considerable erudition and a glowing academic reputation. The fragment had three wives, two concubines, and over thirty children when he died at age thirty-nine. The ninety-fourth life was spent in Malta, the Priest was male, the son of poor parents who went out into the world on his own at age eight. He worked around the quays and was killed at age sixteen when an off-loading crane broke and dropped its load on the Priest. The ninety-fifth life was spent in Greece, where the Priest early became the leader of a splinter-group, all-male religious cult. The Priest was killed by his own followers at age twenty-one. The ninety-sixth life began the fourth level, or, given the nature of validated perceptions, the mid-cycle of the Mature cycle for this Priest, who was born male in what is now the state of Washington. The fragment traded successfully as far north as the Inland Passage, and as far south as Coos Bay. He died in a severe storm at sea at the age of twenty-seven, leaving a wife and four children to the irregular care of his brother. The Priest had now had more than two thousand years of incarnation, and more than three thousand eight hundred years had passed on the physical plane. The ninety-seventh life was spent near the city of Rome, where the Priest, female, was the wife of an innkeeper on the old Appian Way, who made a small fortune in selling "antiquities" to the unsuspecting. The ninety-eighth life began the fifth level of the Mature cycle for this Priest, who was born female on a small island off Korea to a family of pearl-fishers. The Priest died as a ritual sacrifice at age two, in the hope of encouraging more pearl production. The ninety-ninth life was spent in Tibet, female, married to three brothers, one of whom killed her during a dispute. She was fifteen and had two children. The next life was lived in Mexico, the fragment was male and a priest as well as a Priest. This fragment supervised ritual instruction and taught the novices. He died of fever at age twenty-eight. The one hundred first life was spent in western Spain, the daughter of an outlaw who was executed along with the rest of her family when her father was finally apprehended by the "authorities". She was twenty-eight when she died. The one hundred second life began the sixth level of the Mature cycle. The Priest was born in what is now the Czech Republic, a female in a house of "ill-repute". She grew up there and died of "overwork" at age fifteen. The next life was spent in China where the fragment became the author of an almanac known for its accuracy. His prestige outlived him by more than a thousand years. He died near Canton, leaving one wife and five children at age thirty-six. The one hundred fourth life took place in what is now Morocco. The fragment was born with pronounced birth defects and was sold to a market-entertainer, who taught the fragment to juggle. The Priest died of cumulative "distress" at age nine. The one hundred sixth life was spent in Britain, the fragment was female, and she died giving birth to her third child at age seventeen. Life number one hundred seven began the seventh level of the Mature cycle for this Priest, who was born female in what is now Honduras to a family of potters. This fragment was married against her will and was executed for the death of her husband (for which she was, in fact, not responsible) at age twenty-three. Life one hundred eight was lived as a male for thirty-four years in many parts of central Africa. The Priest was a story-teller and went from clan to clan learning and telling stories. He died of snakebite. The one hundred ninth life was spent as a male in Norway, an apprentice ship-builder who died in a village fire at age nineteen, leaving three children behind. Life one hundred ten took place in India, the surviving brother of identical twins. The fragment became a regional religious tax collector and was strangled at age forty-nine, leaving no living family. Life one hundred eleven was spent as a female; the life lasted twenty-seven years and consisted mainly of raising the orphaned children of two of her siblings. Cause of death was a ruptured appendix.

The Old cycle began for this Priest at life one hundred twelve. The fragment was male, born in Malaysia, the son of an herbalist. He died of experimentation with his father's supplies at age eighteen. The one hundred thirteenth life was spent in Egypt where this female established a "haven" for women to live contemplative lives. She is still revered as a saint in the Coptic tradition, and was until recently venerated in the Orthodox Church. The one hundred fourteenth life took place in Norway, in the Lappish region. The fragment, born female, was considered expendable during a hard winter and fatally abandoned at age three. The one hundred fifteenth life was lived in Japan, where the fragment, then male, devoted his life to establishing an aesthetic and philosophy of flower arranging and gardening. He died at twenty-nine, a widower with two living children. The one hundred sixteenth life began the second level of the Old cycle for this Priest, who was born female in South America to an isolated "clan" deep in the rain forest. The female learned about the traditions of the "clan" and was being trained as a shaman when spider-venom struck her down at age eighteen. The one hundred seventeenth life for this Priest was lived aboard a boat at the mouth of the Ganges River, where he served as a male prostitute for most of his twenty-five years. He drowned under "questionable circumstances" which burned two karmic ribbons. The one hundred eighteenth life was spent in Hungary, where the fragment was male, and involved in keeping the barbarian invaders out of the country, although he had left the Church in order to do this. In spite of his best efforts, this did not happen and he died in battle at age thirty-three. The one hundred nineteenth life began the third level of the Old cycle for this fragment, who was born to a caravan family in Mongolia. Being a fifth female, she was sold as a slave while quite young and ended up tending sheep. She died of exposure in her tenth year. The one hundred twentieth life was spent in Antioch and other cities of the region, guiding European merchants. The Priest was known for his honesty and generally profited from his work. He had three wives, eleven children and five camels when he and the merchants he was guiding were killed by bandits when he was forty-one. The one hundred twenty-first life was spent in central India, male, the apprentice to a for-tune-teller. He died of parasite infestation at age sixteen. The one hundred twenty-second life was spent in Africa as a dealer in ancient Egyptian artifacts which she supplied through her associations with grave robbers. She was made to take the blame for blasphemy, and she and her children died in prison under torture. She was thirty-two. The one hundred twenty-third life was spent in North America with the so-called Cheyenne people. The Priest was male and died in a prairie fire at age eight. The one hundred twenty-fourth life for this Priest was spent in the South Seas where the fragment trained as a navigator, only to be lost at sea on his second voyage at age eighteen. The one hundred twenty-fifth life of this Priest took place in northern Europe as a part of a group of monks charged with ministering to the peasants of Germany and Poland. The fragment died at age twenty-four from exhaustion resulting from many self-induced hardships. The one hundred twenty-sixth life began the fifth level of the Old cycle for this Priest, who was born male in Indonesia and was enrolled in a Buddhist monastery while still very young. He died there at age twenty-three, revered for his contemplative manner. The next life was spent in Spain, the fragment was Moslem, and a famed copyist. He died of fungal contamination at age thirty-four. The one hundred twenty-eighth life began the sixth level of the Old cycle, and was spent in Corsica, the son of a horse-breeder who disliked this son, and did little to protect him from bandits, and he died at age eleven. Life number one hundred twenty-nine began in north-eastern Italy, the fragment was female, a religious composer who died of injuries got while traveling at age twenty-six. The next life was spent as a female in what is now Venezuela, the fragment was the daughter of a cooper and was killed at age fifteen during an insurrection. The one hundred thirty-first life was spent all over eastern Europe and into the Balkans, the fragment was female, one of a troupe or "clan" of gypsies. She was married, had five children, and died of pneumonia at age thirty. The one hundred thirty-second life was spent in New England with a group of Puritans. The fragment was a young minister, given to notions of tolerance which got him into trouble. He died of peritonitis at age twenty-eight. The one hundred thirty-third life was spent in China, working as a male attendant in an opium den. The fragment became addicted himself and died of malnutrition at age nineteen. The one hundred thirty-fourth life began the seventh level of the Old cycle for this Priest, who was born in Calcutta to a white father and Hindu mother. She managed to survive as a servant and had one child before contracting Bubonic Plague at the age of sixteen. The next life was spent in Bavaria, where the fragment, female, ran a small academy for upper-class girls. They learned history, French, Italian, and Latin, mathematics, comportment, penmanship, and either music or art. The fragment died at age sixty-two from cancer, and her school was taken over by less scrupulous fragments. The immediate past life, life number one hundred thirty-six, was spent in Manchuria. The fragment was female and died attempting to protect her daughters from the Japanese. In the current life, the Priest lives in Iceland, is male and nineteen years old, studying astronomy and doing independent observations. The Priest has had twenty-one contacts with the Essence Twin, and sixteen with the Task Companion. The fragment has burned three thousand two hundred sixty-six karmic ribbons and has had one thousand eight hundred forty-nine contacts with the six members of the cadence.

The King we will follow is seventh cast in the cadence, and was first incarnate 5,421 years ago. The first life was in India where the fragment was made a kennel boy, assigned to sleep with the village's dogs. He died of exposure at age eleven. The second life was spent in Central America where the fragment, then female, was sacrificed for the good of the "clan" at age twelve. The third life was spent in southern Spain, female, had five children and murdered her "husband" to keep him from selling the children. She was stoned to death at age twenty-six. The fourth life took place in what is now Pakistan, the fragment was male and made the assistant to the village shaman. He died from a disciplinary beating at age eighteen. Life number five began the second level of the Infant cycle for this King in the south of France, where the fragment was born male, became a kind of hamlet "sergeant", enforcing the rules. He had four children before dying of a ruptured spleen at thirty. The sixth life took place in what is now called Sudan. The fragment was female, the child of hunters, who died of neglect at five. The seventh life took place in what is now Siberia. The fragment became the regional coordinator for hunting and froze to death at twenty-seven, leaving two wives and eight children behind. The eighth life was spent on the plains of Hungary where the King was a horse-thief and died for his crimes at eighteen. The ninth life began the third level of the Infant cycle. The King was born male in

the region of the Great Lakes, and was given the role of
hamlet security, work he took very seriously. He had a
"wife" and three children when he died of exposure during
a winter watch at age twenty-two. The next life was in the
Indus Valley, the fragment was female, the oldest daughter
of a clerk who allowed her to badger him into learning to
keep records. She continued to do this for merchants in the
area after her father died and eventually married one of the
most successful of the merchants. She died at age thirty-
one from intestinal flukes, leaving four living children behind. The eleventh life was spent male in what is now
Ethiopia, the fragment was born to slavery, given the care
of horses, and died as the result of a kick to the head at age
fifteen. The twelfth life began the fourth level of the Infant
cycle. The fragment was born male on what you call the
Channel Islands between France and England. The King
was male, a fisherman in a fishing family, who was killed at
age seventeen during a religious festival to place new stones
for a site of worship. The thirteenth life was spent in central
Africa, the fragment was female, had two "husbands",
eleven children, three of whom survived. She died at age
thirty-one of a severe uterine infection following a miscarriage. The fourteenth life was spent on the Malay Peninsula,
where the King, then male, became the leader of a small
fleet of merchants' boats. He had four wives and nineteen
chldren when he was killed by pirates at age thirty-four.
The fifteenth life was spent in central Europe, and the
King, then male, died of epidemic disease at age two. The
sixteenth life began the fifth level of the Infant cycle for
this King. The life was spent in South America, at a
"trading post" near what is now São Paulo. The fragment,
then female, helped to "supervise" the market, making
sure that no child was lost or sold without intent. She
died at age twenty-one while searching for four children
kidnapped at the "trading post". The seventeenth life was
spent in what is now Armenia. The King was male, a
slave-trader in the region. He conducted his business well,
married three times and had four living children when he
was imprisoned and tortured to death for refusing to give

his slaves to the local warlord. The King was twenty-three at the time. The next life took place in China, the King was male, the youngest child of a regional "magistrate". He was killed at age eight in an attempt to frighten his father into making a "demanded" decision. The nineteenth life began the sixth level of the Infant cycle, the King was female, born into slavery in northern Italy. She was given the task of running the household for her master, which she did until her death at age twenty-four from septic boils. The twentieth life was spent in what you call New Guinea, the fragment was female, and badly crippled from age two. The King had to support herself when her family abandoned her, which she managed to do for a time. She died at age fifteen, technically from starvation. The next life began in Egypt, the King was male, became a building overseer noted for the quality of work he could get from those in his charge. He died of sunstroke at age twenty. The twenty-second life began the seventh level of the Infant cycle for this King, who was born female in central Asia. The fragment was married at age ten to a Bactrian camel breeder. She had six living children before he sold her. She died of a punctured lung at age twenty-two. The twenty-third life was spent in China, the organizer of a kind of school dedicated to keeping records of the weather and other environmental "conditions". The King did this so well that he was singled out for reward and was murdered by thieves at the age of twenty-nine. The twenty-fourth life was spent in western Europe. The King was male, a servant's son, who was killed at age nine in a fire. The twenty-fifth life took place in what is now Iraq, the fragment was male, and became a military leader for various "cities" in the region. He had four families and a small fortune when he choked on a bone and perished at age forty-one.

The Baby cycle began for this fragment at life twenty-six. The King was born female in the South Pacific, learned four languages spoken in the region as part of her duties as the principal wife of the "naval commander" of the area. She had two living children when she was killed during a typhoon. The twenty-seventh life was spent in what is now Alaska, the King was born to a whaling family, and was lost on the hunt the first time out, at age twelve. The twenty-eighth life was spent in the region of the Black Sea, the fragment was male, a merchant-traveler who plied his trade through the region. He was killed by soldiers at the age of twenty-six. Although he had no official "wife" he did leave behind nine children. The twenty-ninth life was spent in eastern Greece, the fragment was female, and she died at age seven, sacrificed to the crop gods after two years of failed harvests. The thirtieth life was spent in what is now The Netherlands, making sandals and "shoes". The King became the leader of the village elders and his family was held in high regard. He died of a stroke at age fifty-five, thrice widowed, with eight surviving children and six grandchildren. The thirty-first life began the second level of the Baby cycle for this King, who was born female in the region of what is now Vladivostok. The village and ninety-three percent of the inhabitants were wiped out by a tsunami. The King was then age three. The thirty-second life was lived in Central America. The King was female, widowed with four of her own seven step-children to care for. She did this by maintaining her late husband's farm until exhaustion caught up wth her at age twenty-four. The thirty-third life was spent as a junior officer in the Egyptian army. He died after the loss of an arm at age sixteen. The thirty-fourth life was spent in southern India. The fragment was female and died of fever at age ninteen after giving birth to three children, the product of fraternal incest. The thirty-fifth life began the third level of the Baby cycle for this King, who was born female in central Europe. She had two husbands and ten children by the time of her death from poison at age thirty-one. The thirty-sixth life took place in what is now Iraq, the fragment was male, and served as a "warden" for prisoners of the ruler. He was killed by inmates at age twenty-nine, leaving behind five children to be raised by his late wife's sister. The thirty-seventh life began the fourth level, or mid-cycle, of the Baby Cycle for this King, who was born into servitude in southern Spain. He was trained to make bricks and tiles, and labored in that capacity until he contracted a wasting fever and died at age fifteen. The thirty-eighth life was spent in Mongolia. The King was born male to a family of goatherds. He died of reactions to insect bites at age eight. The thirty-ninth life was spent in western China, the fragment was female, the slave of a religious shaman. She guarded him and managed his affairs until her death at age twenty-one from botulism. The fortieth life began the fifth level of the Baby cycle for this King. She was born in Africa, made the "wife" of a scout, and died at seventeen, the victim of village raiders. Life forty-one was spent as a commander in the Hittite army. The King as successful in battle, and was killed on campaign at age thirty-two, leaving a wife and three children behind. The forty-second life was spent in Mexico. The King was born prematurely, and female. When it became obvious that the child would not thrive, she was exposed and died at age one. The forty-third life brought the King to the sixth level of the Baby cycle. The fragment was born in Japan to a family of fishermen and divers. Trained to retrieve pearls, this female fragment drowned while trying to increase the number of pearls she had taken. She was nineteen. The forty-fourth life was spent in what is now Algeria. The King was the leader of a gang of thieves. He was murdered by rival thieves at age twenty-four. The forty-fifth life was spent in western Russia tending to the horses of his master. He died of a chronic fungal infection at age sixteen. Life forty-six began the Seventh level of the Baby cycle for this King. The fragment was male, the supervisor of a fort in central China. He lived to be thirty, gained promotions and respect for his dependability. His two wives and eleven children sincerely mourned him. The forty-seventh life was spent as a male, a slave, set to building quays on the Nile. He died of parasite infestation at age nineteen. The forty-eighth life was spent as a female, one of twins in what is now Portugal. Separated at birth to off-set the evil omen of twins, the King was not permitted to marry for fear she would have more twins. She became the market "clerk" for the village and never saw her sister again. She died at age thirty-four of infection resulting from the bites of semi-feral dogs. The next life took place in eastern China, the fragment was male and invented several new military machines for defense of cities. For this he was honored and imprisoned so that his skill could not be used by any other power. The fragment had now had a thousand years of incarnation and over eighteen hundred years on the physical plane had gone by since the King started to incarnate.

Life fifty began the Young cycle for the King, who was born female, and became a religious initiate in India. She died at seventeen, having been bitten by a cobra. The fifty-first life was spent as a Mede, a regional military commander who held his fortress against all comers, including Greeks and Parthians. He died of bleeding ulcers at age forty-five. Life fifty-two began the second level of the Young cycle for this King. Born male in the mountains of South America, this King was of "slave" status and assigned to building roads. He died of hypothermia at age nine. Life fifty-three took place in northern Africa. The King was female and ran a brothel catering to Mediterranean merchants. She prospered and died of fever at age twenty-nine. She had no children. The fifty-fourth life was spent as a female, daughter of a leader in a conquered "clan" in Britain. She was beaten to death to serve as a reminder of the capitulation at age fifteen. Life fifty-five was spent male in what is now Laos. The King was male, the commander of the region. He died in battle at age twenty-six, leaving four legitimate and nine illegitimate children behind. The fifty-sixth life began the third level of the Young cycle for this King. The fragment was male, of Algonquin ethnicity. He died at age four from being struck by a "ball" during play. The fifty-seventh life was spent male, of "slave" status, put to building fortifications for his masters, a job he deliberately botched in order to bring about the collapse of the northern Chinese city he loathed. He died at age thirty-four from exhaustion. The fifty-eighth life was spent female in what is now Japan. The King was an oldest daughter put in charge of younger siblings, and she died defending them at age nineteen. Life fifty-nine brought the King to the fourth level of the Young cycle. The fragment incarnated in Siberia, was male, and died of a fall at age eleven. The sixtieth life was spent as a male in western Africa. The King traded in spices and spent most of his life going from village to village with his companions and goods. He died at age thirty-eight, devoured by animals in the river. The sixty-first life was lived in what is now Sweden, the fragment was the daughter of a "slave" in charge of running a household. She was bought by a Dane as a concubine, and carried away to Denmark where she was murdered by the Dane's wife at age twenty-one, after she had borne three children. The sixty-second life began the fifth level of the young cycle for the King. The fragment was born female to a "clan" of beggars in Egypt. She managed the work well enough, but got into a fight with the "authorities" who cut her throat when she was fifteen. The sixty-third life was spent in Indonesia, the King was male, the heir of the regional warlord. The fragment had just taken his father's place when the whole region was taken over by another warlord. The King died at nineteen. Life sixty-four took place in northern Europe where the King was the only surviving member of the royal house, and although female, was the only one with the "right" to rule, which she did very capably until her death at age seventy-two. She never married, and had no children. The sixty-fifth life was spent in the city of Tyre where the King was sold into slavery at birth and then proved too rebellious to keep. He was "disposed of" at age six. The next life was spent in northern Italy, where the fragment was assassinated at age twenty-four by his ruler-father's soldiers for imagined treason. His wife and children were also killed at that time. The sixty-seventh life began the sixth level of the Young cycle for this King. The fragment was born female in Greece, and given in tribute to the local priests. She served as a temple prostitute for most of her fairly short life, succumbing to fever at age sixteen. The sixty-eighth life was lived in southern China, the King was a regional nobleman who promoted the "good" of his people. He sponsored several promising boys for education and the chance of advancement. He also strove to unite the kingdom under his own rule and died in the attempt to take power at age twenty-nine. The next life the King was male in South America, a maker of nets who committed suicide out of "boredom" at age eight by attempting to fly. The seventieth life began the seventh level of the Young cycle for this King. The fragment was born in Persia and made her mark in the world and history by becoming the ruler of her district. She had four children and had all her lovers murdered so that they could make no claim in the throne. The seventy-first life took place in Spain, the fragment, now male, died at age two in a fire. The seventy-second life was spent in central France, the wife of a Roman politician. She did all she could to advance her husband's career, but her ambitions came to an end as the result of an accident on the road which left her with a broken back. She died at age twenty-three. The seventy-third life was spent in the islands called the Philippines. The King was male, the eunuch leader of a group of fighters with the same alteration. The fighters drove many pirate bands from the sea and became powerful enough to have some political "clout". The King died of a kidney infection at age thirty-five.

At life seventy-four the King entered the Mature cycle. That life was spent in south Africa, female, on a small island with nine families resident upon it. She died of neglect at age five. Life seventy-five was spent in Rome as a tribune. Although married, he preferred the sexual company of men. Thus he had no children to console his wife when he was murdered by a possessive lover at age twenty-three. The seventy-sixth life was spent in what is now Panama. The King was male, of a violent disposition which brought him to an untimely end at age seventeen. The seventy-seventh life was spent in south-western France raising livestock and wine. The King was female, and was able to survive a difficult marriage. By the time she died at age eighty-one, she had outlived all nine of her children as well as three of her thirty-one grandchildren. She was survived by another seventeen great-grandchildren. Life seventy-eight began the second level of the Mature cycle for this King. He was born male, of "slave" status, in northern India. Caught stealing jewels from his master, he was executed at age thirty-nine. The seventy-ninth life was near the village that became Kiev. The King was carried off in a raid and killed at age eight. Life eighty was in Sardinia. The King was two, and female, when she was abandoned to her fate by her starving family. The eighty-first life was spent in what is now Albania. The fragment was female and died while successfully fighting off rapists. The eighty-second life began the third level of the Mature cycle. The fragment was male, a monk who established a school on the road between Florence and Vienna. His philosophy did not always meet with the approval of his superiors, and as a result he was burned for heresy at age seventy-three. The eighty-third life brought the King to Manchuria. He improved diplomatic relations in the region and is still remembered for this accomplishment which ended in his murder at age thirty. The next life began the fourth level of the Mature cycle. The fragment was female, living in Byzantine territory and died during one of the barbarain attacks on her village, age three. The eighty-fifth life was spent in the region of what is now northern Arizona. This King studied the history of his people and the region, attempting to make a cultural record. He failed in his task, but achieved more than he had thought possible. He died at age nineteen, leaving one child. The eighty-sixth life was spent in Indonesia, the wife of a "courtier" and his most ardent supporter. She gave him eight children and the benefit of her energies until she died of a heart attack at age twenty-eight. The eighty-seventh life began the fifth level of the Mature cycle for this King, who was born female in North America, where she quickly decided to live on her own, which she did, beginning at age fourteen. She maintained this private way of life until her death at age thirty-six. Among the people of her "clan" she became a figure of legend, more of an archetype than a person. The eighty-eighth life the King was a male, of mixed race, who became a covert courier and spy for the Emperor of China. He kept at his work with tremendous devotion to duty. He permitted himself no family so that he could not be influenced or blackmailed, or, for that matter, rejected because of his origins. He died at the hands of his enemies, as he had long anticipated, at age forty. The eighty-ninth life was spent in Sicily, the fragment was male and died of the results of a dare, inhaling poison gases from a near-by volcano. He lived fourteen years. The ninetieth life began the sixth level of the Mature cycle for this King. Born female, she lived in Greece, daughter of a priest, and died at age six at the hands of her step-mother. The ninety-first life was spent in Wales, the King was male, who gathered legends and songs into a book. He was considered "odd" although today it might be considered "depressed". He was married, had three surviving children when he died at age thirty-one of an "accidental" fall from a bridge. At this point the King had more than two thousand lives of incarnation on the physical plane, and more than three thousand eight hundred years had gone by on the physical plane. The ninety-second life was spent male, in Greenland, the "minister of justice" for a number of villages. The fragment had five surviving children when he died at age twenty-nine of gangrene develolping from frostbite. The ninety-third life began the seventh level of the Mature cycle for this King. It took place in Africa where the King, now female, became a courtesan to royalty, and died in childbirth at age eighteen. The ninety-fourth life of this King was spent in England. The fragment was female, widowed at twenty-two and took over her husband's brewery, becoming a brewster in earnest five years later when she "bought out" the competition. She raised eight nieces and nephews and died of heart disease at age fifty-six. The ninety-fifth life was spent in Tahiti as a female, married to a retarded man for community and karmic reasons. She died while "on the job" at age seventeen.

The Old cycle for this King began at life ninety-six, when the fragment was born female in Sri Lanka, where she became a religious recluse and died at twenty-one of malnutrition. The ninety-seventh life was spent male, a "professor" at a major university in Moorish Spain. His topic was "world affairs". He had two wives and nine children as well as six male lovers. He died at age forty-four of heart disease. The ninety-eighth life was spent as a male in the far north of Canada. This fragment brought four "clans" together into a common unit for a better "division of labor". He fathered eleven children, three of whom survived. He froze to death attempting to pull a companion from the ocean. He was twenty-seven years old. The ninety-ninth life began the second level of the Old cycle for this King and was spent in what was then Bohemia, the daughter of a regional ruler who married her to his oldest crony. She promptly murdered her husband, burning an old karmic ribbon in the process, and was executed at age twenty-one. The one hundredth life was spent in Borneo with a "clan" of head-hunters. He defied a taboo and ended up in the "village collection" at age eighteen. The one hundred first life was lived in India where the King wrote and produced historical-mythic plays for the court of the ruler. He married one of the illegitimate daughters of the ruler and had seven children with her before his death from cancer at age thirty-nine. The one hundred second life took place in Rome and lasted six years. The King, then male, died of typhus. The one hundred third life took place in what is now the general region of Armenia, the fragment, although female, became the rallying force behind an attempt to stem the Mongol expansion of the twelfth century, Common Reckoning. The attempt was successful as long as he was available to lead it. Once she was invalided out of the struggle, the resistance quickly collapsed. She died at thirty, as much from a broken heart as from the effects of her old wounds. The one hundred fourth life was spent on Cyprus, the King was a professional female beggar preying on "naive" Europeans. She died of abuse at age twelve. The one hundred fifth life was spent as a female in the South American jungles, this time as the senior woman of a small "clan" and therefore the one in charge of the children. She fulfilled her obligations, burned four karmic ribbons and died of fungal infection at age twenty-seven. The next life was largely spent aboard ship, the son of a merchant plying the seas from Africa to Germany. The fragment inherited the business and decided to go exploring. His ships and all aboard were lost in an Atlantic gale about halfway to Newfoundland. He was twenty-eight. Life one hundred seven began in Spain and ended in Japan as a sailor. He was executed at age 31. The one hundred eighth life began the fifth level of the Old cycle for this King. She was born in Japan to a family of innkeepers. She died, along with her two-month-old son, in an earthquake at the age of fourteen. The one hundred ninth life took place in Italy, the King was schooled in music, became a composer of madrigals and other vocal compositions, some of which are still sung today. He died at age forty-eight of fever. The one hundred tenth life was lived in Manchuria, the King was male and became a teacher. He had eight children by two wives and died at age thirty-nine of leukemia. The one hundred eleventh life began the sixth level of the Old cycle for this King. Born in South America of mixed parentage, he became a priest and defended his "native" congregation against the demands of virtual slavery by the Church. He died in prison and in disgrace at forty-one. The next life, the fragment was Dutch, a ship's captain, who saved all his passengers and most of his crew after the ship foundered in the Tasman Sea. He went down with his ship at age fifty-two. The one hundred thirteenth life, the fragment was born in Boston, male, to an apothecary, and died in a fire at age ten. The one hundred fourteenth life was spent in Alexandria, the fragment was mixed French and Egyptian, male, a "hustler" and a rogue. He was killed at age twenty-one. The one hundred fifteenth life began the seventh level Old cycle for this King, who was born male in China, taught calligraphy and literature, was married with four children when he and his family had to flee in the face of massive civil unrest. He died in 1931 Common Reckoning of starvation at age fifty-eight. The King is currently female, of Apache ancestry, living in southern New Mexico, raising her five grandchildren. She is forty-seven years old. This King had fewer lives than is "usual" for Kings, but because of the seventh position in casting went about the matter with truly Kingly directness. The King had twenty-seven contacts with the Essence Twin and thirty-four with the Task Companion. The King burned four thousand three hundred sixty-six karmic ribbons and had two thousand five hundred thirty-nine contacts with the six members of the cadence.

Let us assure you no life is more important than any other, or that any life is "better" or "worse". All insights are valid and no evolution occurs without the insights being recognized. But we assure you, the most "mundane" lives are as apt to be filled with insight and intimacy as the most creative, driven ones. The choices made bring their repercussions, and dealing with choice and the ramifications of choice is the entire "purpose" of life incarnate, just as evolution is the "desire" of essence, and the product of evolution is joy.

CHAPTER 7

Coping

By its very nature, life as you experience it on the physical plane makes intrusions and demands. From the basic matters to the most complex, the physical plane is intrusive and its nature "requires" attention, the attention usually manifested as choice. The vast majority of choices are made in responses to these demands, usually from such "automatic" assumptions that you do not recognize them as choices, such as the way in which you lace your shoes, if you have shoelaces. There are many ways you might choose to knot the laces, but the "usual" way is so usual that the choice to tie the laces in that manner is "over" before a coherent "decision" has been made, at least after the age of three. Repetition of movement is part of physical training, and useful as well as valid. All martial arts would be impossible without the ingraining of habit, so that an evaluative choice does not have to be made at the time of conflict. The purpose of instruction is as much to instill habit and make a "state of mind", as to control the assimilation of information. The same may be said for practicing a musical instrument. One of the most "significant" reasons for such repetition is not the notes as such, but the habitual establishment of the means by which the desired sound is produced so that the instrumentalist need not "think" about how it is played in order to play it. This kind of habituated response is not uncommon in many ensouled species, and we would think it is the most basic form of coping with the physical plane. Routine has a very valid function for most fragments, as the disruption of routine quickly reveals, for once the habitual pattern is gone, making choices of any sort tends to become an "exhausting" process, one that requires more time and attention than the fragment would ordinarily wish to give. We would think that any review of a major emergency or disaster would reveal the validity of this, for those who have been through such events often report having difficulty in making up their minds or in trusting their own judgment for a considerable period of time after the event in question has passed. This does not mean that the choices are less valid—all choices are valid—but that some fragments during times of life disruption, lose the "knack" for making daily choices readily and easily.

Above the habitual level there are the matters of dharma, the doing of things, which is where most conscious choices are made. The day-to-day decisions make it possible for a fragment to deal with much larger issues. A fragment who has had most opportunities for choice removed by the nature of culture or karma is often perplexed when faced with even the most "minor" decision. Those who are in a position to make choices frequently manage the business better, by virtue of practice and habit, if nothing else. For example, a fragment who had already decided that the dirty clothing will go to the dry cleaner instead of the laundry, that it is time to get the pet a new flea collar, that the newspaper subscription will be renewed, that the gas bill will come out of the next paycheck, that the menu for the dinner for friends will have to be modified in order to accommodate the allergies of one of them, that the computer printer needs a new toner cartridge, that the birthday present will have to go by express delivery, that a chicken salad will be a more "prudent" lunch than a pizza, that the garage needs a new roof, that the matinee will be a better time to see the new major film than the evening showings, that the camera needs cleaning, that another two sets of

dishes will be needed at the dinner party if everyone is to
match, that the contribution to Amnesty International will
be larger this year, that it is time to rent a carpet cleaner
again, and that the memo about the business merger needs
to be updated, can then more capably and competently
choose whether or not the aged relative is to continue to
receive life support while in a coma. Juxtaposed, those first
choices may seem "trivial" as compared to the decision
about the comatose relative, but the practice of making
these supposedly minor choices is "essential" to developing the competency to address "difficult" choices. Practice
may not make perfect—nothing can do that where matter
is concerned—but it can make the process less daunting,
which aids in the development of competence in the framework of the overleaves and the societal "orientation" of
the fragment. Incidentally, ridiculing the choices of youngsters is one of the surest ways of making that youngster, as
an adult, incapable of choosing "well", for not only has
there been no support of any choice while the youngster
was practicing, but the results were dismissed with deri-
sion, which is more damaging than outright physical abuse
for most fragments. For a fragment to become competent
at making choices, the possibility of that happening to the
youngster "must" be present, and the efforts the youngster
made regarded with respect.

—————

"**M**ichael seems to stress competency. Cound they define
what they mean by competency?"

In regard to decisions, we would think that practice in
making choices is the most crucial step in developing
competence. The process of choosing develops with use,
and we would think that learning to assess the nature of the
problem is the most basic aspect of competence. Of course,
various cultures define problems in various ways, and what
is seen as a social gaffe to one culture would present a
significant choice to another. That aside, we would think

that learning to discern the nature of the problem at hand would be an important part of competence. For example, is the problem with the partner one of clashing overleaves or a question of unrealized "expectations"? Depending on which is verified, the competent fragment would evaluate the choices available in different ways. After all, every choice is unique. We would also think that learning when to avail oneself of specialized knowledge is a part of competence. We would like to point out that it is true that the fragment who advises oneself without competent understanding where such understanding is available is apt to make decisions that lack full "appreciation" of the ramifications or the choice made. That does not make the choice any less valid, or the lesson less applicable; it only indicates that certain considerations have been overlooked.

In regard to the competence of those practitioners consulted for additional advice such as but not limited to legal, educational, and medical, we would think that there are seven levels to attaining competence in this venue. (1) Theory: the fragment "must" comprehend the purpose and "philosophy" of the discipline in question. (2) Practice: the fragment has had enough opportunities to put theory to the test in a "pragmatic" manner. (3) Initiation: the fragment has extended knowledge of the discipline beyond the basics and appreciates the ramifications of using the first two stages of competence. (4) Expertise: the fragment has reached a level of ability where the exceptions to the rule are as readily recognized as those embodying the rule itself. (5) Interaction: the fragment is aware that valid progress is not determined by the practitioner alone, but through a valid exchange of information and definition of a shared purpose. (6) Flexibility: the fragment is able to adapt the specific knowledge to each unique circumstance presented, and to achieve a satisfactory outcome in terms of the consultee's wishes as well as the fragments' own. Standards are useful, but not when they become dogma. (7) Integrated knowledge realized through specifics for individuals in a responsible manner: This is brought about by all fragments involved reaching as much understanding as is possible, not only of context but of methodology as well. We would have to say that for those who regard themselves as experts, this is the most elusive stage of competence, and is revealed in such phrases as, "I am sure you don't want to get bogged down in technicalities", you don't understand the math", or "an explanation would be tedious". When a fragment retreats into jargon with those unfamiliar with the specialized language, it is a signal that the seventh level of competence is not operative. The fragment seeking the information may, of course, choose to accept this, may choose to resent the behavior and as a result question the advice, the fragment may bow to the dogma and be willing to accept the strictures "on faith", the fragment may choose to request that the supposedly competent source of information make an effort to help the inquirer grasp the subject more fully, or any number of other choices. Obviously competence is a very individual thing, and a supposed expert practitioner may be a competent source of advice for one fragment and not for another. Culture, class, and gender lines often come into play at this point of the progression and there may be much "static" influencing communication.

Let us say that in general the competent practitioner places the welfare and demands of the client or patient or student above any personal or "diagnostic" conviction and has enough expertise to be flexible. In dealing with the inconsistency of data that is always present in dealing with individuals, the product of experiential differentiation, any practitioner who seeks to establish labeling as a primary focus of any treatment or information or service ahead of experiential reports of the fragment who is the patient or client or student is not truly competent in our view, even when a clear diagnosis or recommendation presents itself: "Your appendix must come out", "Settle the suit out of court", "Refer to the explorations of the Pacific Islands after Cook's death", et cetera, for every fragment has an individual and unique response that "must" be "factored in" to the treatment or case proceedings or course of study if the advice given is to be efficacious in any valid term. If such is not present, the fragment asking for the opinion or information would do well to insist upon it, if the advice is to be viewed with "tolerance", and assessed with judgment. First and foremost, a competent practitioner must listen without bias and accommodate what the fragment seeking advice is saying, If the practitioner finishes sentences, adds comments, or dismisses information as not valid, the practitioner is not competent for the fragment consulting the practitioner, although for other fragments the competence may be "beyond question". We realize this may cause some distress to practitioners who regard themselves as the "keepers of wisdom" and who use their position to maintain an "elevated posture", but for those seeking to do the patient, student, or client some good, we would think clarity of information would be a high priority, so that the consultant will truly benefit from what is offered by the practitioner. The practitioner does not necessarily "know best", and behaving as if one does runs the risk of karma. The practitioner, demonstrably, knows more, not "better", should the practitioner choose to accept so "heretical" a notion.

━━━━━

"**W**ill Michael give some suggestions as to how to go about finding someone who is competent in regard to the person needing competent help?"

This is an excellent matter for inquiry and we commend you for voicing it. The determination of competence is not always easy, but you have already familiarized yourself with the way in which we perceive competence. So clearly, a practitioner who supports a "party line" is not apt to provide the knowledge sought, or to provide it in any form that is useful. We would also have to say that any practitioner who is known for wanting to "prove a point" is apt not to give the kind of thorough attention sought by the inquirer. It is also of use to note that many fragments are impressed by a display of "confidence" on the part of practitioners, and the practitioners, who are, of course, aware of it, cultivate the manner with the intention of making it clear that the inquirer may repose "faith" in them. We have said before but we will reiterate: faith is silly. Confidence in a practitioner's skill and abilities may be useful in terms of relational rapport, but the practitioner who insists on more than that is fully in the thrall of chief features. Framed diplomas reveal something about levels one and two of competence, but very little about the other five. Being an apt pupil does not mean that a practitioner automatically acquires competence when the learning process is complete. It is useful to keep in mind that the practitioner consulted will have to provide you with the most accurate assessment for your personal case. Insofar as the practitioner fails to do that, the competence in regard to you is lacking. When the fragment assesses all the ramifications, including experiential differentiation, there is a reasonable chance that the insights provided will be competent.

———

"**W**hile we are on the topic of competent advice, would Michael please clarify a remark they made several years ago— that all animal allergies are denials? Because this doesn't sound like a competent remark, based on Michael's own scale of competence."

Insofar as the statement goes, we would agree. But as it was taken "out of context" to the nature of the question, we will explain. This answer was in regard to juvenile-onset allergies, not post-fourth-internal-monad allergies. Often these allergies reflect past lives, such as in the case for this questioner, whose body was invaded by ants before the fragment was quite dead. That was in the seventeenth century, Common Reckoning, and the fragment was male. Today the sight of ants evokes a very unpleasant memory. But to continue. As we have stated before, juvenile-onset allergies for all fragments are in fact associated with denial, often directly linked to the immediate past life or occasionally the most traumatic past life having bearing on the current life. For example, a fragment torn to death by wild bears may well pass its youth seeking to avoid bears at all cost, and having an allergy to them provides the "raison d'être". However, genetic conditions and environmental factors can, in fact, have a cumulative effect on all fragments and that cumulative effect can later in life produce allergic reactions related to the genetic structure of the body itself. Let us remind you here that well over ninety-five percent of all bodies are genetically compromised. When such a genetic condition is exacerbated by juvenile conditions from previous lives, the allergy in that event may prove to be life-threatening, such as the reaction some fragments have to the sting of bees. There is a certain amount of "sideways" effect here, especially once mammals are "left behind", in that, for example, a person abandoned to die whose body was partially devoured by birds before death occurred might in this life subsume all allergic reactions "under one roof" and have a dangerous reaction to all forms of birds and bird by-products—down, feathers, flesh, dander, excrement, and all the rest. Once the genetic system supports the previous life experience it is unlikely that at any stage of the life the allergy will be completely unavoidable. Incidentally, we would wish to differentiate between true allergies and stress reactions, which are often promulgated unwittingly by the parents for "the good of the child" and may lead to systemic distress when the child is in the presence of whatever animal the parent perceives to be most threatening. For example, a parent who is philipophobic has a child who gets sick around horses.

━━━━━

"Never mind allergies to things. What about dealing with people? That strikes me as being a lot harder. In my own case, a relative is doing primal scream therapy and I don't know how to deal with it. Suggestion?"

Let us remind you that you may of course choose to deal with it in any way you decide, and that all choices are valid. You, being a Warrior, and inclined to regard action as the means of accomplishment, are not likely to benefit from this technique, we would agree. Since the relative is not Action Polarity, we would have to say your reservations, in this case, for this fragment, may be "misplaced". In any case, we would think that out-and-out denunciation of the therapy might not bring the results you hope to achieve. But if what you mean is how might you enter into some kind of discussion about his therapy without having the whole "dialogue" becoming a heresy trial, we would wish to observe a few things: One, that this Scholar fragment enjoys outrage now that he has discovered it after a lifetime of ikonographic distortion resulting from being The Child Who Never Causes Any Trouble or Embarrassment. He is now, in fact, having a "rollicking good time" primal screaming at anything that upsets him. Two, that his current partner is well-aware of the fun he derives from this therapy and encourages him to continue it as a means of promoting their ongoing relationship, for it provides a means to deal with ikonographic conflicts without direct personal confrontation. And three, as long as this fragment is screaming about things that have happened to him in the past, he is "immune" to confronting the present and the future, both of which, we are regretfully aware, frighten him "entire". If there is some desire to break the pattern, it may be that instilling some sense of courage in the face of abject terror is the only "reasonable" means to accomplish this perceived goal. This is not to say it is your "duty" to do so. We did not say that and we did not imply it. But should you choose to act, you may decide to keep these factors in mind, for "ballast".

"Michael has warned about self-limiting views on the world. What might I do about it so that it isn't such a problem for me?"

Let us say that the goal of perseverance in this fragment by its very nature tends to focus on specific goals and points of view. When combined, as it is in this case, with the Scholar nature, this tends to create a pattern of study and awareness that is specifically oriented to an established "end". It might not be amiss, should you choose to do so, to consider the works of many of the great landscape painters and with their images in mind undertake easy strolls with the stated intention of finding a vista resonating to the work of one or another of the great landscape painters. Of course, in the literal sense this is not possible but that aspect of the problem will serve to "loosen" the vision and embrace wider parameters. Another exercise you may wish to choose to do, is the selection of the "color of the day", wherein you make a concerted effort to make note of every instance in which you perceive a specific color, whether it is in nature, in manufactured setting or even on television. It is not necessary to do this "religiously", but experientially, so that the exercise itself does not become a tool of limitation. Therefore, we do not set this forth as a rigorous discipline but as an interesting experiment, for you or any other fragment seeking the kind of "broadened" outlook you have chosen to pursue. You may also wish to try taking short walks during which you deliberately look at nothing specifically but try instead to take everything in. There are many other ways for these insights to become accessible, but we would have to say that these suggestions are the ones that can be accomplished most "spontaneously", which is, we would think, an integral part of the insight sought.

"Along the same lines, that is, dealing with perceptions. When people abdicate the fourth internal monad, Michael has implied, they may try to have the experience through others. Will Michael enlarge on this, please?"

Let us observe here that those fragments whose lives are not significantly "interpreted" yet, but who have nonetheless abdicated the fourth internal monad, have an inner awareness of the "closing" of a door, or the resigning of options. There is often a sense of "something being lost," which is many times misinterpreted as innocence, which is a factor in cultural archetypes. The drive to bring other fragments to their overleaves manifestations is very strong in those who have not attempted the transit themselves at all: in those fragments who have begun the fourth monad only to abdicate it, there is a significant level of "resentment" usually unrecognized, for those who have, and therefore, support from these fragments is sporadic at best. For those fragments who have not attempted fourth monad, the perceptions of others "going beyond" is often seen as the "vindication" of a "worthy sacrifice" and is, therefore, often supported when the manifestation of the overleaves of others does not significantly contradict enculturation. The fragment attempting to achieve the insights through others is inclined to perceive him or herself as the "power behind the throne", or the "best thing that ever happened to" the monad transiter. Let us observe here that the general expectation until recently present in the cultural mores was that females would find their "apotheosis" in the achievements and accomplishments of their fathers, brothers, husbands, and sons—only recently has this cultural mythology been generally challenged and questioned, and, as a result of this paradigm, until recently it has not been uncommon for females in this and all Occidental societies to "abjure" the fourth monad for reasons of societal expectations which regarded such transitions as "unfeminine". By the same token, males preferring communicative, creative, and/or contemplative lives choose to do so in the face of cultural ikons that imply such pursuits are not "manly".

———

"According to family members, I don't 'appreciate' them. I think I do, but I haven't found a way to convince them of it. Will Michael make some suggestions, please?"

The question of "appreciation" is never an easy one, but we will make some recommendations. First, there are essence-specific ways to show appreciation, and they can be metaphorically adopted for many purposes. Slaves recognize appreciation in the form of civic citations. Artisans recognize appreciation in the form of structural awards. Warriors recognize appreciation in the form of campaign ribbons. Scholars recognize appreciation in the form of "academic" degrees. Sages recognize appreciation in casting "advancement". Priests recognize appreciation in the form of religious hierarchies. Kings recognize appreciation as suzerainty. Finding ways to express the appropriate form of appreciation directly or indirectly can do much to enhance the sense of appreciation. We would think that many fragments are prone to assuming that the way they are appreciated "ought" to work for everyone, which is demonstrably not the case. We would think that trying the appropriate gesture could achieve much of what is sought in this inquiry. For example, a Scholar given a campaign ribbon might be "flattered" but will not feel "appreciated", and vice versa. And those seeking to show appreciation to the fragment asking the question had "best" be willing to make this fragment a "star" if appreciation is to be recognized.

"What about frustration? Does Michael have any suggestions about how to handle frustrations?"

The obduracy of the physical plane itself makes frustration unavoidable, but that does not mean that it is "necessary" to endure it stoically, for that would obviate choice. There is also a question of the level of frustration. Frustration at failing to find a parking place is not the same order of magnitude as anxiety about a wayward teen-ager who is unwilling to listen to familial advice. There is also the frustration inherent in family ikonography. We will address each of these in turn.

Let us discuss the "parking place" frustration first. This is a "fast burn" frustration, in that it comes on suddenly and is quickly ended—when the parking place is found. The build-up of expectations—that a parking place is available—in contrast to the "reality"—that it cannot be found—tends to bring to the fore all manner of chronic disappointments to fuel this situation. For example, the fragment may recall many similar frustrations from the past and compare those frustrations to the current one. The fragment may engage chief features and be persuaded it is because of something negative in the fragment that causes the parking places to "evaporate". Let us suggest that whenever possible a finite amount of time be assigned to the parking task, and if a space is not presented, then alternatives be considered. This is the strategic use of "Plan B". When postponing the parking is not prudent, then consider other ways to accomplish what is needed, such as the use of public transportation or errand "carpooling" making it possible to have the car "circle" while errands are run. If these are not viable, it is possible to arrange for shipping of desired items, or other forms of delivery. What will "short-circuit" the frustration the most is being able to decide when "enough is enough", and to stick by that decision so that the frustration cycle will not easily start up again. When such a technique is used, or other similar techniques, the chief features have less opportunity to become fully engaged and the fragment is likely to be able to proceed without feeling that the gods/luck/fate/the world, et cetera, are "against" the fragment. In fact, it may be possible, over time, for a fragment to develop similar methods to all forms of frustrations. And while we are aware these techniques will not be very successful if the fragment is stalled on a bridge behind a bad accident, it is worth noting that all other fragments share the frustration and are not doing it to make anyone—themselves included—miserable. If the delay affects many fragments, there will be some public announcement in this regard and we would think that the delay would be "understandable," even to the most "compulsive" hostess or boss.

On the second level of frustration, we would think that

there are two related techniques, and ones that can provide
relief in continuing areas of frustration. The first step in
this is to decide what the frustrating "messages" are, and
to make a list of them, as the messages are preceived. To
say "Gina is driving me crazy with her unreliability" will
not gain much in the way of frustration alleviation. Phrasing
the message in this way: "Everyone has to make allow-
ances for Gina", "I always buy into Gina's shenanigans",
"Gina is entitled to misbehave and I am not" or something
along those lines, will be useful in ending the perceptual
pattern these frustrations reflect. When an assembly of
these messages has been made, then, should you choose to
continue, decide if the message is a burden—something
you are expected to deal with no matter what, and that you
have tended to accept as a valid expectation, or an intrusion; that is, something imposed upon you by external
events or changes in personal situations. In the case of a
burden, we would recommend purchasing a very inexpensive set of crockery dishes—at a thrift store or flea market
or garage sale or some function—and write a single message
on each dish, and then read each message aloud before you
smash the plate to pieces. If possible, leave the broken
crockery in place for at least twenty-four hours and take a
photograph of it, for this will make it easier to remind
yourself of what you have done, although you are, of
course, at liberty to make any choice in this regard you
wish to make. While this will rarely end the expectations
that have brought about the frustrations, the impact of the
frustrations is apt to diminish if you are willing to choose
to release the burden represented in the messages. As to
intrusion, the process is similar, but not quite the same. In
this instance, the messages are written—again, one message at a time—on balloons. The balloons are then blown
up, their messages read aloud before they are popped. We
must stress that this is not a cure, nor do we or anyone else
"require" this of you but, should you choose to address
the frustration in a context that will provide some interrup-
tion of habit, the techniques we have outlined may prove of
use if you are willing to choose to validate the experience.

Yes, we agree this is a symbolic act, and we would think
that as a symbol-using species this manner of dealing
with frustration can do much to "resolve" inner conflicts
without creating karma and legal problems in the process.

On the third level of dealing with frustrations, such as
family ikon frustration or chief feature frustrations, we have
a few techniques that may provide a degree of mitigation to
the stresses should you choose to inculate the insights
provided by the process. That is not to say that the discipline "must" or "should" be undertaken, but for those
who are in the process of working with problems inherent
in chief features and/or family ikon, we would think this
proposed exercise might help in bringing the insights to
bear, should you choose to allow this to happen. We must
also point out that those who have not completed the third
internal monad will derive little or no benefit from these
techniques, and those who have completed the fourth internal monad are apt to have the most noticeable results
of all. Of course, all the rituals, disciplines, meditations,
contemplations, spiritual exercises, or therapies will not
assist the fragment who does not choose to validate the
insights made accessible by these various activities. There
are two approaches to the problem, one being slightly less
"involved" than the other, and we will describe it first. On
a very large sheet of paper, draw a picture in as vivid colors
as possible of chief features or family ikon. If you choose
to include speech balloons with messages inherent in the
chief features and/or family ikon, it can assist in identifying
the thing more completely for your purposes. When the
picture is finished, talk to it. We are aware that most
fragments find this awkward or even foolish, but we assure
you that the more you tell the picture about what it is, the
more you may be able to release its hold. Incidentally, it is
not likely that this or any exercise will completely eradicate
chief features or family ikons, but a lessening of the death-
grip these functions tend to have can be a genuine achievement if it is validated. You may think of the difference of
being entombed in cement to having your leg in a cast.
Neither state is perfect, but the lesser condition does have

certain advantages to members of an independently mobile species. To continue: having told the picture all that it is, now write a list of "complaints" against its work. For example, although this is not intended to be anything more than a guideline: "You've made me feel incapable of doing anything right", or "You make me afraid to succeed because I'm sure to lose it all". This list may be as long or as short as you wish. Then, when you are satisified you have summed up all the negative impact of chief features or family ikon, take the picture and burn it. Make sure it is all turned to ash. If possible, you may choose to photograph the process so that you will have a record of having done it. And while, as we have indicated this process does not usually extirpate the culprits, it does lessen their impact. Incidentally—and we must stress the importance of this caveat—this procedure tends to have diminishing effectiveness if done oftener than once a year. Of course you may choose to do this once only, not at all, or on a schedule of your own choice, but we must remind you that frequent use of this technique will not tend to "speed up" the lessening of the holds involved. In some instances we would think that, in fact, over-use of this technique has tended to "blunt" or even reverse the purpose of the technique.

The more complex version of this technique may be found in a similar but more involved exercise. First, it is important to choose one chief feature or the family ikon and use just that one form to address. Then make a poppet out of paper and cloth [a poppet is a ritual doll, the corn-husk dollies in Pennsylvania Dutch country or the images of Ganesa over shops in India] in the symbolic image of the chief feature or family ikon. The poppet may be any size but we would recommend that it be at least as tall as your arm is long. Select a fabric that most cogently represents the way in which you are "expected" to present yourself. You may make this figure quite elaborate, with garments or accessories indicating the way in which chief feature or family ikon manifests in your life. It is of use to include strips of paper for the things the chief feature or family ikon bears as messages. When the figure is complete, again, talk to it,

tell it what it is and what it has done to you and what part
of this you want to end, and what you like to change to. It
is important to include changes desired within yourself as
well as those wanted from others, for, of course, the chief
feature or family ikon is "built in" to your "personality".
Burn the poppet, again, should you choose to do so, with
photographic evidence, and remove the ashes from the
home, if burned in the family hearth or barbecue, as soon
as they are cool. If you choose to keep the ashes near at
hand, you may find that the burning does not have much
impact. Again, we must caution all fragments that to repeat
this exercise with any frequency serves little purpose but
to diminish the effectiveness of the process. In this case,
we would think that two years at least might be allowed to
go by before another poppet is undertaken, to derive the
benefit sought. Again, this is a symbolic act, and if you
choose not to release the family ikon or chief feature being
dealt with, then the chances are good that the process will
not bring about the desired "results". If you are willing to
choose to permit the symbolic act to have impact in your
life, then there can be a lessening—not a banishing, a
lessening—of the hold of family ikon or one chief feature.
We would also encourage those choosing to try this technique not to expect something "dramatic", for that is
rarely the case. Instead, a "refocusing" takes place over a
period of days that may enable the fragment to pursue life
with fewer fears and "expectations" hampering the
fragment.

―――――

"This is going to sound nuts, Michael, but we've been told our
one hundred and twenty-four-year-old house is haunted. Is it,
and if it is, what can we do about it?"

First, yes, we would agree there is an echo present in the
dwelling left over from the owner-before-last who inhabited
the structure for a period of sixty-two years and in that
time impressed a "presence" on the building which is

detected by some of those who visit you. The presence is not potentially harmful, but it may prove "upsetting" to some. We will offer more than one way to eradicate the presence without "charging" the house with distress. First, we would suggest, should you choose to do so, that you purchase a medium-sized, inexpensive mirror and expose it to every part of the house, including cupboards, attics, basements, closets, pantries, garages, and staircases, and at each exposure, invite the presence to enter the reflected part of the house as "his own". We are aware that most fragments feel "silly" or "foolish" or even "idiotic" doing this, but it provides a necessary focus for this symbolic act and is part of working of the "exorcism". When this is finished, take the mirror some considerable distance from the house—we would think that five miles would be a reasonable distance—and smash it. Do not bring the pieces back to the house, unless you choose to have some portion of the presence linger.

The second way is a bit more extreme, but if the presence is associated with a person still living, is slightly more efficacious: should you choose to undertake this process, take a number of saucers and pour enough salt into them to cover the bottom. Place the saucer on the inside of every entrance to the house—front door, back door, side door, patio door, garage door, basement door, et cetera—and leave the salt out overnight. In the morning, pour the "used" salt into a bag and take it some distance from the house and dispose of it. This is not as "convenient" a "fix" as the first mentioned, but it can "clear the air" quite handily [another joke Michael thinks is very clever] We would add a note of caution here—those with small children or pets may find this process impractical, and where either are present we would think another technique would be preferable, although, of course, you may choose any technique—or no technique—in dealing with the presence.

The third method is "slower" and less "obvious" in its results, but it is also in many ways the easiest, and that may prove to be the most cogent reason of all to select it, should you choose to try one of these processes. This involves planting rosemary near the entrances of the house, or, if one lives in a place where this is impractical, growing rosemary in pots near the entrance to the living area. There is an added bonus that rosemary, being a culinary herb, may be harvested for cooking, should you choose to do so. This brings about a gradual "house-cleaning" over time and lessens the accumulation of "negativity" in any area. It is, for most fragments, pleasing to the senses, as well.

Please understand we are not telling anyone to do any of these things. This information is presented so that if you choose, you will have some notion of how to go about it. We would think that should you choose any of these processes, you might want to record your responses as a way of validating the information we present. For we readily acknowledge that not all fragments choose to hear the words, and for some it would not be appropriate for the task at hand to do so. Those with goals of caution and repression do not tend to be drawn to these techniques or teaching of this sort. Those with goals of rejection and retardation are also disinclined to pursue esoteric studies, except as a form or rejection. Those with attitudes of stoic, skeptic, and cynic are not generally attracted to information of this sort although, if it stands up to the scrutiny of the skeptic, there may be validation and recognition "achieved". We would think that those who choose to follow teachings of our "sort" [another Michael joke, according to Michael]. We have said before but we will repeat yet again we are not the only mid-causal teacher, and our current three groups of students are, as has been announced earlier, not open to inquiry from the general public. There are many other teaching entities on the mid-causal plane, some of them using non-verbal communication to bring the messsage to bear in the life. We would remind those seeking to follow a teaching that any so-called teacher who requires certain action or behavior from any student is not a teacher but a bully, and any so-called teacher who abrogates your choice is not a teacher but a demagogue. You are, of course, free to follow any teaching you choose and to reject any teaching you choose, including, we remind all here present, this one. We do not require agreement or any "complicity". There is no benefit to us if you turn this to dogma, for then evolution does not occur. We encourage doubt, but we remind you that flat dismissal is not doubt, it is intolerance and fear.

All fragments on the physical plane are evolving, as the universe itself is evolving. Nothing about evolution can be "lost" or "misled" or "perverted"—only perceptions can do those things. Evolution goes on within essence as it does within all other planes of existence through validated contact, which, of course, becomes easier as physicality—and by that we mean matter itself—becomes more tenuous. And while you cannot "speed up" evolution or "skip" certain stages of the lessons, we would have to say again that nothing is wasted. You may choose to abdicate every contact, monad, karmic ribbon, and other "pre-arranged" part of the life, and still you will evolve, for essence is incapable of fear, and evolution is the source of joy.

All fragments experience their lives "personally", that is within the context of experiental differentiation and the overleaves, and as long as this is not "disrupted" by karmic intrusions, the purposes of the life-tasks will "inevitably" lead to evolution, and all evolution will eventually bring all to the Tao, which, we remind you, is not a deity any more than gravity is. There is nothing you can do or not do that will "please" or "displease" the Tao, for there is no judgment at that level of existence, and the love that is the nature of the Tao is not predicted on any expectations or goals, but on existence itself. Therefore there is no way you cannot complete the journey, although you may choose indirect ways to reach the goal. As the context of culture is transformed, the nature of experiental differentiation will be found within the changing cultural context. Some will choose to live in less "hectic" societies as a way to "balance" the experience as "mercurial" [another Michael pun] a culture as this one is becoming. This does not mean "approval" or "disapproval", only choice and experiental differentiation, and is, of course, valid, as are all choices.

Let us also remind you that dates, as compared to days,

are common labels and as such are general personal truths, not world truths—except to the extent that your planet rotates and so has day and night. The impact put upon any date is a cultural artifact, not a cosmic event, and while it is not amiss, from time to time, to review experience and the "state of society" if you choose to do so, there is no set "time" when this is more "auspicious" than any other, which includes the day you have designated to begin what you have defined the third millennium.